# The New Shop Class

## Getting Started with 3D Printing, Arduino, and Wearable Tech

■ ■ ■

**Joan Horvath**
**Rich Cameron**

Apress®

**The New Shop Class: Getting Started with 3D Printing, Arduino, and Wearable Tech**

ISBN-13 (pbk): 978-1-4842-0905-9

ISBN-13 (electronic): 978-1-4842-0904-2

Trademarked names, logos, and images may appear in this book. Rather than use a trademark symbol with every occurrence of a trademarked name, logo, or image we use the names, logos, and images only in an editorial fashion and to the benefit of the trademark owner, with no intention of infringement of the trademark.

The use in this publication of trade names, trademarks, service marks, and similar terms, even if they are not identified as such, is not to be taken as an expression of opinion as to whether or not they are subject to proprietary rights.

While the advice and information in this book are believed to be true and accurate at the date of publication, neither the authors nor the editors nor the publisher can accept any legal responsibility for any errors or omissions that may be made. The publisher makes no warranty, express or implied, with respect to the material contained herein.

Managing Director: Welmoed Spahr
Lead Editor: Michelle Lowman
Editorial Board: Steve Anglin, Mark Beckner, Gary Cornell, Louise Corrigan, James DeWolf,
    Jonathan Gennick, Robert Hutchinson, Michelle Lowman, James Markham, Matthew Moodie,
    Jeffrey Pepper,  Douglas Pundick, Ben Renow-Clarke, Gwenan Spearing, Matt Wade, Steve Weiss
Coordinating Editor: Kevin Walter
Copy Editor: Corbin Collins
Compositor: SPi Global
Indexer: SPi Global
Artist: SPi Global

Distributed to the book trade worldwide by Springer Science+Business Media New York, 233 Spring Street, 6th Floor, New York, NY 10013. Phone 1-800-SPRINGER, fax (201) 348-4505, e-mail orders-ny@springer-sbm.com, or visit www.springeronline.com. Apress Media, LLC is a California LLC and the sole member (owner) is Springer Science + Business Media Finance Inc (SSBM Finance Inc). SSBM Finance Inc is a Delaware corporation.

For information on translations, please e-mail rights@apress.com, or visit www.apress.com.

Apress and friends of ED books may be purchased in bulk for academic, corporate, or promotional use. eBook versions and licenses are also available for most titles. For more information, reference our Special Bulk Sales–eBook Licensing web page at www.apress.com/bulk-sales.

Any source code or other supplementary material referenced by the author in this text is available to readers at www.apress.com. For detailed information about how to locate your book's source code, go to www.apress.com/source-code/.

*In memory of Hope Frazier, editor extraordinaire,
without whom we never would have started
on the winding road to this book.*

# Contents at a Glance

# Contents

# About the Authors

**Joan Horvath** is a cofounder of Nonscriptum LLC in Pasadena, California. Nonscriptum consults for educational and scientific users in the areas of 3D printing and maker technologies. She also has an appointment as Core Adjunct faculty for National University's College of Letters and Sciences. She has taught at the university level in a variety of institutions both in Southern California and online. Prior to that, she held a variety of entrepreneurial positions, including VP of Business Development at a Kickstarter-funded 3D-printer company. Before becoming an entrepreneur, she spent 16 years at the NASA/Caltech Jet Propulsion Laboratory, where she worked in programs including the technology transfer office, the Magellan spacecraft to Venus, and the TOPEX/Poseidon oceanography spacecraft. She holds an undergraduate degree from MIT in Aeronautics and Astronautics and an Engineering master's degree from UCLA. She is also the author of *Mastering 3D Printing* (Apress, 2014).

**Rich Cameron** (known online as "Whosawhatsis") is Joan's cofounder at Nonscriptum LLC. Rich is an experienced open source developer who has been a key member of the RepRap 3D-printer development community for many years. His designs include the original spring/lever extruder mechanism, the Reprap Wallace, and the Deezmaker Bukito portable 3D printer. By building and modifying several of the early open source 3D printers to wrestle unprecedented performance out of them, he has become an expert at maximizing the print quality of filament-based printers. When he's not busy making every aspect of his own 3D printers better, from slicing software to firmware and hardware, he likes to share that knowledge and experience online so that he can help make everyone else's printers better too.

# Acknowledgments

Although just the two of us are shown as the authors of this book, we had the backing of a great team. The community spirit in the maker and hacker world is an amazing thing (particularly in the RepRap and Arduino communities), and we never cease to be amazed at how generous people will be with their time to help a new entrant learn the ropes. We hope we have created a guide here that will take some of the front-line questions off their shoulders going forward. Particular thanks for in-depth discussions go to Metalnat Hayes on wearable tech, and Karen Mikuni, Ethan Etnyre, and Quin Etnyre for the student point of view on making in schools.

We want to thank our editorial and production team at Apress, including the infinitely patient and cheerful Kevin Walter, copy editor Corbin Collins, editors Michelle Lowman, James Markham, and Jeffrey Pepper, Dhaneesh Kumar and the rest of the production team. Coco, Mosa, and Nancy Kaleel were instrumental in helping us frame this book, and we enjoyed working with them on the foreword they kindly contributed. Thanks, too, to Mosa Kaleel for the back cover photo.

Joan would like to thank Doug Adrianson, who, along with his late wife Hope Frazier, co-edited an earlier work that was reborn as Chapters 12 through 14 of this book. The two of them were amazing writing mentors to Joan. She would never have been able to write her recent works without their coaching and the discipline enforced with Hope's trademark "SW" (for "says who?") plastered all over Joan's writing seven or so years ago.

We have relied heavily on the staff of the Windward School In Los Angeles for inspiration and the use of some of their many great ideas. We particularly want to thank Simon Huss, Regina Rubio, Glen Chung, Lyn Hoge, Tom Haglund, Cynthia Beals, Geraldine Loveless, Julie Gunther, Ernie Levroney, Jim Bologna, Larisa Showalter, and Dawn Barrett for discussions that helped us frame many of the issues in the book in a way that we hope will help teachers understand these technologies. In the same vein, we thank the many people we interviewed for their thoughts and in some cases pictures to help convey our message. Angi Chau at Castilleja School, Kathy Rea and Andy Wittman at Marlborough School, and John Umekubo at St. Matthew's Parish School in particular spent a lot of time helping us understand their world. The team at MatterHackers generously allowed us to use their MatterControl software in Chapter 3.

Finally, we are grateful to our families, who had to put up with the two of us commandeering their respective kitchen tables for brainstorming and pizza sessions when they would have rather been eating a civilized dinner. We hope everyone finds the final result was all worth it.

# Introduction

Arduino. 3D printing. Wearable tech. What *is* all this stuff? If you are a parent, teacher, or school administrator, you may be aware of a wave that the young people in your life are riding, but you may feel like you are caught in a riptide of terminology and being towed farther and farther from land. As technologists working in this sphere, we became aware of many people who felt like you do (and we got tired of answering the same questions many times). To try to make information available more broadly than we could in person, we have written this book to answer your critical questions. What does it cost to get started with these technologies? What do I have to learn to get started? Beyond that what will I (or my kids) learn by taking on these challenges?

The technologies we talk about in this book for the most part arose out of a do-it-yourself, "hacker" or "maker" culture. This culture (which you will read more about in Chapter 1) frames learning as something you do yourself, usually online or by making things with like-minded people. A disconnect between this culture and traditional education has developed. The authors are a traditionally educated aeronautical engineer-turned-educator (Joan) and a self-taught hacker and 3D printer expert (Rich, known online as "Whosawhatsis"). In this book we come together and explore the gaps and similarities in our world views. Through our partnership, we try to show a model of how traditional education can merge with the makers and hackers of the world to create a much richer learning experience than is possible to have by learning passively.

Chapter 1 gives you an overview of the difference in mindset between the two of us and provides a road map for the rest of the book. Chapters 2–4 go into some detail with regard to some of the basic technologies: an easy-to-learn microprocessor called an Arduino, 3D printing, and robotics. Chapter 5 shifts a little and talks about how people are creating spaces to learn by making things, both in public spaces and at schools. Chapter 6 talks about building on these base technologies to do "citizen science" (real science projects with general-public participants). Chapter 7 is an introduction to the world of wearable technology—creating clothing that can light up, react to the world around it, or just do things that seem like magic. Chapter 8 is an overview of some easier technologies and explains our view on why you may not want to start with these training wheels.

Chapters 9–11 take a step back to talk about the cultures that grew these technologies. Chapter 9 gives you some insight into the open source world—a technology community in which everyone shares ideas and builds on them. Chapter 10 discusses how to bring girls and women into the maker community, where they are wildly underrepresented. Chapter 11 explores the case study of a community college program focused on having students make things, including a project to create 3D-printed objects for the blind.

Chapters 12–14 shift to talking about some of the motivation for bringing a maker style into a classroom, including the fact that it is a good way to encourage students to become scientists. These three chapters discuss how scientists actually work and think and tell stories of how many of them came to science through a love of taking things apart. You may see some of your young makers in these stories.

Finally, Chapters 15–17 bring it all together and discuss how the other chapters all bring evidence that some of the best learning comes through actually creating something with your own hands, arguing that this is a particularly effective way to learn science.

Before all that, though, we start with a foreword by some of the friends who inspired us to write this book. Coco Kaleel came into our lives when she was about 11, and we were working at a 3D-printer company. Her parents were not technologists, and they desperately needed a guide to all things maker. They will tell you about their journey, and we hope we can make yours easier than theirs was!

Use this book as a starting point to guide your own explorations or those of a young scientist in your care. We have tried to give you pointers to many other references without being overwhelming. Of necessity, this means we have made choices about what to include and what to leave out. There are many other ways to do most of the things here, and we made the choices we thought opened the most doors. We only ask that you start stepping through those doors and out into new worlds that you will help create.

# Foreword

## By Coco, Mosa and Nancy Kaleel

When our daughter Coco was very young, she wanted to play with robots and servos and soldering. We were lost. As filmmakers and writers with backgrounds in animation and romantic comedy, we understood her creative desire but immediately became intimidated by the complex terminology and technology that she wanted to learn. We needed subtitles to help us understand and guide her into this amazing world of makers and truly innovative people.

This book was written for parents like us, teachers, and others.

But first, let's start with Coco's story from her (currently) 13-year-old point of view.

## The Maker

My maker story started one sunny morning when I, a preschooler in pink footie pajamas, was playing with my Tinkertoys. My parents were preoccupied with painting a room, so they couldn't be disturbed. A very ambitious child, I was trying to make a carousel for my stuffed animals, but I didn't want to push it with my hand. Frustrated, I asked my dad for help. He told me I'd have to wait because he was covered in paint, so I went back and figured it out myself. An hour later, I had built a crankshaft-equipped "carousel" above a "toy store." In the end, the carousel didn't seat any stuffed animals (it only turned), and the toy store was just an empty wireframe of a cube, but we had all learned a very important lesson—I was a maker.

I was the kid who went as an astronaut on Halloween and got LEGOs instead of dolls for her birthday. The Christmas of my 9th birthday was my first introduction to LEGO Mindstorms, a version of a robotics kit equipped with a basic programming environment. A few months later, I informed my bewildered dad that I wanted something more complicated. Shortly thereafter, my father took me on my first trip to a robotics club, where I eventually learned to solder and program Arduinos.

This is where my story took a turn. I got a 3D printer kit, and I taught a soldering class at the Los Angeles Public Library. I started a website (www.veryhappyrobot.com) to inspire others and share my experiences. I was invited to present at my first conference, where I gave a speech called "Girls and Robots." Joan Horvath, one of the authors of this book, invited me to give a poster presentation at the 3D Printing World Expo. I also spoke at the Texas Linux Festival, all with the goal of inspiring kids to learn technology. Currently, I co-chair a 3D-printing club at my school. We are working to design 3D objects that will help blind kids learn math, a challenge presented to us by Joan.

Having this book five years ago, when I told my parents I wanted more, or ten years ago, when I had just finished my "carousel," would have been a big help to all of us. There was no beaten path for them to take. When they discovered the robotics club or when I built that printer from a kit (I am still the youngest person to ever assemble it), they knew they had found something special for me.

Luckily, the amount of resources for maker kids has increased. Toy manufacturers have created building kits for girls and boys. People and groups and companies are creating things all the time and often give away their "secrets" in the name of open source, so I, or anyone, can take it and make it work for me. And if I ever get stuck on something, I am not afraid because I know there will be someone who got stuck the same way and will help me get unstuck. And someday, I'll help the next kid get unstuck.

I also look forward to the day when shop classes come back, and technology is a key focus in learning, and there is a 3D printer in every school, and C++ is taught just like a foreign language. Developments like these will inspire my generation and all the generations to come and show that makers and programmers aren't scary beings that can hack into your phone from a mile away. Makers are problem-solvers, thinkers, and bi-linguists. You can see me being one in Figure F-1.

**Figure F-1.**  *Coco at work. Photo courtesy of Mosa Kaleel*

# The Parents' Perspective

If a child has an early proclivity for sports, music, or leadership, parents can easily find T-ball or American Youth Soccer Organization (AYSO) teams at the local park for their young athletes. Music teachers, choirs, drama and dance academies, and youth orchestras abound for kids passionate about the performing arts. There's scouting for kids with community interests.

But what about the kid who wants to build robots, program, solder a circuit board, or take everything apart to just see how it works? Oh, how we wish there were peewee leagues for science, technology, engineering, and math (STEM) when Coco was in preschool. Or maybe you're a teacher or an artist or an interested adult? There is often nothing available to kindly guide and inform you through this daunting process.

# The Next Thing?

After the Tinkertoys, LEGOs, and Mindstorms, we were clueless about "the next thing" for our daughter. It seemed so simple to her that there would be something else, but we had no idea what, or whom to ask. All we could say to anyone was that our daughter wanted to code (okay…), to take everything apart (as evidenced by our insistence that, moving forward, the TV remote is used to change the channel *only*), and to make robots (who wouldn't want that?).

Unfortunately, her elementary school could offer no support. There was no space in the curriculum, no physical space on campus and no money in the budget to explore technology. Worst of all, despite a lot of teacher curiosity none of the teachers really understood the technology. If we'd been scientists or engineers ourselves, things might have been different.

Although we were able to learn a lot piecemeal on the Internet, we craved a centralized authority to guide us when it came to making. Then we found out about hackerspaces and robotics clubs that were close to our house. These places are explored by Joan and Rich in Chapter 5.

By happenstance, a lecture promoted by a local robotics group about Raspberry Pi (see Chapter 2) was being held at a local hackerspace. When Coco first set eyes on the venue for the presentation and met the membership of that group—all adults—she immediately said, "My people!" They seemed to see a bit of themselves in Coco, too, and eagerly helped start to teach her what we couldn't. We can't thank all of the people that we met there enough.

The robotics group counted aerospace engineers and graduate students among its membership. Coco learned about the Arduino, the basics of electronics, and how to solder alongside many adults. She discovered she was quite good at it (that fearlessness of a then ten-year old). Ask someone over 55 about soldering, and they'll tell you the projects they made as a kid in shop class in school. Ask someone under 21, and most don't even know what soldering is.

# Creating a Maker

One thing we did realize along the way was that although there is a lot of ready-made equipment out there, a great way to learn something is to make or assemble it yourself. We found that kits were perfect for Coco. This was especially true of the 3D printer. We knew that consumer 3D printers were in their infancy and that Coco would have to fix it if it broke because, in case it's not obvious yet, her parents would be useless. She loved kits and started a website to help people get started and to chronicle her journey.

We decided to invest in a 3D printer, and Coco assembled it herself as a kit (at age 11). Not only did she learn about the engineering, software, and mechanics, she also met Joan and Rich in the process. Their knowledge base, from both traditional and new perspectives, as well as their amazing willingness to openly share was a turning point for Coco. They set the stage for Coco to start to put together the various aspects of technology that she had been learning.

Coco got very comfortable printing and making things. She then wanted to learn about quadcopters, so she built a kit. The owners of a (rare) brick-and-morter drone store near our house encouraged our daughter to learn about drone technology. When Coco noticed that the camera mount on her drone didn't fit properly, they encouraged her to find a solution. As an eager 12-year old, she learned a 3D-modeling software, used it to design a proper camera mount, and printed it on her 3D printer. It took a bunch of tries, but eventually she got there, along the way learning one of the most valuable lessons a child could learn—perseverance. She then uploaded the design to a sharing website where it's since been downloaded several hundred times. You can see the three of us taking a break from all that in Figure F-2.

*Figure F-2.* *The Kaleel family. Photo courtesy of Mosa Kaleel*

# Your Turn

Coco's camera mount, a small simple piece of plastic, brought together the cumulative efforts of soldering, electronics, 3D printing, and sharing. Joan, Rich, and a community of engineers and makers pushed a 12-year old to problem-solve and learn far beyond what we could have imagined for her. But not everyone can be so lucky to have mentors and experts in robotics, 3D printing, and drones all in the same community. Joan and Rich recognized this and decided to provide you with this resource by filling in the gaps and connecting the dots that took us years to find and understand.

Our hope for the future is that schools and communities will build the same support systems and infrastructure for kids who love robotics, programming, and 3D printing just as they've done for baseball, soccer, music, dance, drama, and scouting. We can look at all the advantages that athletics, the arts, and community service do to enhance a child's life experience. We look forward to the day when technology will be assimilated in the school curriculum and at community centers to benefit the makers and innovators of tomorrow.

We wish that Joan and Rich's book had been available to us ten years ago when we first discovered Coco's desire to be a maker. We didn't even have a name for it back then—we just knew she loved to build, tinker, and discover what made things work. Even a decade later, the infrastructure to support kids with this passion is just now getting started. This book is an excellent resource to ensure that a young child's inclination for technology, engineering, and making is fostered and fully realized.

# PART I

■ ■ ■

# The Technologies

This first section of the book introduces you to Arduinos, 3D printing, and the mindset of the community that has developed the consumer versions of these techologies.

Chapter 1 is an overview of the differences in mindset and views of learning between the maker/hacker community and the traditional, educational one. It is also a guide to the rest of the book. In Chapter 2, you learn about the Arduino microprocessor and the low-cost ecosystem of sensors, motors, and other electronics that has sprung up based on the Arduino. One of those ecosystems is the low-cost, open source 3D printer, introduced in Chapter 3

If you take Arduinos, some motors and sensors, and maybe a few 3D-printed parts, you can make yourself robots and other things that move on their own. Chapter 4 discusses the basics of robots and gives you some entry points into the overwhelming number of kits, ideas, and online tutorials.

Taken together, these chapters provide the material you need to know before moving on to the more complex applications of the technologies covered in the rest of the book.

# CHAPTER 1

■ ■ ■

# 21st Century Shop Teacher

The words *shop class* conjure up a messy place where sawdust and metal shavings pile up on the floor as awkward birdhouses are built up on the tables. *Computer lab*, on the other hand, brings up images of white floors and walls, whirring fans, and overly-good air conditioning. It is also the last place on earth that you would want sawdust and metal shavings. School districts have been closing out their shop classes, because of perceived lack of student interest or liability concerns, as computer labs become ubiquitous.

However, a new hybrid of machine/wood shop, computer lab, and electronics bench is emerging. These are variously called hackerspaces, makerspaces, fab labs, or perhaps robotics labs. They might be spaces open to the public as a place for learning skills or using tools, or focused on some specific activity like building robots or creating fantastical costumes. They may have equipment that runs the gamut from glue guns and fabric to 3D printers, hand tools, laser cutters, and computer-numerically-controlled (CNC) machine tools. For the most part, we will use *makerspace* as the general term for this type of space, since it seems to be the commonest term in school, library, and museum settings.

When a makerspace is set up in a school, will it become the site for 21st century shop class? What will students learn there? Who can run one of these shops? If you are a teacher, how can you get past the intimidating complexity so that you can learn to use the equipment and get your students using it, too? If you are a parent, what will a home version of these spaces look like?

This chapter talks about the resurging interest in making things, enabled by the combination of low-cost 3D printing and (relatively) easy-to-program electronic components. It introduces the technologies that we talk about extensively in later chapters and what you can do with them. Finally, we introduce ourselves—a traditional engineer/educator and a hacker—and start the conversation we want to have with you throughout this book about how to reconcile these different approaches to learning and how to become conversant with what these technologies make possible.

## What Is "Making?"

Being a maker is more of a state of mind than a well-defined activity. In the next section, we lay out our (different) perspectives on what being a maker *should* be and how someone should become one. For the moment, though, we will define *maker* as someone who makes something because they want to, even if they could buy what they are making. A maker also typically wants to learn how something works and learns this best by making it.

There are various levels of difficulty of making, and some are closer to fine art or crafting. In this book, we focus on the technology-oriented side of making, while recognizing that often a love of design may come from woodworking or sewing initially and then cross over into electronics, or the other way around. (Figure 1-1, for example, shows an electronic maker's foray into holiday tree design.)

***Figure 1-1.*** *A maker's holiday tree of wooden dowels. Courtesy of Luz Rivas*

Even narrowing down making to the technological options leaves an overwhelming number of different possibilities. You may have had the experience of searching online for "Arduino," for example, and getting dozens of example of things to do with an Arduino board but no explanation of what one actually *is*. (For the record, it is a microprocessor that can control physical things, which we will meet in depth in Chapter 2.)

This book is intended to be a field guide for you to see where good entry points are for a beginner, and how to move from beginner to more advanced if you do not have a handy community around you already. In the last chapters, we talk about how making can be a good route into learning science, technology engineering, and math (STEM) subjects.

---

■ **Tip**   If you live near a public makerspace, it likely has beginner classes (try an online search for "makerspace" and "hackerspace" plus your city name). Call them up and tell them your situation. For example, are you a parent with a kid getting interested in these technologies? They are likely to know about resources that are available regionally. If you do not live near one, search online for forums (see Chapter 9's discussion) and post about what you are trying to do. You will usually find someone willing to help, even if that person happens to live on the other side of the world.

---

# Who Is a 21st Century Shop Teacher ?

One of the challenges of starting up a makerspace is finding people to run it. It requires a mix of skills that are rarely found in one person—a combination of comfort with traditional shop class methods plus electronics plus competence in computer programming. If a school's IT department is asked to set up a makerspace, they may not have any experience with the issues that arise with making physical things. On the other hand, the shop class or art teacher may not have a lot of experience with the computing aspects of these new hybrid skills.

The authors (Joan and Rich), shown in Figure 1-2 at New York Makerfaire, came into this space on very different trajectories. We worked together for a time at a small 3D printer manufacturer. Now we collaborate on figuring out how to teach just about any subject through hands-on creation of physical objects.

*Figure 1-2.* *The authors at 2014 New York Makerfaire. Apress PR photo*

Joan is a traditionally educated baby-boomer aeronautical engineer with a strong computing background. She came into the maker world in early 2013 with almost no hands-on electronics or shop experience. Rich, on the other hand, is a millennial, self-taught electronics hacker and 3D printer guru who has been involved in open source 3D printing since its earliest days (around 2008). This makes him the old-timer of the two of us. In this book, we will give you both sets of insights about how these two communities can best work together. The next section gives you our two first-person views about this community, and how we each think about traditional education and hands-on making. We want you to feel like this book is a conversation with the two of us that will help you figure out how to navigate this new world.

## Joan: An Engineer and Educator Meets Making

I learned engineering from university classes at MIT and UCLA, culminating in a Master's degree in engineering from UCLA. For 16 years I was an engineer at Caltech's Jet Propulsion Laboratory (JPL), which makes spacecraft that go to other planets. In those environments, the critical skill is being able to learn things quickly. I am used to learning things top-down. Usually a first introduction would be from a book or manual, with a lot of equations. In a professional engineering research environment, particularly in aerospace, people become very specialized. I am primarily a software person, and it would have been unthinkable for me to plop down in a spacecraft electronics assembly area and touch *anything*. In the course of 16 years, I was probably in the same room with actual flight hardware two or three times, if you do not count looking down on it from a glassed-in viewing gallery.

Like most people at JPL, I always had a special relationship with the robot spacecraft I worked with. They almost felt like children, or coworkers. I worked on software that told the Magellan spacecraft what to do. Magellan was the first spacecraft to create radar images of the surface of the planet Venus, which is covered with dense clouds. The software absolutely, positively could not have bugs.

We had to be very creative and deal with situations that no one had ever really thought about before. After all, how many people think about what happens in Venus orbit every day at work? Despite that, excruciatingly careful planning and fanatical attention to detail was also necessary, and JPL in the 1980s and 1990s was probably the last place in the solar system one would exercise a "let's see what happens" maker mentality. I left JPL in 2000 and consulted in the entrepreneurial aerospace world for a decade. Then I started to spend more and more of my time as an adjunct faculty member at several institutions.

I came into the maker community early in 2013 when I was looking for material for online undergraduate interdisciplinary studies classes. By this time, I was an adjunct faculty member teaching students who were training to be elementary schoolteachers. I wanted them to see science and engineering as a process of discovery, rather than as an exercise in vocabulary worksheets. As it turned out, we decided that the learning curve was too steep at the time to fit it into that particular program, although we piloted one of the first online teacher professional development classes in 3D printing.

By then, I could see the power of 3D printing and other maker technologies and joined a small 3D-printer company. It horrified my new colleagues that I was a rocket scientist who had worked on several interplanetary spacecraft (Galileo to Jupiter and Cassini to Saturn, in addition to Magellan, and some studies of things that never flew), but had not really built anything with my hands since my undergraduate lab days. I felt uneasy touching electronics, even though intellectually I knew it was all hobbyist stuff and if I messed up it would not result in the failure of billions of dollars worth of spacecraft.

Most of my new peers could design and build a consumer 3D printer from nothing but what was in their heads. Some of them (Rich excepted, of course!) did not see the point of all my formal education if I could not sit down and just build something. Specialization seemed some sort of abdication of responsibility to them, given how alien it was to think that you would focus on just one piece of a much bigger project and rely on hundreds of colleagues to know the rest. Makers prided themselves on building something all themselves and on knowing everything about it. Having been part of a team that flew a spacecraft to map Venus seemed inconsistent with the fact that I could not wire a terminal block competently. (Note to anyone over 40 taking up making: go up a half diopter on your reading glasses—some of this stuff is *tiny*.)

## Learning by Doing—Are There Limits?

When it became clear to me that using these 3D printers was pretty complicated (even by recovering rocket scientist standards), I started to develop training materials to make things easier for our customers. When I tried to teach myself how to use open source 3D printers, I found a lot of detailed information scattered online. But there was almost nothing that stepped back and walked through the overall process of creating a 3D print or that defined terms and general concepts for a new user. There were user forums, but they were organized somewhat randomly around whatever order people had asked questions. They were searchable, but you needed to know what questions to ask and what terminology to use. Often that terminology was different than conventional engineering terminology.

When I asked about this, the reaction often was that the detail was there, so what was the problem? Or, secondly, that learning on my own was sort of a rite of passage—that unless I figured everything out myself, I probably was not ready to use the technology anyway. After an extensive period of pestering experienced users (particularly Rich!) and trial and error, I slowly became competent and moved on from there. However, the way I did it was very inefficient at the community level. I saw person after person spend days dragging together the same information from scattered and inconsistent sources.

I had started my career working with early supercomputers at JPL (which had about the same computer power as the $25 processors we will talk about in Chapter 2, but that's a different story). There are some similarities between 3D printing today and the early days of computing, but even then specialization in hardware or software was pretty common, and there was less of the maker expectation to be good at all aspects.

There is an old joke that says that the difference between scientists and engineers is that scientists like to be surprised but engineers hate it. This implies that engineering is the process of working largely to apply existing knowledge. However, the maker process seems to assume that makers need to discover everything for themselves and thus be engineers who like to surprise themselves.

If you ask a maker about this, they will insist that people learn better by learning everything by doing. To me, though, it seems like this philosophy limits most people to learning only what they can invent themselves and makes it unlikely they will create new knowledge. It is all about how things work, but not about general theory and bigger picture behind it. I call this type of learning *icicles*—very deep knowledge in some areas, but with gaps in between.

In the end, I wound up writing a book (*Mastering 3D Printing*, published in 2014 by Apress) with Rich in a technical reviewer role. Writing the book and structuring material for it the way I would like to have learned it brought me up to a level where I felt competent—unless something involves one of those miniscule terminal block connectors (Chapter 2).

## Global, Virtual Apprenticeship

If you are traditionally educated in a technical field, you are likely nodding your head now about how "these makers" are reinventing the wheel and avoiding doing the hard work of learning math and science the usual way. You may have been resisting having a makerspace in a school because it is "just playing." But, notwithstanding everything I have just said, it's not that simple.

I know that I am a very structured, top-down learner. Given that I am a female engineer who went to school when female engineers were a single-digit percentage of most fields, I am a bit bemused by being the "traditional engineer" in this book. However, I will accept that I have been taught traditionally. Almost all technical fields are taught in a way that favors visual learners and top-down learners.

But if someone learns bottom-up, will they be better off deriving the top-level knowledge themselves? Makers learn things by working in a makerspace and hanging around others, or by doing the same thing virtually by hanging out on forums and discussion boards. But most of all, they learn by trying things and seeing what happens. Is becoming a maker a new way of having a global, virtual apprenticeship if only learning from books is not for you? Or are they a new type of artist? Or are they creating a new discipline altogether? We will try to address these questions as we explore the examples in later chapters of this book.

Not long ago, what you could learn about electronics by cut-and-try experimentation was fairly limited because of cost of the hardware, its complexity, and access to information. The critical piece that is new is the availability of sophisticated but easy-to-use electronics and tools like 3D printers, plus nearly infinite (overly infinite?) web-based information. As we will see in later chapters, these new electronics were designed with either students or hobbyists in mind. Some of the most powerful uses of these new, accessible electronics are *in combination with* 3D printing. Both students and professionals who need to prototype or make one-of-a-kind things quickly (like product designers, or scientists, or artists) can very quickly and relatively inexpensively turn out a pretty sophisticated first version of an electronic device or a scientific instrument or a piece of kinetic art.

Many students learn best if they can immediately apply what they have learned to something concrete in front of them. Some of these students are ones who might have excelled in shop class when that was an option for them. (As mentioned, most shop classes in the United States are being shut down, for perceived lack of interest or liability reasons.) Others are fascinated by the virtual world and come into making from the programming side—also an area that is not supported well in all school districts. What does maker learning look like?

I will now hand this over to Rich to describe his path into making, and the hacker-versus-maker approach. There he is in his typical work environment in Figure 1-3.

**Figure 1-3.** *The hacker in his element*

## Rich: The Hacker Path

I learned engineering from the single greatest repository of knowledge humanity has ever produced: the Internet. Like many hackers, I am an autodidact. In school, I excelled at tests but still only passed some of my classes by the skin of my teeth. I couldn't stand to waste time on assignments intended to teach concepts through mindless repetition when they were clear to me when they were first introduced. Instead, I liked to spend my time learning C and similar programming languages to develop various software projects.

I've always found that the best way to learn anything is to first have some project that the knowledge is required to accomplish. Of course, unfettered access to information is crucial, but the Internet makes that easier than it's ever been. With the exception of one basic electronics class and the standard set of math and science classes where the students complained about needing to learn things they'd never use, I haven't gone to school for any of the knowledge I use on a daily basis. I developed one of the first low-cost 3D printers (Chapter 3) and became vice president of research and development at a small 3D-printer company on the strength of what I have been able to teach myself.

My basic electronics class taught me Ohm's and Watt's laws (Chapter 2) and other concepts over the course of a semester, but I learned far more during the first week that I sat down with an Arduino and something to accomplish (Chapter 2 talks about Arduinos). I started designing circuits and fabricating circuit boards, at first using things like perf board and conductive ink, then using free computer-aided design (CAD) software and mail-order prototyping services.

I began building robots with Arduinos as controllers, and when I needed more complex and precise mechanical parts than I could produce with hand tools, I decided to use one of these Arduinos to build a CNC mill to cut the shapes I needed automatically from CAD drawings. When looking for software to use with such a machine, what I found was the software for controlling open source 3D printers. A 3D printer, as you will learn in Chapter 3, is a robot that can make things, including other machines, and in many cases even copies of its own parts or improvements for itself. This quickly became more interesting than my robots or the CNC mill, and I've been working on open source 3D-printer designs ever since.

## Hacker vs. Maker

Though the situation has been improving in recent years, the term *hacker* has been much maligned and misunderstood more often than not in the media and in popular understanding. Hacking does not consist of writing computer viruses, defacing websites, and breaking into computers for mischief or personal gain, though hacking is usually a necessary precursor to these activities.

One of the several definitions (and my personal favorite) for *hacker* is in the Jargon File (www.catb.org/jargon/html/H/hacker.html), probably the oldest and most complete reference for the terminology used by hackers. It says: "One who enjoys the intellectual challenge of creatively overcoming or circumventing limitations." Hacking uses and develops a person's creativity, critical thinking, and problem solving, the three most universally important skills one can have.

Some people do not like to use the word *hacker* to describe the types of activity in this book, because they think of the word in the sense of a *black hat* (as opposed to a *white hat*) computer security hacker. A stereotypical black hat hacker overcomes or circumvents obstacles imposed by computer security systems because they want to damage or steal something, whereas a white hat does so to find security holes so that they can be fixed. However, a true hacker's motivation for overcoming these obstacles is simply for the challenge (and possibly the bragging rights) of doing so. Whatever shenanigans they may get up to after the barriers are broken do not define what it means to be a hacker.

Only a small but sensationalized minority of the larger hacker community is involved with breaking computer security systems. The inherently constructive types of hacking we describe in this book have nothing to do with this type of hacking. The limitations we try to overcome are often simply the limits of what anyone has ever figured out how to do, or even thought possible. In this sense, almost everyone who ever invented some new technology was a hacker of some sort.

The maker movement grew out of this hacker culture as well as the do-it-yourself (DIY)/hobbyist and avant-garde art/sculpture scenes. Type **kinetic sculpture** into your search engine of choice to see some particularly impressive examples of what makers do. Although hacking is occasionally used for destructive ends, making is a constructive pursuit by definition. Though both terms are equally applicable to most of the things that people like me do and what goes on in a hackerspace (I prefer that classic term into over makerspace), *maker* is often seen in language that has been sanitized for those who may still misunderstand what hacking is all about. There is a subtle distinction that hacking is motivated primarily by the enjoyment of creative problem solving, whereas making is directed more toward the end product. In this sense I am a hacker first, and a maker second.

## Learning by Doing: Overcoming the Limits

There is age-old knowledge that will always be useful, but in a field as fast-moving as 3D printing, the most important thing to learn is whatever was discovered yesterday. Traditional education can teach the old stuff, but when it comes to keeping up with new developments, you're on your own. The open source communities make this information available to find, but learning to learn is an essential skill. Just as a picture is worth a thousand words, knowing how to recognize and fill the gaps in your knowledge when you need to is worth more than a billion memorized facts and formulae.

There is one kind of knowledge that is more valuable than what was discovered yesterday, and that's what will be discovered tomorrow. Learning how to find information is critical, but you'll never contribute any new knowledge if you can't figure things out for yourself. Classically educated engineers tend to look down on what self-taught hackers like me do as "just playing" and think it's foolish to discover things for ourselves that are already known and could just be taught to us. However, by reproducing past inventions and discoveries for yourself without the prior knowledge, you are also learning how to invent and discover new things.

People don't become great musicians by listening to a lot of music, but by practicing simple pieces of music before they can perform difficult ones, and although watching a lot of baseball on TV might make someone more likely to get a seat at the World Series, the players on the field started in Little League. Things that are easy to discover have already been discovered, and things that are easy to invent have already been invented, but to discover or invent more difficult things that are new to the world, you need practice discovering and inventing simpler things that are new to you. If a man learns how to make a wheel, he'll be able to get to the next town. If he learns how to invent the wheel, he might make it to the moon.

Joan likes to talk about top-down vs. bottom-up learning, but I think of my method as more of a middle-out strategy, more like ice crystals spreading out in a supercooled liquid (search for videos of that online if you haven't seen it, it's pretty impressive) from various nucleation points rather than the icicles that Joan envisions. I learn best by gathering disparate, seemingly random bits of information when I need them and then get the deepest understanding by integrating and filling in the gaps between them on my own. New bits that are close enough to something I already understand just make sense and are easy to absorb, and if a gap is too large, a quick Internet search allows me to find the bit of information in the middle until all the gaps are small enough to bridge easily.

At the same time, I like to ponder the edges of my understanding and figure out related things, practicing expanding my knowledge. Unlike the way the same subjects might be taught in a school, these new areas of thought may cross into a different subjects and back, and some of the most interesting and unique topics are ones that fall between typical class subjects, and may even be things that a traditional education would fail to cover. I sometimes spend hours at a time pondering things that nobody really understands, like the connection between quantum physics and general relativity.

## Physical Software

I was always more of a software hacker and never had much interest in taking a shop class when I was in school. It may seem odd then that my most well-known contributions to the open source 3D-printing community are hardware projects: 3D-printer and component designs, and other printable objects. The fact is, the tools of digital fabrication turn hardware and mechanical designs into a software problem. CAD software allows circuits, components, or entire machines to be designed and sometimes even simulated in software before any of the physical parts are made. Then the computer-controlled machines can turn those designs into physical products with minimal human interaction.

These 21st-century shop tools aren't yet the simple IT devices that 2D paper printers are (though some less honest 3D-printer manufacturers make them out to be), but they're a lot closer to it than the human-operated machine tools that they replace, and they're getting closer. This fact made it possible for me to do hardware design and fabrication within the software realm that I was comfortable in, allowing me to think of hardware design as a physical extension of software hacking.

The first CAD program I learned to use was CadSoft EAGLE, a program popular in the Arduino community for designing circuit boards. I taught myself how to use it to design my own Arduino-compatible development boards and robot controllers. Then I uploaded my designs to online PCB prototyping services so that I could order my custom boards and receive them in the mail. Once they arrived, I would solder in the components, try the circuit, and (if necessary) modify the design and re-order.

The tool that enabled me to use software to create real things the most was OpenSCAD. OpenSCAD is the quintessential "physical software" tool, billing itself as "the programmer's solid 3D CAD modeler." In OpenSCAD, you build up complex 2D and 3D objects from simple primitives in a process called *constructive solid geometry*. To do this, you write code in a language with a C-like syntax (which my prior programming experience allowed me to pick up in a matter of hours). This approach to design isn't for everyone, and there are many more mouse-oriented CAD options, but for someone with a software hacking background like mine, it's ideal. I can quite literally code physical objects the same way I would code a computer program.

## How the Paths Merge

So who will be a 21st century shop teacher? Our answer is that it will take people like the two of us coming together to create bridges between the traditional education and the maker communities. Those of us who know book-learning science will continue to pass it on. But for relevance and application, 21st-century shop will need a big dose of actual making things. As Rich says, much of what we know now did not exist a few years ago, and learning to learn will be the high-value skill as many barriers to prototyping and manufacturing fall.

However, it is also necessary to learn accurate material. Currently the maker community manages this by being small and an everyone-knows-everyone type of group, but of necessity this is changing. Not everyone has the ability to recapitulate Isaac Newton and other greats to reinvent everything as they go, either.

Given that, how will people learn five or ten or twenty years from now? As Joan found when she tried to learn 3D printing from unstructured materials, even a very good technical education does not necessarily make it easy to learn a whole new field from scratch. However, it did help her organize what was known to make it easier for everyone who comes after.

To take that to the next level, a much closer collaboration between educator and hacker is required, and the result is this book. We argue a lot and do not see entirely eye-to-eye on the best path for education. However, we have mutual respect and can see we each learned best in our own ways. We also have a shared love for plain cheese pizza, which helped create common ground in the beginning and now is just a plus.

---

■ **Note** Industrial and product design education has traditionally immersed its students deeply in the creative process and what we describe here as "hacking." If you are trying to create coursework for more advanced students in a hacker style, some seminal books in this field are from the design or psychology literature. One classic is Mihaly Csikszentmihalyi's *Creativity: Flow and the Psychology of Discovery and Invention* (HarperCollins, 1997). Csikszentmihalyi is best known for his concept of "flow"—a state in which people are working right at the upper limits of their abilities and are very happy and productive because they are learning and pushing their limits. Makers almost by definition will be in this state often. Figure 1-3 could be an illustration of the concept of flow.

---

# Defining Your Problem

Many who are reading this book likely are parents or traditional educators. This book is designed to help with situations like the following:

- Your child has asked for an Arduino starter kit for her birthday, and you were embarrassed to discover that it was not a dog breed, as you originally assumed.

- Your principal has announced a maker initiative for your school and asked you to coordinate it and produce a budget. You have little or no idea how to proceed.

- You are a school administrator, and parents are asking what practical skills their children are learning. Or perhaps parents are asking about when you will include 3D printing and maker technologies in the classroom.

- You bought a 3D printer to teach math and science either at home or in a classroom, unboxed it, printed a Star Wars figurine, and wondered, "Now what?"

- 25 Arduino starter kits have just been delivered to your school courtesy of a donor, and you had no idea so much wire and so many fragile small parts would be involved. And no one has the least clue what to do with them or how to teach with them.

- You already are into this type of learning but need some evidence to convince dubious colleagues to introduce maker activities into your curriculum.

To address situations like these and more, we have structured the book into a chapter for each of the major types of maker technologies. Table 1-1 is a survey of what we address in this book. We also list the basic skill sets that you will need to learn concurrently if you are going to use these technologies and the chapter that goes into each area in more depth. In each chapter, we give a rough indication of how much it costs to get a "starter set" and get going with it. These skill set and costs summaries appear at the end of Chapters 2 through 8.

***Table 1-1.*** *Typical Maker Technologies and Activities*

| Technology | What It Is/Does | What You Need to Learn | Chapter |
|---|---|---|---|
| Arduinos | Microcontroller that controls lights and/or sensors, motors, etc. | Programming Wiring Possibly soldering | 2–7, 15–17 |
| Raspberry Pi | A basic computer | Linux operating system | 2 |
| Circuit stickers* LittleBits* LightUp* LEGOs* | Make circuits by drawing or magnetic attachment or other simple connectors | A bit about circuits | 8 |
| 3D printing | Makes physical items based on 3D models | 3D computer modeling or scanning, software that slices model into layers, physical interaction with printer | 3–7, 15–17 |

*(continued)*

*Table 1-1.* (*continued*)

| Technology | What It Is/Does | What You Need to Learn | Chapter |
|---|---|---|---|
| Robotics | Design/assemble robots | Wiring, programming Possibly soldering and/or machine tools | 4 |
| Wearable tech | Clothing that uses Arduino-like devices to make clothing that lights up, senses things, etc. | Arduinos plus sewing | 7 |
| Cosplay | Costume creation | Sewing and glue Possibly Arduinos | 7 |
| MakeyMakey* | Boards that plug into computers and allow anything to be an input device | Circuit design basics | 8 |
| Citizen Science | Using maker tech to do science | Arduinos, sensors, science | 6, 16, 17 |

*Starred items have shorter learning curves, at least in the beginning.*

Part of the point of playing with these different technologies is to learn the skills listed here (versus thinking that you would need to learn programming or soldering first, for example). The learning curve can be pretty steep, as we will see when we go into Arduinos and 3D printing in Chapters 2 and 3 respectively, and it is hard to learn these skills in isolation without a project to help you focus on what to learn first, as Rich noted in his backstory earlier in this chapter. For that reason, these skills are often taught in project-based ways that teach a little bit of each of the skills needed (say, programming and wiring just a few components, in the case of the electronics-oriented spheres). You can do progressively harder projects as you build the many skills needed to get started.

---

■ **Tip** It can be frustrating to embark on electronics projects if you're not sure what parts you will need. One way to get around that is to buy a beginner's kit to get started. "Learn how to…" kits are sold by many vendors, notably Sparkfun (www.sparkfun.com) and Adafruit (www.adafruit.com). These companies also have tutorials on their sites for a wide variety of skill levels. Each chapter in this book will give you some ideas of what to buy to get started more specifically, but these two sites are a good place to look around in general to see what is possible.

---

# Making a Scientist

Let's take a step back now and ask: why are we rushing around trying to figure out how to use these maker technologies in education? Making is good training to be a scientist. If you just absorb preexisting knowledge without some discovering of it yourself, you will not appreciate or be able to see it as a process. All too often, Joan encounters someone who thinks science is too hard for the average person to understand, or who thinks that the best way to teach science is as a vocabulary lesson, with worksheets that match a concept and word. This kills the idea of science as exploration and inquiry, which is what makes it fun (and hard).

Scientists, though, are usually makers. Anyone doing laboratory work might need to make or modify equipment. By the nature of their work, typically scientists are doing something for the first time. For the most part, they need to design experiments that can be done by existing equipment. More and more, though, these same low-cost electronics that allow you to learn in the first place can be used to create simple equipment capable enough to do a new type of experiment, or to collect vastly more data than was possible before. We talk about this aspect in Chapter 6, when we discuss citizen science and open source labs.

More fundamentally, though, the maker (or hacker) mindset—the *let's see what happens* attitude—is a crucial part of being a scientist. To prove that, in Chapters 12–14 we have collected a lot of short vignettes about working scientists, engineers, and mathematicians, with some explanations of their thought processes. Some stories are about the professionals as children, getting in trouble by blowing something up (or in one case putting a fork in an outlet). Others talk about the practicalities of what they do all day. All of them, though, will give you some idea of why it is a good idea to use some precious formal education classroom time to actually make things.

The final chapters of this book tie together the maker concepts in Chapters 2–11 and the stories of technologists in Chapters 12–14 to make some recommendations about how to teach by making with a combination of 3D printing, maker electronics, and some old-fashioned tools, too. We also talk about how important it is to try things and fail. If you have to succeed all the time (as Joan saw at JPL), it limits the pace of learning. Low-cost making means you can have low-stakes failed projects, which is critical for learning engineering and science.

## Making and the Common Core

If you are involved in education in the United States, you are probably very aware of the Common Core Initiative (www.corestandards.org). These new standards incorporate problem-solving and critical-thinking skills as central requirements for how students learn. We do not explore those links explicitly in this book, but note them here as something to explore further in the many resources available to teachers about the Common Core. If you search on the name of a technology and "Common Core," you will find a lot of aligned materials.

## Educational Implications

Over the last several decades, manufacturing in the United States has gradually declined (although there is a lot of recent effort to change that). Because this means there are fewer jobs in manufacturing, traditional shop class has been languishing at many schools. If you couple declining interest with the liability issues of machine tools, you can see why schools with budget problems have been shuttering their shop classes. See, for instance, this article in *Forbes* by Tara Tiger Brown (www.forbes.com/sites/tarabrown/2012/05/30/the-death-of-shop-class-and-americas-high-skilled-workforce).

Creating a makerspace is a way to walk back into offering some sort of hands-on class, even if it is not a full-on shop class. The very things that make it hard to get started—that you do need to learn about the physical world—mean that students who have learned this way have a leg up over those who have never actually put anything together.

---

■ **Note** If you want a book to accompany design-focused learning in your classroom, Henry Petroski's books about the process of engineering design, most notably *To Engineer Is Human* (Vintage, 1992), focus on the role of trial, error, and failure in good engineering practice. Chapter 15 talks about this subject in depth. Donald Norman's design books, such as *The Design of Everyday Things* (Basic Books, 1988), are classics about how to observe the world and invent to meet real needs.

---

# Broader Social Implications

The other impact of maker technologies (particularly 3D printing) has been to vastly lower the cost of making a prototype. Reducing the cost and raising the accessibility of a technology essentially democratizes it. This means that it is now possible for a seventh grader to create a prototype of a physical object that a few years ago would have required a professional modelmaker. 3D printing is the physical equivalent of low-cost computer graphic tools. This is nice for the seventh grader and may get her an A, but it is transformative for many professions, like product design. It also changes how those professionals work. If you are in the business of training people to be product designers, or engineers, or entrepreneurs for that matter, it is important that students learn how they will later work.

## Making Prototyping Cheaper

If prototypes are cheaper and faster to make, the design process itself also becomes more iterative and more tolerant of failure along the way. Manufacturing may experience a broader sea change soon. A piece in *Harvard Business Review*'s blog by Peter Acton speculated that the ability to manufacture in small lots at home could create sweeping social change, as mass manufacturing starts to lose both its appeal and its price edge. (`https://hbr.org/2014/12/is-the-era-of-mass-manufacturing-coming-to-an-end`). These shifts imply that jobs will be shifting too—which means students need to be prepared differently for this emerging economic model.

## Intellectual Property Issues

One of the biggest issues for these technologies is that making copies of physical objects becomes very easy. Intellectual property law will take a while to catch up with 3D printing in particular. How do we think about sharing (or selling) files that are then used to print physical things? When scanning technology gets more readily available, what will the rules be for copying something for your own use, or to sell it, particularly if you then build on the design and change it a lot? If you search on "intellectual property 3D printing," you can see the various discussions out there on these topics.

# Summary

In this chapter, we introduced the concept of a maker and told you how the two authors came to be writing this book from their respective points of view (educator/engineer and hacker). We introduced the different technologies that are explained in depth in later chapters and pointed out that each chapter talks about the technology as well as summarizes what it can be used for, what you need to learn to use it, and how much it costs to get started. We also introduced the educational and broader social implications of these technologies.

# CHAPTER 2

■ ■ ■

# Arduino, Raspberry Pi, and Programming Physical Things

In Chapter 1, we discussed the different ways to think about using hands-on making to learn various subjects. In this chapter we introduce the basic nuts and bolts of commonly used open source electronics (microprocessors, single-board computers, and other components) and suggest paths to get started making things with these technologies.

Some of the components in this chapter (Arduino and Raspberry Pi) can and have been used for extremely sophisticated projects, up to and including an Arduino-controlled small spacecraft (the *Ardusat*, www.ardusat.com). We cover slightly less-ambitious applications of Arduino class microcontrollers in Chapters 4, 6, 7 and 8. An *Arduino* is a microcontroller, which means it is not a whole computer. It is not intended to run multiple programs, drive a screen, and so on. It is meant just to control or monitor one or more devices. *Raspberry Pi* boards, on the other hand, really are full-blown computers and can run (moderate-sized) programs, handle a keyboard, and do many other things.

The big challenge of learning to use these technologies is that you have to learn several things at once. In most cases, you will need to write computer code in an appropriate integrated development environment (IDE) and be able to wire physical circuits, not to mention try to figure out what your system should actually do (Figure 2-1). If you are learning all that at the same time, it can be hard to figure out what is wrong if things do not work.

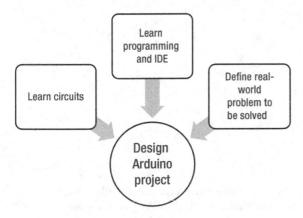

*Figure 2-1.* *Learning Arduino*

This chapter is largely Rich's world, but Joan has jumped in quite a bit to try to make things simpler. Some of this chapter might be a little more detailed than you want at this stage; in a few places, we've given you permission to skip to the next section if you want to. Since this chapter was a very tight blending of both our points of view, we just say "we" in this chapter rather than jump back and forth between our points of view. We are sure you will see a bit of both hacker and educator in the coming sections.

This field has a lot of terminology, and it is difficult to unravel it in an orderly way. So, we may use a word before we define it in depth. When we do that, we will give you a pointer to later in the chapter, so you can hold the term in your mind and see it discussed just a little farther on.

We have tried to minimize jargon as much as possible, but you will see a lot of the words here when you go to buy supplies, enroll in a class, or buy more detailed books, and we did not want to underprepare you, either. At the end of the chapter, we summarize what you need to learn for the different paths through this space and discuss what different key components typically cost so that you can budget as you get started. This is not so much a how-to chapter (we reference other books for that) as it is a why-would-you chapter. We want you to understand what you might do with a Raspberry Pi or Arduino and develop a basis of understanding that will carry you through the later, more specific application-focused chapters.

Some of the other electronics we talk about primarily in Chapter 8 (Circuit Stickers, LightUp) are intended to be used in more traditional classroom or home settings. They are geared toward simpler aspirations such as being able to design a basic circuit safely and as a gateway to more difficult programming.

One way to avoid having to deal with everything at once is to first learn how to write programs in a computer language called (confusingly) Processing. *Processing* is a programming language and development environment that is similar to those used by Arduinos. We introduce that here first as an option.

More typically, though, people learn how to use the technologies in this chapter by creating progressively more complex projects and thus learn incrementally more about each of the aspects. If you have some guidance, this is fine, but if not it can be difficult to know the difference between a "hard" and "easy" project before you embark. Figure 2-2 shows how we walk you through the possible learning paths. First we talk about Processing; then we backtrack a bit to give you some material about circuits so the rest is comprehensible; then finally we move on to the Arduino ecosystem itself. In later chapters we talk more about where else you can go with all this.

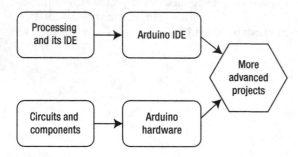

*Figure 2-2.* *The paths we follow in this book*

# Processing and Arduino

One way to avoid trying to go in too many directions at once is to learn some basic commands in the computer language called Processing and then learn how to program an Arduino. Programming an Arduino is very similar to programming in Processing. Processing lets you use computer code to draw things on a screen in an animated way, so it could let students program an animation of a moving lever, for example. Arduinos allow you to control physical objects such as making a simple actual machine move.

## Learning Processing

The Processing computer language is a simple language that is built on Java and is a lot like the C programming language. It is very good for creating animations. To test it out, go to the Processing tutorials page at https://processing.org/tutorials/overview/ and download the Processing IDE.

An IDE is software that allows you to develop and run code. The Processing IDE has a simple interface for writing and running code in the Processing language, and there is a reference for the IDE's interface (https://processing.org/reference/environment/). Once the IDE is installed, paste in some of the examples. Doing so will get you comfortable programming simple animations. If you then want to take the next step up and incorporate physical hardware into your simulations, you would then move to the Arduino IDE, covered in the next section, which is based on Processing's and is laid out very similarly.

# Arduino and Its Ecosystem

Arduino is an open source platform comprised of a family of microcontroller boards and an IDE used for programming them. A microcontroller is an integrated circuit (IC), or computer chip, that includes a processor core, programmable input/output (I/O), and memory used to store the programs and data being used by the processor. To develop a program to run on an Arduino, you install the IDE on a laptop or desktop computer (a Mac, Windows, or Linux machine). Once you have written the code for the Arduino, you send it to the board via USB.

You can download the IDE from the Arduino main page (http://Arduino.cc). Figure 2-3 shows an Arduino and a Raspberry Pi next to each other for scale. The Arduino has been screwed down onto some acrylic next to a *breadboard*, which we talk about later.

*Figure 2-3.* An Arduino (top) mounted with a breadboard, and a Raspberry Pi

An Arduino is essentially a computer built into a single chip that—although much less powerful than a desktop computer, or in most cases even a modern cellphone—is much more powerful than room-sized computers were in the 1970s. The Arduino's IDE is a text editor used for writing programming code to instruct the microcontroller on what to do, with built-in functions for compiling code written by the user into a series of simple instructions that the microcontroller will understand, and for communicating with the microcontroller to copy those instructions to its internal flash memory. An Arduino lets you interact with the physical world in some way that you program. You can program it to read data from a light sensor and start up a light-emitting diode (LED) if it gets dark, for example.

There are a variety of boards available with different shapes, sizes, and capabilities. Some of these are officially endorsed by the Arduino team and carry the Arduino name, though many are based to varying degrees on the open source designs that have been published for one of the official Arduino boards, or on one of the other unofficial boards. These unofficial boards are allowed to use the Arduino designs, but not the Arduino name except to say that they are *Arduino-compatible*. Many have names that include either the *Ardu-* prefix or the *-duino* suffix as shorthand for Arduino-compatible.

Official Arduino boards come in a range of prices starting around $20 (costs in this book are in U.S. dollars), whereas clones start at around $10 for the basic versions. Some counterfeit Arduino boards (ones that use both the open source designs that they are allowed to and the trademarked names and appearance that they are not) can be found for as little as $2.50. Although they usually work, they are likely to include inferior components, and our community discourages people from buying them for this reason—and because counterfeiting is an abuse of the spirit of open source (see Chapter 9).

---

■ **Tip** There are many good books and websites about Arduinos. However, it is important to find some beginner projects first. Just as you would probably not start teaching someone to drive at the Indy 500, it is best to learn these environments with relatively simple projects and work your way up. *Beginning Arduino* by Michael McRoberts, 2nd Edition (Apress, 2013) starts with a project to blink one LED and goes up from there. The Instructables website (www.instructables.com) has many different DIY projects; if you search on "beginner Arduino" or "beginner Raspberry Pi" on the site, you will find appropriate projects (although the definition of "beginner" on that site might be a little aggressive in some cases).

---

Arduinos and Arduino-compatible boards may not have as much computing power as a typical personal computer, but they can do some things a laptop computer cannot. If you want to connect to any electronic devices that are too simple to have a USB port or equivalent interface, your Mac or Windows computer probably will not be able to do it without something like an Arduino that is programmed to translate that data for it. Arduinos are commonly used for a variety of programmable electronics projects, including robots (Chapter 4), drones and other autonomous or semi-autonomous vehicles, 3D printing and other computer-controlled manufacturing (Chapter 3), translating and relaying or logging data from sensors (Chapter 6), wearable electronics (Chapter 7), playful computer interfaces (Chapter 8), and many other tasks that involve linking simple electrical interfaces either with their limited computing power or translating that data into the more sophisticated protocols required by a more powerful computer. Arduinos are also smaller and cheaper than a typical laptop or desktop, and use less power, which makes them better for embedding in projects. (See the next section for more detail.)

An Arduino, unlike a Mac or Windows computer, does not run an operating system or multitask between multiple programs. It has a single program that begins running when it powers up, after a brief pause for the bootloader to check whether you are trying to upload a new program, and continues until the power is switched off. This makes it better for certain operations where precise timing is critical, such as sending commands to move stepper motors. (A stepper motor is a motor which turns a shaft in discrete, precise increments, often used for robotics projects, as opposed to a brushed motor that just turns continuously when a voltage is applied; see the section on stepper motors later in this chapter.) Computer-numerically-controlled (CNC) machine tools like mills and lathes, which use stepper motors to move their tools, are typically built with a computer controller, but using an Arduino-equivalent to control them might work better for precise timing. Open source 3D printers are typically built this way.

All the current Arduino boards use chips made by Atmel Corporation, but there are other similar products. As of this writing, most Arduino boards and their clones use 8-bit microcontrollers from Atmel's AVR family of products, but Microchip Technology's PIC family of products has similar capabilities, and Parallax Inc.'s BASIC Stamp is also comparable. Religious wars are fought on the Internet over which is best, and each product line (as well as each individual product) has its own strengths and weaknesses compared to the rest of the ecosystem. It is our opinion that the ubiquity and beginner-friendliness of the Arduino environment makes it a clear winner, even when the others might be more powerful. Although the others might be better for specific uses, the wealth of free information and shared projects make the Arduino much more useful for those just getting started.

## Interfacing an Arduino with the Real World

The power of an Arduino is that it can interact with the physical world. This section talks in some detail about how that works. Figure 2-4 illustrates the general idea.

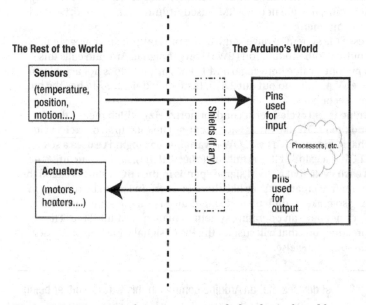

***Figure 2-4.*** *How an Arduino interacts with the physical world*

*Pins* on a computer chip are electrical contacts facing down toward the circuit board that are either soldered directly to the board or connected to a socket that is. Some pins are used to provide power to the chip, but most are used to either take a signal in from something (*input pins*) or send a signal to something (*output pins*). Arduinos process the signals coming in and then send out signals based on what they perceive. This part is a little technical, but if you are doing a first pass through now, we suggest you come back to this section later, because some of the insights here will be important in later chapters that talk about how to use Arduinos and associated technologies in bigger projects. We give you our permission to skip ahead to the section "Circuit Design and Components" if you feel like you do not need to know details right now.

Arduinos have General Purpose Input/Output (GPIO) pins that can be configured either as inputs that can read things like analog voltages and pulse frequencies that various sensors produce, or as outputs that can trigger LEDs, motors, small display modules, and so on. Any of the GPIO pins on an Arduino can be configured for use as either a digital input or a digital output. You can change which mode is being used at any time. Each program generally sets each pin's mode at the beginning and does not change it, though there are exceptions.

People typically think of digital hardware as being binary systems that have just two values (think *on* and *off*). Depending on context, these values might be *true* and *false,* or 1 and 0, or HIGH and LOW. The Arduino has some tricky ways of finessing this to get other values in between to emulate a continuous (analog) signal. You need to do this if you are trying to control a heater to be between 60 and 75 degrees, for example. In this section, we talk about this for output and input pins, which are handled a bit differently. This topic is, of necessity, a bit complex, and we are just giving the general flavor here of what is possible and what is easy and hard.

## Output Pins

If a pin is being used as an output pin, it will be set either to LOW (0 volts, which is known as *ground* or GND), representing the value 0 or *false*, or *HIGH,* representing the value 1 or *true*. Setting pins to HIGH means the Arduino raises the pin to its *logic voltage*, either 5V or 3.3V, usually referred to as VCC for historical reasons. In either case, the amount of current that can travel through the pin is limited. Typically it is around 40 milliamps, but may be less for some, like the newer ARM-based Arduino boards. To drive loads that need more power requires additional components.

We mentioned that is possible to finesse the system to have some of the pins output an analog signal. They do this by using a technique called pulse width modulation (PWM) on the signal. Arduino calls this function `analogWrite`, which allows it to put out a value between 0 and 1. The Arduino does not actually put out a lower voltage (you can't set a pin on a 5V Arduino to put out 2.5V). Instead, it quickly switches the pin between 0 and 1 several hundred times per second.

A typical PWM frequency for an Arduino is 490 cycles per second, or hertz (Hz), which means that for any PWM setting, the pin will go HIGH and then LOW 490 times each second. The total time of each cycle is fixed, but the proportion of that cycle that it spends HIGH vs. LOW is variable. `analogWrite` uses a scale of 0–255, so a value of 0 is fully off (100% LOW), a value of 255 is fully on (100% HIGH), and a value of 127 is 50% HIGH, 50% LOW. The percentage of each cycle that a PWM signal spends in the HIGH state is called the *duty cycle*. Although you can write a program that creates pulses like these of a certain length by running in a loop (a method called *bit-banging*), doing so makes it difficult to do anything else at the same time. This is particularly true because an Arduino does not have an operating system to manage multitasking. The microcontroller is equipped with hardware functions that will sustain the PWM signal while the processor does other things until the pin is told to do something else.

---

■ **Note**   Why not output an analog voltage? Most devices that an Arduino controls in this way are either being powered directly by the pin (if they can be powered by the Arduino's logic-level voltage and use a low enough current for the pin to source, such as an LED) or are having their power switched off and on by the Arduino's digital signal through a device that allows it to switch higher voltage and current, such as a that required to run a brushed DC motor. In either of these cases, the response to a decreased voltage is less linear than the response to a decreased duty cycle. An LED will not light up at all if the voltage is too low, and does not rise in brightness proportionally to the voltage of its supply, but by turning it off and on at a speed much faster than the human eye can perceive, the apparent brightness will be reduced. Likewise, if you want to control the speed of a brushed (not stepper) motor's rotation precisely, you can make that speed proportional to the duty cycle of a signal turning the motor power either full on or full off. Common motor drivers controlled this way are digital devices that, like the Arduino itself, do not even have the ability to drive an analog voltage. This process works better than using an analog voltage for a variety of reasons.

---

Only certain pins have hardware PWM capability, though any pin can be used for bit-banging, which is often called *soft PWM* because it is a software implementation of the protocol rather than the built-in hardware implementation. Other protocols that are not natively supported in hardware can be implemented in software, such as Pulse Frequency Modulation (PFM), in which information is encoded as the frequency of a series of pulses, rather than its duty cycle.

# Input Pins

If a pin is configured as an input, it will not try to provide a HIGH or LOW voltage digital signal. Instead, it will stop pulling strongly in one direction or the other (a state called *floating*) and allow whatever is connected to it to determine the voltage. If the voltage is close to the Arduino's logic voltage, a digitalRead will tell you that it is HIGH, and if it's close to ground, it will read as LOW. digitalRead always returns one of these two responses, and there is a zone of uncertainty in the middle where the output is less predictable. Therefore, the circuit should have a voltage that is close to one of these values, but never higher than the logic voltage level or lower than ground.

Certain pins can be used to read analog voltages between these two values with analogRead, and unlike analogWrite, the chip's analog-to-digital converter (ADC) actually does use analog voltages, which it converts into digital values. ADC readings have a range of 0–1023, so on a 5V Arduino board, 5V reads as 1023, ground reads as 0, and 2.5V reads as 511.

The Arduino's chip has another way to interface with other components. Although many simple components are controlled by switching power on and off, many components useful as sensors simply reduce a voltage by a variable amount relative to what they are sensing. Some components are smarter and do some processing on their own. Several data protocols have been designed to allow these simple devices to talk back and forth. These are similar to protocols like USB that a PC uses to talk to other devices, but they are simpler and slower because they are designed for devices with minimal processing power.

The microcontrollers used for Arduino boards have hardware implementations of *Inter-Integrated Circuit* (I²C) and *Serial Peripheral Interface* (SPI) for communication with other components. They also typically use the RS-232 protocol to talk to another chip that translates a computer's USB connection for programming the Arduino and for communicating with the program running on it. Some newer Arduinos are built with microcontrollers that have native hardware support for the USB protocol as well.

# Shields

An Arduino on its own is not good for much. Most Arduinos have a single LED connected to one of their digital outputs that they can turn on and off. The canonical first project on an Arduino is to make this LED blink to test that the hardware and software work, but a single blinking LED is not very useful on its own. Doing more useful things requires connecting to other devices. You can do this by attaching wires to the individual sockets on the board, but many projects are common enough that people have designed other circuit boards to connect to the Arduino for that purpose. In general electronics terminology, such a board is known as a *daughterboard*—an ancillary board that connects to a main board, or *motherboard*, to extend its functionality or capabilities.

Most Arduino boards share a common layout for the I/O pins, and there is a special type of daughterboard known as an Arduino *shield* that matches this layout. A shield is designed to plug in to the top of an Arduino board (look back at Figure 2-4 for a visual). Shields use all their pins to mechanically join it to the Arduino board, though some pins may not be electrically connected. A shield typically has at least one chip that is either a sensor or that changes the Arduino's output. For instance, it might be switching higher voltages or more current so that the Arduino can control motors, brighter lights than the single basic LED described in the previous paragraph, speakers, or anything that is not directly compatible with the logic-level signals that the microcontroller puts out.

Some shields do some processing of their own and use low-level protocols and translate signals for the Arduino in the same way an Arduino can translate them for a PC's USB interface, but most simply use an analog voltage or a pattern of digital pulses. A shield may do more than one of these things, such as a motor driver that allows the Arduino to control the power going to a motor. The motor in turn has an encoder that returns one or more pulses to one of the Arduino's inputs every time the motor completes a rotation so that the Arduino can sense how fast the motor is turning. Each shield generally does not use all the Arduino's pins for its own function, but because a shield covers up all the I/O pins, it typically has another set of the same connectors on the top so that the rest of the pins will be accessible. If you have two shields that do not use any of the same I/O pins, you can usually stack one on top of the other and use both at the same time. There are also several *proto shields* available that simply have space for you to build your own circuit, either on a breadboard (discussed later in this chapter) attached to the shield or soldered to a similar grid of holes.

For example, the ArduSensor Shield (see www.qtechknow.com for more) shown in Figure 2-5 connects to an Arduino and gives a user the ability to connect up to four sensors (breakout boards that detect flex, force, light, and temperature).

***Figure 2-5.*** *A shield (courtesy of Qtechknow.com)*

## Stepper Motors

Arduinos are often used to control stepper motors, which are discussed in detail in Chapter 4. For example, 3D printers (Chapter 3) typically use a modified Arduino-compatible controller. A stepper motor is designed to hold something in a fixed position. By cycling the polarities of the two or more electromagnetic windings, the motor transitions from one position to the next, turning the shaft a bit more with each transition to make it rotate. These polarity changes must be precisely timed to ensure smooth movement of the motor. A microcontroller like the one an Arduino board uses is designed for that type of application, so although it is a slower processor than you would find in a PC, it is doing less and its timing is more predictable, making it better suited to the job.

# Circuit Design and Components

Understanding electronics requires that you also understand a little bit of the physics behind the hardware. What is voltage? What is current? What about resistance? These measurements describe the movement of electrons through a conductor.

*Voltage*, measured in *volts* (symbolized by the letter V), is a pressure that causes electrons to move through a conductor, like water being pumped through a closed loop of tubes with something that resists the flow somewhere in the system, such as a valve. The pump pulls water in, creating a low pressure at its input, and pushes it out of its output end, creating a higher pressure. When you connect these high- and low-pressure areas, water flows from the high-pressure area to the low-pressure area. A greater pressure through a pipe causes more water to flow from one end to the other (or the same amount of water to flow faster), and a greater voltage causes more flow of electrons.

*Current*, measured in *amperes* (symbolized by the letter A), or *amps* for short, is the flow of electrons. *Resistance*, measured in ohms (symbolized by the Greek letter omega, $\Omega$) resists the flow of current, like a valve resisting the flow of water. If the valve is mostly closed, the resistance is high, and very little water will flow. But an open valve is like a low-resistance path that allows more current to flow. The relationship of these three terms is calculated using Ohm's law: voltage equals current times resistance.

In order for current to flow, a circuit must have at least two different *voltage potentials* (levels of pressure) so that there can be a voltage or *potential difference* across the *load* (whatever the circuit is powering). These voltage potentials have very little meaning except in relation to one another, and the zero point of the measurement is arbitrary. By convention, one voltage level in a circuit, generally the lowest, is specified as 0V (zero volts), and all other voltages are measured in reference to that one. This reference point is known as *ground*, which is not to be confused with the *earth ground* connected to the third prong of a wall socket.

# Resistors

To build your own Arduino projects, you will need some additional components. Which components you need depends entirely on your project, but you are likely to need some components more than others. The most basic electronic component, and the one your project is more likely to require than any other, is a resistor. Resistors are available in a wide variety of resistances, but assortments are available with all the values that you will need for most projects. LEDs are also very common components, and you are likely to want a few for your projects, especially as you are learning. Each LED should be connected through a resistor to limit the current running through it, and to build a circuit with multiple components wired to one another, you will want something to connect them. The best way to assemble these simple, experimental circuits is to use a breadboard and jumper wires.

---

■ **Tip**  In your Arduino projects, you might need to use breadboards or terminal blocks. A *breadboard* is a flat piece of plastic with rows of holes in it. There are conductors inside linking groups of those holes together in a specific pattern. (In Figure 2-4, the back has residue on it from when it was glued to a backing board, like the breadboard in Figure 2-2.) You can poke two components and/or jumper wires into the same group of holes to create an electrical connection and hold them in place. If you make a mistake, want to change your circuit design, or decide that you are finished with that project and want to reuse the components for another one, you can easily pull them back out of the holes. This is much easier and less permanent than soldering your components in place, but for projects you want to keep, a soldered board is preferable. Some suppliers, like Adafruit, sell printed circuit boards (PCBs) with holes and connections matching a breadboard, making it easy to transfer your breadboard circuit to a more permanent medium. Sometimes you will need to connect bigger wires than will fit in a breadboard, or it will be easier to split out the wiring and connect them through a terminal block (Figure 2-5). *Terminal blocks* are intended to be more permanent connectors than the temporary ones in a breadboard, but are still less permanent than soldering.

---

**Figure 2-6.** *(L) Front of a breadboard; (R) back, with backing pulled off*

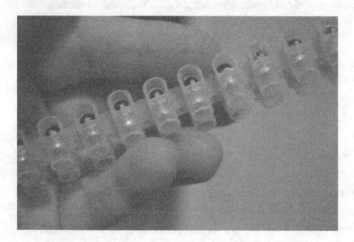

**Figure 2-7.** *A terminal block*

Resistors have many uses. The most common things you will use them for in conjunction with an Arduino are as a pull-up or pull-down, as a voltage divider, or for current limiting. A *pull-up* or *pull-down* uses a fairly "strong" resistor (one with a high resistance), almost always at least 1 kiloohm (a kiloohm is 1000 ohms, abbreviated kW or K) and usually 10–200K so that when there is a voltage across it, very little current will flow. When connected to an input pin, a pull-up resistor connects the pin weakly to VCC until something connects it more strongly to a different voltage by using a lower resistance. A pull-down resistor does the same, but pulls the voltage down to GND instead of up to VCC. This prevents an input pin from floating, keeping it in a known state until it is activated by another device.

What happens if you have a pull-up and a pull-down connected to the same pin? When this happens, current flows between VCC and GND, and the voltage drops across each resistor. The total voltage dropped is equal to VCC, but each resistor drops a different amount of that voltage, which is inversely proportional to its proportion of the total resistance. This is called a *voltage divider*. In a 5V circuit with an 82K resistor connected to VCC and an 18K resistor connected to GND (for a total resistance of 100K), the point where these resistors connect to each other measures 18% of VCC, or 0.9V. The same would happen if you used an 82Ω resistor and an 18Ω resistor, but 1000 times as much current would run through the resistors, being wasted as heat. Without a pin connected to the center, these two resistors would function in the circuit just like a single resistor with a resistance equal to the sum of the two resistors.

A *potentiometer* is a special type of resistor with a third conductor in the center that can slide along the resistor to connect to it in different places, usually attached to a knob. With VCC connected to one end, GND to the other, and an analog pin at the center, you can turn the knob and use the analog pin to read the position of the potentiometer's knob.

# LEDs

An LED is a component that lights up when a current runs through it. Diodes have the unique property of a forward voltage drop, a specific amount of voltage that they will block, which depends on the type of semiconductor used to make them. Beyond its forward voltage drop, an LED has very little resistance, and it may allow enough current to damage the LED. If the LED is controlled by an output pin, this current can damage the microcontroller, too. Because each resistor in series increases the total resistance, a resistor can be added in series to limit the current flowing through a load. How much resistance is required depends on the voltage that it needs to drop (supply voltage minus the LED's forward voltage drop) and the desired current. Figure 5-6 shows a typical LED and resistor side by side.

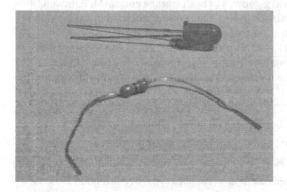

***Figure 2-8.*** *An LED (top) and a garden-variety resistor*

# Power Supplies and Batteries

Arduino circuits need to be powered somehow. Often an Arduino is plugged into a USB port on a laptop and gets its power from there. Arduino boards also include voltage regulators that can be used to power them from a battery or a *wall wart*-style power supply.

---

■ **Tip**   Tools like Fritzing (www.fritzing.org) and 123D Circuits (www.circuits.io) allow you to design your circuit as a virtual breadboard or a circuit schematic and then turn them into a design for a custom circuit board. Once you have a circuit board design, you can look for online services that will fabricate your PCB and send it to you, so you can solder your components on.

---

# Raspberry Pi

A Raspberry Pi is a small computer that can run moderately sized programs. It is the most well known of a class of devices known as single-board computers. A Raspberry Pi is about the same physical size as some Arduino boards, but it has a lot more processing power. Unlike the 8-bit microcontrollers from the ATmega family on most Arduino boards, which typically run at 16 Mhz, a Raspberry Pi has a 32-bit ARM processor running at least 700 Mhz, making its performance roughly equivalent to a desktop PC from the late 1990s.

ARM chips like the one that runs a Raspberry Pi are also found in smartphones, tablets, smart televisions, and television set-top boxes. Unlike these devices, a Raspberry Pi does have a few general purpose input and output pins, but they are not quite as versatile as those on an Arduino. Unlike an Arduino, the Raspberry Pi is intended to be used with an HDMI monitor and a USB keyboard and mouse like a desktop PC, though there are uses for a Rasberry Pi that require neither.

Single-board computers like the Raspberry Pi usually run the Linux operating system, an open source PC operating system based on Unix. Linux is free, relatively easy to modify, and capable of running on a wide variety of processors. It also has the advantage that graphical desktop interfaces comparable to those of Windows and Mac OS X, are available but optional parts of the operating system. Whereas the modern versions of those operating systems require several gigabytes of both storage and RAM, lightweight distributions of Linux are available that fit into a few megabytes or less. One commonly used Linux version optimized for the Pi is called Raspian, which is available for free from www.raspbian.org.

Why would you use a Raspberry Pi instead of a desktop? In a word, cost. A Pi runs about $35 as of this writing, and can perform many of the functions of a minimalist desktop. If you want a utter bare-bones computer that can run several programs at a time with a real operating system, the Pi is appropriate for you.

---

■ **Tip**    There are a lot of books about using Raspberry Pi. Some focus on how to connect it to other components or sensor networks (along with an Arduino), and others focus on the Linux programming aspect of it. This is a rapidly expanding field, and a web search at your favorite online bookseller should reveal a lot of options. More generally, the Raspberry Pi Foundation's website at www.raspberrypi.org is a good place to get more information.

---

# Starting More Simply

If all this seems too intimidating and complex, there are simpler packages designed for beginners that avoid wiring altogether. Some have resistors and other components on stickers (such as Circuit Stickers, circuitstickers.com), which you can then connect by drawing around them with a copper ribbon or conductive-ink pen. Other systems enclose the components in sturdier plastic packages and have magnetic connections, like LittleBits (http://littlebits.cc) and LightUp (www.LightUP.io). LightUp has an app that allows learners to take a picture of their magnetically connected circuits and get feedback on whether they are connected correctly or not. Their circuits can connect to an Arduino, too. Chapter 8 discusses these products further, with other innovative interface and augmented reality products.

# Things You Need To Learn

As you have gathered if you have read this chapter, learning to use these devices is not a simple process. However, the flip side of this is that you (and your students, if you are planning on using these technologies to teach) will learn a lot in the process. There are several ways to go about scaling up. Probably the commonest way is to start with very simple projects that require you to learn a bit about each of the aspects as you go. (See the upcoming "Where to Learn Online" section for more on where to learn about these technologies.) However, if you want to build a full-up curriculum, probably the way to go about it would be to teach some circuit basics first, followed by a bit about how computer coding works in C (the language used in Arduino programming) or something similar. If you want to cut to the chase, however, and jump right in to Arduino projects, buying a kit that comes with an instruction book might be the way to go.

---

■ **Tip**   It is tempting to find a project that you want to do and to try to work backwards from that to figure out what to learn. This can be a good approach in the long run, but you need to figure out how to break out some simpler pieces to start with to build up your knowledge in an orderly, bite-sized way. This sounds obvious, but we have found most people starting out see a spectacular project and want to start there without any first steps. You may need to play scales a little bit before you try that concerto, but by all means use your big goal as an inspiration and guide!

---

## Adult Supervision

The single best safety device is a competent adult who keeps an eye on beginners of any age. If you are an adult beginner and in charge of teaching children, our suggestion is that, to paraphrase the airline safety video line, you attend to yourself before trying to help others. As general good practices, use appropriate eye protection, have a fire extinguisher that works, and be sure you know how to use it. Avoid loose and/or flammable clothing and ventilate work areas well. Read manufacturer's suggestions for use of any particular device or process.

## Learning About Circuits

One good entry point into this space is to learn about the basics of circuit design. You can do that by playing with an Arduino project, or you can buy one of the circuit-sticker or other simplified alternatives. The intent of the Arduino itself was for it to be a good beginner platform, so there are some limits on how low you can go first.

## Learning to Code

Using processors requires that you learn how to write code. As noted at the beginning of this chapter, you can learn Processing and its environment as a step toward Arduinos. Or you can start out teaching yourself C or one of the similar languages in its family such as C++, Java, or Python. Unfortunately, there are no shortcuts in learning to code, but a good way to get started is to do progressively harder projects, starting with having your computer print out "Hello World."

As you saw in Chapter 1, Joan and Rich both came into this sphere from the software side (Joan pretty much has stayed there, learning enough about the hardware to get by). Depending on the types of projects you want to do, learning to code or at least becoming computer-literate is the first gateway you will need to pass. There are many learn-to-code classes out there, both in person and online; you might check your local community calendar to see if one is being offered at an appropriate level, or ask at a local makerspace. You will need to load some sort of development environment onto your Mac, Windows, or Linux computer to get started.

## Learning to Solder

If you want to have projects around for a while, you probably want to advance away from projects on a breadboard (which are pretty fragile) and solder your projects together. You can try to find a "learn to solder" class at a makerspace or community college nearby, or if that is not possible, do what Rich did: learn from online tutorials and a lot of practice.

If you go that route, though, be sure you get a soldering iron that has temperature control (a dial for temperature, not wattage) because otherwise you will have no temperature regulation, which makes it a lot more difficult to keep the iron from damaging components or itself. Solder contains lead, which can be dangerous, and there are various opinions out there about how old you need to be to solder. Obviously, you should not eat and solder at the same time, and you should ventilate the area (there are some soldering fans with a filter made specifically to help manage solder fumes). Eye protection is always a good idea during any project.

## Electrical Safety

The electronics in this chapter are designed to run at a low voltage. However, any system should be unplugged and unpowered (even from a computer) when you are working on it. If some part of the system is ultimately plugged into a wall, never assume that everything is at 5V. Be careful to avoid getting the circuits wet.

It also helps to be neat. A rat's nest of wires is never a good thing, besides being hard to debug. Plan your project ahead and think about your wiring before you start to hook it all up.

## Where to Learn Online

Community colleges and makerspaces are probably the best bet for a class in the near term; you might also try your public library, since libraries in many municipalities are exploring adding hackerspaces. If you prefer to learn on your own versus taking a class, online Arduino forums are good places to start , Check out http://forum.Arduino.cc, letsmakerobots.com, instructables.com, and hackaday.com. The vendors noted in the next section have forums, too.

# How Much Does Getting Started Cost?

The price of getting started depends somewhat on what you are doing. If you buy a kit from Sparkfun (sparkfun.com), Adafruit (adafruit.com), or the Makershed (makershed.com), you can get started for $50–$100 for one kit. Be sure you buy a kit that includes the processor you want to learn (Arduino or Raspberry Pi, as the case may be). Some starter kits include everything *but* the processor, assuming that you bought it elsewhere. The software is open source and free—but you might budget for a few books, manuals, and add-on shields as well. If you decide to also learn to solder, you can find beginner kits for that too. You might get an experienced friend or recommendations in a forum when you start to buy this next level of tool. Later chapters discuss projects that use these basic processors, and we give you a general idea of costs for beginner projects in each end-of-chapter section.

# Summary

In this chapter, you learned about the Arduino and Raspberry Pi ecosystems and how to get started learning how to use them. We noted that Arduinos are particularly good for taking signals from sensors or controlling motors, LEDs, and other physical objects. A Raspberry Pi, on the other hand, is a small but full-function computer on a credit-card-sized board. Using them requires learning a bit about circuits, computer code, and your application. The chapter concluded with some notes about how to acquire that knowledge. Chapters 3 through 8 will now talk about applying these technologies, or similar ones, in applications ranging from 3D printing to electronics-infused clothing items.

# CHAPTER 3

■ ■ ■

# 3D Printing

Chapter 2 covered low-cost electronics that can sense the world around them and control objects that move. There is another side to this makertech movement: the ability to create just about any physical shape that will fit on the build platform of a 3D printer. If you combine these two sides, you get the capabilities for robots, drones, wearable tech, and the very low-cost science fieldwork described in later chapters in this book.

In this chapter, we talk about what 3D printing is, what varieties are appropriate for consumer use, and what is involved in using a 3D printer. We also get into materials you can use, what you have to learn, and a bit about the difference between these tools and traditional shop-class machine tools. Figure 3-1 shows a typical consumer-level 3D printer along with a roll of *filament*—the feed stock used to make a 3D-printed object.

***Figure 3-1.*** *A small consumer 3D printer*

The two of us worked together at a small 3D printer company for a while, and so are used to finishing each others' sentences on this topic. First, we introduce 3D printing and give you a sense of what it is. Next, we give you an overview of the field and then narrow it down to the consumer-level printers that you are likely to buy. Finally, we talk through the workflow of actually using one of these machines, which unfortunately is still more complex than we would like.

# What Is 3D Printing?

A *3D printer* is a device that creates an object by building it up one layer at a time. The materials a 3D printer uses vary from plastics to chocolate to concrete. In many ways, the *printer* part of the name is misleading; there really is not a lot in common with conventional printing. Joan prefers to use cooking as a metaphor, or you can use the more technical term—*additive manufacturing*—which is somewhat more descriptive of what the printers are actually doing.

## Additive vs. Subtractive Manufacturing

A lot of conventional manufacturing (and old-fashioned shop class) is *subtractive*. That means that you start off with a big block of material (wood, metal, or anything else), and a machine tool shaves off pieces to create what you want. Additive manufacturing techniques like 3D printing instead add material a little at a time to create something.

There is a third set of manufacturing techniques, such as pouring concrete (although there is now concrete 3D printing, as we describe later), sculpting clay, metal-bending, or casting metal, that do not fit neatly into either the additive or subtractive category. In those cases, a tool, such as a mold or form, is used to shape a material. A malleable material is poured or pushed into the tool, and it conforms to the tool before hardening. Alternatively, as with a metal bending tool or the hands of someone shaping a clay pot, a harder material can be selectively forced into a new shape. Some of these techniques can be used in conjunction with 3D-printed parts to enable very fast prototyping.

A 3D printer starts off with an empty build platform and piles up material onto that platform one layer at a time. To figure out what should be in each layer, software takes a computer model and slices it into very thin vertical layers, like a precooked sliced ham set on end. Then, a computer controls a robotic head that creates one layer at a time in a variety of ways, depending on the type of 3D printer.

Figure 3-2 shows a visualization of layers in software used to create models for a 3D printer (MatterControl, discussed later in this chapter), and Figure 3-3 shows the part being printed.

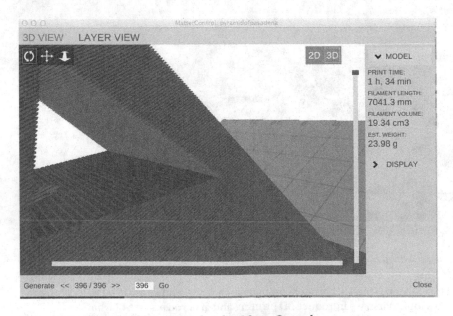

*Figure 3-2. 3D-printed layers simulated in MatterControl*

*Figure 3-3. 3D printed layers in reality*

## Does 3D Printing Live Up to Its Hype?

You have probably heard a lot in the news lately about 3D printers and the many applications of the technology. How big an advance is this technology, really? And what new things will it enable? We think it is unfortunate that the technology has been so heavily hyped and suggested for a variety of applications where it might not be as good as incumbent techniques, because this misdirected hype distracts from the areas where it really is transformative.

3D printers are tools. You do not see people writing breathless papers about the crescent wrench and how many applications it has, because wrenches (or spanners, if you are from the eastern side of the Atlantic divide) have been around a long time. But when a new tool comes along, there is a period when things that were not really possible before become possible. We are in this phase with 3D printing, which is genuinely transformative for the following applications in particular:

- *Learning how to make physical things*: Using a 3D printer is a good gateway to using traditional machine tools. Although it is possible to burn yourself, they are a lot less intimidating than traditional shop-class machine tools.

- *Product prototyping*: It is now a lot cheaper and easier to prototype a physical product. In the past, either SLA or SLS printers (described later in this chapter) were used to make fragile, very expensive prototypes; or a prototype might have been cut out of foam board. It is now feasible to have a cheap printer at each office of a design firm and avoid shipping around physical models and prototypes altogether. Colleagues can literally email around a design.

- *Design iteration*: If it is easy and cheap to prototype, then it is also easy and cheap to try out different designs. This can allow for a more "quick and dirty" style of design, rather than perfecting a design before making a (formerly time-consuming) prototype.

- *Visualizing complex abstract concepts*: The ability to make a complex shape at low cost means that mathematicians, scientists, and engineers can print out a 3D representation of a complex shape to help with insights beyond those possible on a screen.

- *Custom items*: Medical, fashion, and other unique or small-run manufacturing items become more economical with 3D printing.

- *Biomedicine*: It is possible to lay up complex tissues involving scaffolding structures and living cells. This area is just beginning to come into its own.

People often ask us what a 3D printer is good for. This is always a slightly weird question for any tool. (Answer: what are you trying to make?) A better question is to ask what sorts of things they are *not* good for. 3D printing is still pretty slow (it takes hours to make a print of any size), and so at the moment it is not appropriate to make more than a few hundred of something. Beyond that, you want to think about mass-manufacturing techniques, like some sort of molding.

## Types of 3D Printers

3D printers have been around since about 1984, when Chuck Hall developed the first 3D printer based on using a robotic mechanism to control a laser. The laser was used to solidify a tiny area in a vat of liquid resin, thus creating an object out of the resin. This technique is known as stereolithography (abbreviated SLA) and was first commercialized by 3D Systems in 1989. Since then, other technologies have evolved. This section categorizes them by the type of feed stock they use: powders, resins, filament, or other things.

## Printers that Use Powders

Many commercial grade printers use one of a set of technologies that will we lump into a category we call *selective binding*. In these printers, fine powder (such as gypsum, nylon, or even metal) is fused either by using heat to *sinter* or melt the fine particles to fuse them together, or by depositing a binding agent (a glue or solvent) to make them adhere.

Typically, the process starts with an empty build platform, which is coated with a fine layer of the working powder. A print head (usually consisting of either a lens and set of mirrors to focus a laser onto the surface of the powder or an inkjet for depositing binding agents onto it) fuses one layer's worth of the material, sometimes laying down ink to color the object at the same time. Then another thin layer is laid up on top of this. The process continues from there. Once the print is done, the user has to dig it out of a bed of powder and vacuum off the powder. This method generally produces porous objects, and some sort of sealing or post-processing is often needed to make the part stronger.

Selective Laser Sintering (SLS) printers work this way, as do direct metal laser sintering (DMLS) and most full-color printers. Generally speaking, powder-based printers are not going to be suitable for consumer (home or school) use because of cost, the mess, and the hazards of the extremely fine powder. Printing metal is complex and for some technologies requires filling the build chamber with argon or nitrogen.

## Printers that Use Resin

Another class of printers operates by a means we call *selective solidification*, in which a liquid is selectively turned into a solid, typically by using ultraviolet light to catalyze polymerization. SLA (described earlier) was the first example of this, and the Form 1+ printer is a lower-cost example now on the market. DLP digital light projection (DLP) printers use a projector to harden an entire layer at once. There are now several DLP printers aimed at the consumer market (a search for "DLP 3D printer" on your favorite search engine should give a list). The resin is expensive and cures (hardens) on exposure to sunlight. While liquid, it is an irritant and flammable and has to be handled carefully—think chemistry lab issues more than shop class ones.

## Printers that Use Filament

This brings us to the commonest type of consumer printer, in which the machine extrudes material in a sticky, viscous form through a moving nozzle before allowing it to harden. Consistent with our other classifications, we might call this *selective deposition*—depositing material only where you want it to create an object. The most common form of selective deposition involves pushing a thermoplastic filament through a heated nozzle. Because the filament is typically wound on a spool or in a cartridge, the materials are pretty easy to handle (see Figure 3-4). This type of printer (often called FFF, for fused filament fabrication) is the most practical for average educational applications. There are many FFF printers available at or below the $1,000 price point in the United States, and this combination of convenience and relatively low cost is why filament-based printers dominate the home and educational market.

***Figure 3-4.*** *Filament spools*

Many FFF printers come from a design heritage referred to as *RepRap*, short for self-*rep*licating *rap*id prototyping machine. For a long time, most 3D-printing technology was covered by patents. When those patents expired, Adrian Bowyer decided it would be interesting to design a 3D printer that could (mostly) print itself. He printed the first one on his commercial machine, and then made the designs for the parts freely available online. People who "evolved" the design in turn posted their new designs, and progress has been pretty rapid since. We describe these printers in detail shortly in "The Consumer 3D Printer" section.

## Hybrid Technologies

A number of technologies don't fit neatly into one of these categories. There are printers that use sheets of flat material like paper that they cut (subtractive manufacturing) into shapes and then adhere to one another additively. In some new processes, a solution is deposited onto a powder that doesn't bind it together, but prepares it for another process by selectively either promoting or inhibiting a sintering process that occurs later. There are even machines that spray powder, use a laser to fuse it on contact, and then use a cutting tool to subtractively machine fine surfaces—all in one very expensive machine. Such hybrid technologies constitute a rapidly developing area, and new categories may emerge in the coming years.

---

■ **Tip** There are many resources that go into far more detail about the types of printers and their applications than we have room for here. Wikipedia is a good place to start (http://en.wikipedia.org/wiki/3D_printing). There is also a RepRap wiki that discusses the ongoing open source efforts (www.reprap.org). There is a rather spectacular photo gallery of printers linked to the RepRap page. MIT's *Technology Review* online (www.technologyreview.com) is a good place to search for clearly written and unbiased descriptions of advances on the higher-tech end, and academic researchers sometimes publish their work in the open-access scientific journal PLOS One (www.plosone.org). There are also several trade websites to choose from, such as 3D Printer World (www.3dprinterworld.com) and 3Ders (www.3ders.org).

---

## Printers That Use Other Materials

Nearly every day it seems there is a news article about a new type of 3D printer that prints chocolate, sugar, pizza, body organs, concrete, or paper using one of the techniques mentioned earlier or some new combination of techniques. There are too many kinds to be able to go into detail here, but a little searching around technology websites and magazines will reveal many types. If you are interested in the medical applications, type "bioprinting" into your favorite search engine to get started.

# The Consumer 3D Printer

We assume for the rest of the book that you are using a filament-based 3D printer and refer to these printers as just *3D printers* going forward. This section talks about how these printers work and discusses some decisions you need to make if you decide to purchase one.

## Hardware

A filament-based 3D printer is a robot, designed to do a few repetitive tasks very precisely. Typical consumer machines can print features around 1 millimeter in size. Usually, these machines extrude plastic from a nozzle around a third to half a millimeter in diameter, which limits the smallest feature that can be drawn in the plane of the platform to about twice the nozzle diameter. In the vertical direction, each layer height can be less than this (down to tens of microns for the better precision printers). Fraction-of-a-millimeter precision is good enough for many applications at any rate.

These printers are often tethered to a Windows or Mac computer but also have an onboard microprocessor to control the printer's mechanisms—often, this is an Arduino processor (Chapter 2) or something similar in capability. Some printers can run off an SD card, or you can configure a Raspberry Pi (Chapter 2) to act as the host for many printers.

The microprocessor controls three or more stepper motors to drive the axes in three dimensions. For many printers, like the one pictured in the figures in this chapter, the build platform moves in one or more directions. Another stepper motor turns a drive gear that pushes filament into a heater. The molten plastic is thus forced to extrude from a precision nozzle. Figures 3-5 and 3-6 are a pair of closeups of a 3D print in progress. The nozzle is the small conical piece right above the part being printed.

*Figure 3-5.* A 3D printer in action

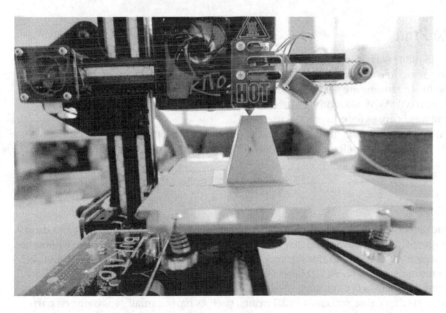

*Figure 3-6.* Later, that same print, now from the front

# Firmware

Each 3D printer has to run control software on its microprocessor to process the commands that direct the movement of the printer's mechanical parts. The software that runs on the microprocessor to do this is called *firmware*. Many open source 3D printers run a variant of a program called Marlin. If you buy a printer, your manufacturer will tell you whether your printer is open source or not and provide details about your firmware that you may need to know.

# Using a Consumer 3D Printer

A 3D printer is closer to a machine tool than to a regular paper 2D printer. The use of the word *printer* is in many ways unfortunate, because it creates unrealistic expectations about how easy it is to use. To make an object on a 3D printer, you need to use a workflow with three steps.

First, you need to somehow get a 3D model of your object, either by creating it yourself, 3D-scanning something, or downloading a model created by someone else. Next, you need to take that model and convert it into 3D-printer commands with one of the software programs available for this process. Finally, those commands need to be loaded onto the printer.

These steps vary some from printer to printer. The programs we discuss in this section run on a Windows or Mac machine (or in some cases, on Linux). They do not run on the printers themselves. You are creating files that will then be downloaded onto a printer. Some 3D printers use software that hides this intermediate file from the user. Most offer some utility for visualizing this data, which is sometimes known as a *toolpath*. Visualization allows the user to verify that the object will be printed as expected before beginning the (usually hours-long) printing process.

## Creating a Model to Print

You can create a 3D model in many ways. First, you can use just about any 3D computer-aided design (CAD) software. Some CAD packages are free and very simple, like Tinkercad, maintained by Autodesk at www.tinkercad.com. At the other extreme are very complex and expensive engineering packages, like Solidworks (www.solidworks.com). As of this writing, Autodesk has a whole suite of packages for various levels of user and is offering free licenses for educational use.

The main requirement for creating a 3D print is that you need to have a program that generates a file in STL format. (STL stands for Surface Tessellation Language or STereoLithography, depending on whom you ask).

### Beginner Packages

Two good free beginner packagers are the already-mentioned Tinkercad, which allows you to drag and drop simple basic shapes, and OpenSCAD (www.openscad.org), an open source programming interface where the user writes code to create objects. The two programs are very different, so you might try both to see what you think. Tinkercad has video tutorials, and OpenSCAD has a very good downloadable manual with examples.

The architectural program SketchUp is often suggested, too. However, our experience has been that SketchUp tends to create objects that cause problems in 3D prints, such as having small gaps between parts of a model or overlaps that have two parts occupying the same virtual space (an impossibility in real, physical space that confuses the printer's software). Software later in the 3D printing workflow (see "The Next Step: Slicing" later in this chapter) is getting better at handling these "non-watertight" and "non-manifold" 3D models, but the results can be unpredictable and require cleanup in yet more software packages.

## More Advanced Packages

Higher-end (more capable and more expensive) software packages tend to split into "artist" and "engineer" camps. Generally speaking, the artist-oriented software systems are aimed at drawing organic, curved things: creatures, people, and so on. Engineering systems tend to be aimed at making it easy to create parts that are built to precise, numerical specifications and that have to fit in with other parts. Both groups need to be able to do both types of model, but if you are doing mostly one or the other, you should consider this if you are embarking on learning a package from scratch.

For artists, the open source Blender program (www.blender.org) is a program that users can and do use to create animated feature films. Blender has a big community of collaborative users, but Blender has the drawback that nothing else is particularly like it, so learning Blender doesn't help you pick up something else later on. Maya (www.autodesk.com/products/maya/overview) and Z-Brush (www.pixologic.com/zbrush) are common (expensive) animation-oriented programs that generate either STL files or files that can be converted to STL.

Engineers can purchase Solidworks (expensive), try one of the Autodesk 123 options, or perhaps try the open source program FreeCAD (available at www.freecadweb.org).

# Scanning an Object

If designing something yourself sounds too intimidating, you might wonder whether you can "copy" an object somehow. Unfortunately, 3D-scanning technology is lagging behind 3D-printing technology, at least at the consumer level. Most scanners work by illuminating an object with one or more beams of light and then measuring the distance to points on the object by seeing how long light takes to reflect ("time of flight" measurement) or how a known pattern of light is distorted by the surface ("structured light"). These scanners then generate an approximate model of an object, which requires manual intervention with the software to clean up.

Anything with internal surfaces can be very challenging to scan (because it is hard to illuminate inside something), and transparent or reflective objects usually need to be sprayed or coated with something matte to be scanned.

Because the process is slow, often inaccurate, and time-consuming, many people will just try to get a rough scan, import it into one of the 3D CAD programs described earlier, and then draw over it. This is an area of very active research, so by the time you read this, such a method may be getting better. Read reviews of any scanner before purchasing it or, if at all possible, try to see it operating on objects like those you will be working with.

# Downloading an Object To Print

If all that fails, you can also get started by downloading STL files that other people have designed and uploaded onto databases. Be sure to note the license on the objects, particularly if you are going to use your print in some moneymaking endeavor. Some creators may not allow modification ("derivatives"), and some may not allow commercial use. Two large databases are Thingiverse (www.thingiverse.com) and YouMagine (www.youmagine.com).

Instructables (www.instructables.com) is not primarily an STL repository, but it does have some 3D-printing projects with downloadable files. Leopoly (subscription required for most features, www.leopoly.com) has tools that allow a user to start with a design from the Leopoly site and modify it, as sort of a halfway solution.

There are more-specialized archives, too. The U.S. National Institute of Health (NIH) is developing a centralized database of medical-interest 3D-printing files at http://3dprint.nih.gov.

# The Next Step: Slicing

Once you have your 3D model that you have created, downloaded, or made from a scan, the next step is to "slice" it. This is something of a misnomer, because a lot more happens than just cutting the model into layers, though that is usually the first step. The 3D model is just the surface of the object to be printed. The shape might be very complicated, but what is created in these files is just an infinitely thin layer that covers the whole surface (imagine painting an object and being able to magically remove the object, leaving only the paint.) For technical reasons, this thin layer is broken up into triangles. So, the computer file with your model in it is just a very long list of points making up the corners of each triangle and information about how that triangle is oriented in space. This has to get translated into movement of the 3D printer somehow. This process is called *slicing*. A slicing program does indeed slice the area within this surface into layers. However, it also figures out how to move the extruder head within each layer to lay up the plastic for it.

The slicing programs also figure out how to add *support*. When a 3D print is created, if there is a part that is overhanging empty space (imagine the outstretched arm of a statue), that part would just fall down if it were printed where it needs to be, because nothing is holding it up. The slicing programs figure out how to add some supporting material for all the layers below that one so that it does not fall down. Creating support and managing the various settings for it are studies in and of themselves, and Joan's book referenced in the upcoming Tip covers this in depth.

For open source printers, the program MatterControl (www.mattercontrol.com) has a choice of three different built-in slicing programs and also incorporates features to load a file onto a printer. For printers that have proprietary software, the manufacturer provides something equivalent that may present fewer options to the user to make the process of printing simpler. Typically, these printers can still accept STL files from any CAD program. Figure 3-7 shows an STL file created in Tinkercad that is now being prepared for printing. It is the same file that is shown in the model and closeup prints in Figures 3-2 and 3-3, and actually printing in Figures 3-5 and 3-6.

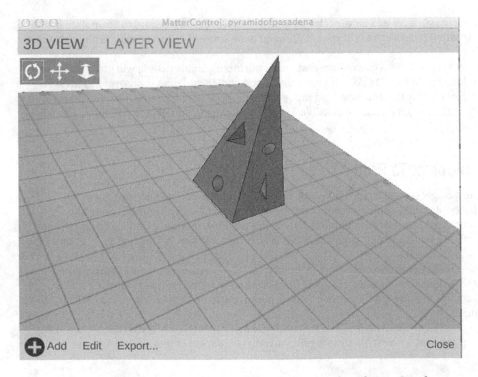

*Figure 3-7.* *An STL file in MatterControl, ready to be sliced and made into G-code*

## Sending the File to the Printer

When the slicing program is finished, the resulting file is usually in a format called G-code, though some printers have proprietary formats that serve a similar function. This file is a very detailed list of mechanical and thermal settings for the printer and a list of the motions for the print head to perform a layer at a time. The file is then executed by transmitting it a few commands at a time over a USB connection or loaded onto an SD card on the printer and run from there.

---

■ **Tip**  If you want to go more deeply into the workflow and issues touched on in this chapter, there are two good books available to get you started. For more detail on 3D printing workflow, you can read Joan's previous book *Mastering 3D Printing* by Joan Horvath (Apress, 2014.) If you want to get into more depth on the hardware aspects of consumer filament-based printers, you can check out *Maintaining and Troubleshooting Your 3D Printer* by Charles Bell (Apress, 2014).  Unfortunately, using 3D-printer software is not easy (yet). There is a long learning curve at the moment for any printer.

---

## Materials

Consumer 3D printers need to use materials in the form of a filament that melts below 280 or so degrees Celsius. The material also has to stick to a build platform reasonably well. These two constraints are a bigger challenge than one might think. There are three common thermoplastics used for 3D printing: polylactic acid (PLA), acrylonitrile butadiene styrene (ABS), and nylon—plus many more exotic ones coming along at what seems like nearly a daily basis.

Figure 3-4 shows a few rolls of filament—a one-pound roll of nylon and a one-kilogram roll of PLA. You may have noticed that the nylon was wrapped in plastic. Most filament tends to absorb moisture from the air, so keeping it sealed up is important. Rich likes to use five-gallon home-improvement-store buckets or very large Ziploc bags to store his filament at little cost.

## PLA

PLA is the easiest material to work with and is therefore one of the commonest. It melts at a relatively low temperature. This is a plus for the printing process but something of a minus for the finished pieces, because they also can warp and melt on the dashboard of a car on a hot summer day. PLA is biodegradable and made from corn, and tends to have a sugary odor when printing that has been compared to pancakes. As such, it is a frequent choice for classroom printing. It can be used on printers that do not have heated build platforms.

## ABS

ABS is a very common plastic, used to make LEGOs (and many other things). It is strong and does not melt in normal consumer environments. It requires a heated build platform, though, and warps and splits pretty easily while printing if not kept warm enough throughout the process. It also often has an odor when printing that bothers some people.

## Nylon

Nylon is very strong and flexible when printed in thin structural components. With care, you can print parts of variable flexibility. Typically, nylon comes only in white, but can be dyed. Nylon does not need a heated bed, but it does not like to stick to anything, so it usually needs a dedicated platform made of an appropriate material.

## Elastomers

Some printers are able to handle elastomers, which are flexible mixes of rubber and other materials. One example is the proprietary material NinjaFlex. Your printer manufacturer can tell you what will work with your printer.

# 3D Printer Limitations

A consumer 3D printer can do pretty amazing things, but it does have its limitations on how large an item is realistic to print and how finely detailed the print can be. Also, most 3D printers require some fiddling. This section talks about some of the realities of the consumer-printer state of the art as of this writing.

## Print Time and Print Size

As mentioned earlier, it takes a while to 3D print something. This may not be a long time compared to the process of hand-machining a similar object, but somehow the expectation is different with these printers. This time lag can be challenging if you are using one or two printers in conjunction with a group of 30 or 40 students. Significant prints can take hours to more than a day.

Given this, most 3D printers have limits on how large an object they are designed to print. If something that is 8 inches on a side can take a day or more, you can see why consumer-level printers typically are that size or smaller. So, if you are making something 6 feet tall and 3 feet long, 3D printing all of it will require a lot of thought and glue. 3D printing just strategic parts that would be hard to make any other way is often a good solution.

## Layer Lines And Feature Size

Consumer 3D printers leave *layer lines*. We like to compare these to brushstrokes on a painting—that is, they are an inherent feature of the medium. However, they bother many artists. There are post-processing techniques to deal with layer lines, and printing thinner layers helps, though it increases the time it takes to print. For some materials, notably ABS, there are ways to smooth the surface and/or paint it after printing.

The smallest feature that a consumer 3D printer can make is typically around one millimeter. Printers may quote "resolution," but this is not a very well-defined term in the 3D printer world. For a 2D (paper) printer, dots per inch is a pretty good metric. However, because most printers lay down material in one 2D plane and then extrude the next layer on top of it, typically there are two natural "resolutions" for a 3D printer.

Within a layer, typically a feature needs to be about twice the nozzle diameter or larger. Layers are always thinner than the nozzle diameter. The material is smooshed down as it comes out and generally must be thinner than the nozzle diameter in the vertical direction (thickness of the layer), but must be slightly larger than the nozzle diameter in the horizontal direction. A decent printer can place the head much more precisely than the limitations of nozzle width.

Figure 3-8 is a closeup of an actual print of the pyramid we have been using as an example in this chapter. If you look near the peak, you can see some wobbliness of the last few small layers coming to a crisp point due to the plastic being unable to cool and solidify fast enough.

***Figure 3-8.*** *The completed pyramid print*

## Printer Mechanical Issues

A significant issue with current printers is that the nozzles tend to clog or jam, and unclogging a nozzle can be a time-consuming and frustrating experience. Producing high-quality filament at competitive prices is difficult, and sometimes the filament diameter or composition is inconsistent, leading to debris in the nozzle or filament that is too wide to even enter the heater block, causing the filament to shred and jam.

Printers also need to be *trammed*—have their moving parts made square relative to the build platform. Misleadingly, this is often referred to as *leveling*. Leveling would imply that you wanted to have the printer bed level in the sense of using a bubble level, meaning level relative to gravity. You do not. You want the bed level relative to the rest of the printer's moving parts. If you have a tilted table on an uneven floor, you want to have an internally consistently tilted printer on it.

Often the metaphor is made that 3D printers now are like computers were in the 1980s, just emerging from a phase where hobbyists made them from kits, and "normal people" did not really know what they were. There is some truth to this, although as Rich likes to say, 1980s PCs did not have nozzles that clog, so perhaps the barriers are a little higher at the moment than they were then.

## Suppose I Want a Metal or Glass Part?

A 3D printer that can directly print metal is not a consumer item. Suppose, though, that you really want to create metal objects, or that you already are familiar with small-scale metal casting? You can still 3D print an object and then use it in the mold-making process. The process of lost-wax (or investment) casting can be adapted to work with PLA, and printed models can be used as patterns for sand casting. This is beyond the scope of the introduction in this chapter, but Joan's Mastering 3D Printing book introduces how casting works in general (but not at the how-to level).

# Purchasing Considerations

If you are planning on buying a consumer 3D printer, you have the problem of too much choice. There are many already on the market, and new ones come out practically every day. We don't recommend any particular type here, because the landscape changes continuously. However, we have a strong preference for open source 3D printers. Printer companies that support the open source community (see Chapter 9) as a rule are keeping costs down for themselves and everyone else by not patenting and protecting aspects of their printers. By adhering to open standards, they also don't force their users to use only expensive, proprietary materials. The flip side of this is that open source hardware and software usually give a user a lot of power and choices, but typically at the expense of a long learning curve.

## Heated Bed

Some 3D printers have heated build platforms and some don't. Some materials (notably ABS) will not stick well to an unheated platform, so if you need to print in a material that requires a heated bed, that need will drive your choices.

## Bed Size

Generally speaking, the larger the print bed, the more expensive the printer. Larger prints also take a lot longer to make. Consider how large a build volume you really need for your explorations. Smaller printers tend to be sturdier and easier to move around.

## Filament Cartridges vs. Spools

Some 3D printers require that you buy filament only from the manufacturer, typically in a cartridge. Open source printers use filament on spools that typically hold either a kilogram, half-kilogram, or sometimes a pound of material (as shown in Figure 3-3). The minus of open source printers is that you need to know a bit about temperature and other settings to use a particular filament. Rich is a member of a group that is setting a standard for machine-readable labels on filament, which should simplify the process for the user. The drawback of cartridge filament is that it tends to be vastly more expensive, and often changing the printer settings is not possible if the hardcoded ones are not working well.

---

■ **Tip**   If you are considering a cartridge-based printer, look up what it costs to buy a kilogram of filament before you buy.

---

## Should I Buy a Kit?

Many 3D printers are sold as kits. The virtue of building a kit yourself is that after you have done so, you will deeply understand how it works. If, however, you are relatively new to the electronics side of 3D printing, getting a kit to work may be overwhelming. Your success may depend on what sort of assistance you have available. If there is a nearby makerspace where you can drop in and pick experts' brains when you get stuck, then you might be in a better position.

Both of us have worked at a company that made kit printers, and building a printer made people more sophisticated users. Kits also tend to be cheaper, and if something breaks, you will be more able to fix it. However, if you are geographically isolated and are unable to ask questions easily, you may not want to invest the energy in trying to figure out a kit as a first step.

## Community Support

A final consideration in selecting a printer to purchase is how well the printer is supported. Check reviews (by searching on "3D printer reviews"), and if the manufacturer has physical stores or locations near you, drop in to see how helpful they will be. At this stage of the industry, a small company that supports its printers well might be a better bet than a large one who leaves you mostly on your own.

# 3D Printing for Educators

Our purpose in this book is to show you how to use making things to encourage a budding engineer or scientist. From the material in this chapter so far, you can begin to get ideas about how 3D printing might be incorporated into curriculum. There are some caveats, though: as mentioned, 3D printing takes a long time. This means that in a typical classroom setting, at best a teacher may be able to print out one thing in a class session. However, building something up layer by layer often looks magical, and students really enjoy seeing something materializing. Team projects or contests or some other way of reducing the object flow may be a good idea.

3D printing enables creating many of the types of projects described in later chapters. This ability to make a complex object at relatively low cost has been critical to lowering the barrier to allowing students to actually make fairly sophisticated robots, costumes, wearables, and so on, instead of just learning about it hypothetically. We give many examples of using 3D printing alone and in combination with electronics in later chapters.

Another issue is that the learning curve is significant. As we have mentioned, the reality of the state of the art right now is that you need to know a bit about what is going on under the hood to be successful. If you think of the printer as a new machine tool to learn versus a printer you just plug in, you will be a lot closer to understanding what you are embarking upon.

# Safety

Unfortunately, thinking of these 3D printers as "printers" loses sight of the fact that they are tools. The nozzle will be hot (typically above 210 C, which is 410 F), and heated beds can be 115 C (239 F). Hobbyist-oriented printers or printer kits may have some exposed wiring, and all printers have moving parts. As with any tool, common sense, the presence of trained adults, and good shop practices with regard to eye protection and appropriate clothing and hairstyles are important. The area where you run the printer should have adequate ventilation.

Users need to be aware that 3D printers are precision devices, at a relatively experimental stage of design, and usually cannot take rough handling. Recently we heard a story about some students shaking a printer that was not giving them good results. Needless to say, this did not improve their print quality.

# Using a Service Bureau

If all this sounds too intimidating, but you want to have some 3D-printed parts for a project, it is possible to have someone make them for you. Companies that do this are called *service bureaus*. These companies usually print your part and offer prints of parts that others have designed. If you are a designer, you can always explore putting your creation on a service bureau site and seeing whether anyone pays to have it made. Some of the bigger providers offer printing in metal and more exotic materials and bigger parts than a consumer machine allows.

Typically, service bureau prints are expensive, but emerging networks of printer owners are making this option cheaper. Some of the established bureaus are Shapeways (`www.shapeways.com`), iMaterialize (`http://i.materialise.com`), and Sculpteo (`www.sculpteo.com`). Solid Concepts (`www.solidconcepts.com`) has been around for quite some time, providing rapid prototyping and additive manufacturing services. Some of these bureaus can print in metal. Two emerging community sites are `3dhubs.com` and `makexyz.com`.

## How Much Does Getting Started with 3D Printing Cost?

A consumer-level 3D printer is about $1,000–2,000 as of this writing. There are printers that cost a lot less and a lot more, but $1,500 is a reasonable budget for a decent machine. Software for slicing typically is included or is open source and available for free. 3D-modeling software is available at many price points, starting with free. Open source PLA spools typically cost around $35–40 per kilogram (and a kilogram makes a lot of small parts). Cartridges typically cost more.

If you start from nothing at all, you will probably need to buy some basic tools, say $100–200 worth. So, getting started can probably happen for around $2,000, by the time you buy a printer, filament, and some miscellaneous items. If you are in a school, a sculpture or shop area may have the tools you need. Obviously, the more 3D printing you plan to do, the more printers you should have, and the more filament you will use.

Having a print made by a service bureau is typically a lot more expensive than printing it yourself. For a print that measures a few inches on a side and is reasonably complex, expect to pay $50–100 for a hard plastic or nylon part at a large service bureau.

Scanners are a bit of a wild card as we write in early 2015, and scanning services are expensive, but all that is changing rapidly. Look online for some reviews or ask more-experienced colleagues for suggestions if you want to be able to scan and copy objects, because by the time you read this, scanning may have improved.

## What Do I Have to Learn to Use 3D Printing?

As mentioned earlier, you need some combination of computer skills and comfort with some physical tinkering with a printer. We have found that a combination of a computer-literate person comfortable with 3D-modeling software and a shop class teacher or sculptor often works well. Robotics uses similar combinations of skills and is a good background skill set, too.

## Summary

In this chapter, we reviewed the landscape of 3D printing and offered more resources if you want to understand the field in greater depth. We saw that consumer 3D printers are evolving rapidly, and still have challenges and a steep learning curve. The chapter briefly reviewed why you would want to use a 3D printer, as well as the technology's role in an educational setting and the realistic limitations on the capabilities of a consumer-grade 3D printer.

■ ■ ■

# CHAPTER 4

# Robots, Drones, and Other Things That Move

Robots have intrigued people long before it was possible to build one. Joan can remember reading Isaac Asimov's *I, Robot* when she was little, but low-cost electronics were not available to make them. Now, however, it is entirely possible to build fairly capable robots for a reasonable cost, based on the technologies discussed in Chapters 2 and 3.

We use the term *robot* in this chapter pretty loosely, more or less thinking of it as a mechanical device that moves, driven by a combination of one or more microprocessors and computer code. Typically we think of "a robot" as something anthropomorphic—it has a head, maybe sensors for eyes, and some way of walking or rolling around. However, it is also accurate to think of a 3D printer or a little flying drone as a robot.

In this chapter (mostly written by Rich, who will be the one speaking) we give you an idea of how simple hobbyist robots work and then talk some about how people are using them to teach engineering and other subjects.

Joan has been a judge for FIRST Robotics for about 12 years. FIRST (For Inspiration and Recognition of Science and Technology, www.usfirst.org) is an organization founded by entrepreneur Dean Kamen and (now emeritus) MIT professor Woody Flowers to encourage kids to learn about engineering by making robots that would compete against each other. FIRST now has a "little league" using LEGO robots and often is the reason schools create their first makerspace-like areas (Chapter 5). As such, FIRST arguably presaged the maker movement with its dueling robots, which we talk about later in this chapter.

## Types of Robots

Building a robot yourself, even a simple one, can be quite challenging for several reasons. The software that runs a robot has to keep up with what engineers call *realtime control*. That is, if your robot is rolling along and its sensors say it is going to smash into a wall, it does not help very much to find that out ten minutes after it happens. This ability to sense something and act on it is called *feedback*. Some simple robots that cannot alter their paths, even if they are marching squarely up against a wall, for example, are called *feedforward only machines*. That means that they cannot act much or at all on whatever limited sensing they are doing.

Robots can be *tethered*. A tethered robot trails a USB cable or other data (and possibly power) line behind it, with a reasonably powerful computer or power source at the other end. This limits the robot's mobility and range, but might allow it to be a lot smarter and more capable, or able to run a lot longer than it could if it were self-contained. They also can be *human-in-the-loop*, meaning that a person is standing around with a joystick, radio-control console, or other controller, or *autonomous*, meaning the robot is running its own software and acting on its own. Particularly at the hobbyist level we are talking about in this chapter, autonomy is typically limited both by the available sensors and by an Arduino-level processor's throughput.

---

■ **Note**   You may have heard about Internet "robots," or just "bots." These are not physical robots—they are pieces of software that do something on the Internet, such as indexing web pages or (unfortunately) sending out spam emails. We are not talking about that sort of robot in this chapter.

---

# The Technology of Hobbyist Robots

Hobbyist-level robots can vary from the very simple (LEGO Mindstorms, or any of the simple projects we point out at the end of the chapter) to complex flying quadcopters. Robots are very good ways to learn about how hardware and software have to work together in the real world. The main reason to use them of course is that they are fun. It's quite the feeling of accomplishment to put something together, turn it on, and watch it move under its own power!

## Making Robots Move

If you want to make things move, you'll need at least one motor. Direct-current (DC) electric motors, use electrical current that doesn't reverse its direction. Aside from a few exotic types you're not likely to use, DC motors create rotation by alternately powering two or more electromagnets placed near one or more permanent magnets. They power each electromagnet (called a *winding*) to pull it toward one pole of a permanent magnet and away from the opposite pole of the same or another permanent magnet. As the motor turns, the polarity of each winding is reversed in sequence, pulling the *rotor* (the part of the motor that turns) to a new position relative to the *stator* (the part of the motor that doesn't). The polarity of the windings is changed in one of two ways, depending on the type of motor.

A brushed DC motor uses *brushes*, springy pieces of metal, that are held against a commutator to reverse the polarity of the windings as the motor turns. A *commutator* is a ring of segments around the rotor that conducts current from the brushes into the windings. As the motor turns, these segments move, causing the brushes to jump from one to the next so that the power takes a different route through the windings, so that the motor can continue to turn with just a DC voltage across the brushes.

A *brushless* motor is built the opposite way, with one or more permanent magnets on the rotor and stationary electromagnetic windings on the stator. The lack of brushes and a commutator allows it to operate with less friction, noise, and mechanical wear, but it means that a smarter circuit is required to drive the motor. A brushless motor will have at least three wires, and they require a driver circuit that will pulse these wires in sequence. Electronic Speed Controllers (ESCs) for brushless motors are generally designed for running propellers on radio-controlled aircraft, and don't have the ability to reverse direction. These drivers send pulses at a specific speed in order to precisely control the speed of the motor.

A *stepper* motor is essentially the same thing as a brushless motor, except that it is designed to control position rather than speed. Rather than using an ESC that pulses the motor windings at a defined speed, the driver circuits that control a stepper motor advance the motor in discrete steps. By counting the steps, you can tell how far the motor has traveled. 3D printers generally use stepper motors to provide precise position control and coordination of their movement. This method works well if you use a motor and driver circuit that are powerful enough for the job, but if you push hard enough against the mechanism, the motor will skip a step and get out of position. When this happens, there is generally no way for the controller to know. The controller tells the motor to move, but there is no signal back to the controller to tell it whether the motor has moved as expected. This is called *open-loop* control, because the signaling only goes one way.

Like a stepper motor, a *hobby servo* is designed to control position, but it is controlled differently and only functions in a limited arc, usually of about 180 degrees. It contains a small brushed DC motor, a set of gears, and a control circuit. These servos have three wires—two to power the circuit and one for a control signal. As the motor turns, the set of gears reduces the speed while increasing the torque, so that a very small motor can move things that require more force. Also attached to these gears is a *potentiometer,* a variable resistor. By sensing the resistance across this potentiometer, the control circuit built into the servo reads the position of the output shaft and will always move toward the position designated by the control signal. This is a *closed-loop* system, and if the motor gets out of position, it will automatically correct itself.

Closed-loop control can be added to any of these motor types by adding an encoder. An *encoder* consists of a pattern and at least one sensor to detect the movement of that pattern. The pattern can be a series of light and dark lines detected by an optical sensor, or the encoder can be built to sense the rotation of a magnet. An encoder produces a series of pulses as the motor turns. The rate of these pulses tells the controller how fast the motor is turning, and by counting the pulses, the controller can know how far it has turned.

In order to tell which direction the motor is turning, and to tell the difference between moving quickly in one direction and jittering back and forth, you need at least two of these sensors offset from one another. By seeing which sensor is triggered first, you can tell which direction the motor is turning. More complicated encoders use a larger number of sensors along with a more complicated pattern known as a Gray code so that they can always tell their position, without the need to count pulses.

Gearing can be added to any of these motors to trade speed for torque (or vice versa), but it's most common with brushed DC motors. For most applications using a brushed DC motor some gearing will be desirable. These motors are commonly available with a gearbox included. The gear ratio determines how much speed is traded for torque. For instance, for a motor that is geared down with a 2:1 ratio, the output shaft turns at half the speed of the motor itself and has twice the torque (though a small amount of torque is lost to the friction within the gearbox). Choosing the right motor and gearing for your application is important for optimizing the strength, speed, and efficiency of your project.

---

■ **Tip** If this speedy tour of motors seems overwhelming, you might step back and read the Wikipedia entry on "electric motors" at http://en.wikipedia.org/wiki/Electric_motor. The article has very good illustrations and a lot of examples. Figure 4-1 shows an assortment of motors that Rich had lying about.

---

***Figure 4-1.*** *Just a few motors from Rich's collection. Top: brushless. Right: brushed. Bottom: servos. Left: steppers*

To get started with building robots, both full kits and modular kit parts are available for some types of robots, particularly robots with wheels or treads to move around (check out sparkfun.com and pololu.com) and multi-rotors (try hobbyking.com and 3drobotics.com). These are designed to allow you to mount some kind of controller, which can be a receiver for a remote control, a programmable microcontroller (such as an Arduino—see Chapter 2) for autonomous functions, or both.

## Controlling a Robot

Some hobbyist robots are remote-controlled. The user guides them with a joystick like any other remote-controlled toy. It gets more interesting, though, if you want to build a robot that partially or entirely guides itself. To be able to do that, the robot has to have some *sensors* to make it aware of terrain and obstacles around it. Actually giving robots even rudimentary vision is a very sophisticated undertaking, but there are some simpler "pinger" sensors on the market that just detect when something is in the way. These sensors might transmit an ultrasonic or infrared pulse and then analyze how long it took for the pulse to come back, thus determining distance to obstacles.

The robot then needs to decide what to do with this obstacle information. This analysis is typically referred to by roboticists as *navigation*; a toy robot will probably just keep making right or left turns to get away from obstacles, whereas a more sophisticated one might be trying to get to a particular place and will need to do some *path planning* to get there. A robot needs to break down a trip from A to B into commands to move right, left, forward, speed up, and so on, depending on how it is programmed.

All of that needs to be coded, either by the user or by whoever made the kit (in the case of toy robots). Many robot designs can be controlled with a program running on an Arduino-compatible board. Figure 4-2 shows entrepreneur Quin Etnyre (a.k.a. Qtechknow, of Qtechknow.com) with a small Arduino-controlled robot, and Figure 4-3 gives a closeup of the robot and its control box.

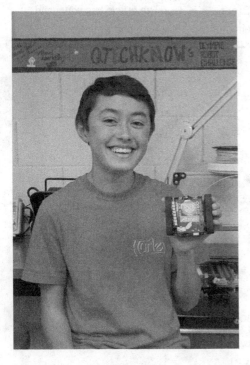

**Figure 4-2.** *Entrepreneur Qtechknow with his robot design*

The robot in Figures 4-2 and 4-3 was designed to be used on a course with Radio Frequency Identification (RFID) tags. The driver can play a game with it to try to cross as many tags as possible. Instructions for building this robot are available at http://www.instructables.com/id/ Qtechknow-Robot-Obstacle-Course. The enclosure for the controller was 3D printed.

*Figure 4-3. Robot and controller*

## Powering a Robot

Not all types of robots need to move around, but those that do need batteries. Batteries come in several different types. Common single-use alkaline batteries are usually not a good choice for a number of reasons. Besides the fact that they're not designed to be recharged and used again, they have a high internal resistance that limits how quickly you can get the power out of them. Even single-use lithium batteries tend to have a higher internal resistance than their rechargeable counterparts.

---

■ **Caution** Lithium-ion and lithium-ion polymer (LiPo) batteries are a common choice for their high energy density and ability to charge and be discharged quickly. They're lightweight and can deliver a lot of power when you need it. A single lithium-ion cell has a nominal voltage of 3.7V, but multi-cell LiPo battery packs are available that put out several times this voltage. These batteries require special chargers to balance the charge of these cells and should be monitored while discharging to make sure that none of the cells drops below about 3.2–3.4V while being used. You can get an alarm that plugs into the balancing connector of these batteries and emits a tone to let you know when this happens to avoid damaging them. Special care must be taken when charging these. You have to use the right type of charger. I know someone who set his bedroom on fire trying to charge one with the wrong type—fireproof charging bags are available for additional safety. If a LiPo swells, often called getting "puffy,", you should not try to charge it again. Look online for instructions to fully and safely discharge damaged batteries so that you can safely dispose of them.

Nickel-metal hydride (NiMH) batteries are available in the same standard shapes and sizes as alkaline batteries, and though their nominal voltage is a little lower (1.2V instead of 1.5V), they maintain a steadier voltage as they discharge. Devices intended to use alkaline batteries that drop to around 1V before needing to be replaced usually work fine with NiMH. NiMH batteries also need specific chargers to detect when they are fully charged and should not be charged with chargers that are not intended to be used with them.

For larger robots and vehicles, scaled lead-acid batteries are sometimes used. These are larger and heavier than lithium-ion or NiMH, but they are simpler to charge safely and can be less expensive than an equivalent battery of these other types. When buying a lead-acid battery, be sure to get a deep-cycle battery. Electric and hybrid cars generally use lithium-ion or NiMH batteries, whereas a golf cart or electric wheelchair is likely to use deep-cycle lead-acid batteries. Gas-powered cars use batteries that are designed to use a short burst of power when starting and then immediately start charging again from the alternator. These car batteries are not a good choice to power a robot.

As with any type of energy storage, uncontrolled release of the stored energy in a battery can be very dangerous, and precautions must be taken. Puncturing these batteries, especially LiPo batteries that lack a metal casing, can cause them to burn violently or even explode. Short-circuiting the batteries can cause sparking and can heat the wires enough to cause a fire. I've even heard stories about a particularly powerful LiPo battery with exposed contacts shorting across a gold ring worn by someone handling it, resulting in the ring being vaporized and the finger being amputated and cauterized in the process. Consumer LiPo batteries come with connectors that insulate the contacts from one another to help protect against this type of accident.

## Quadcopter Drones

Advances in control for small, lightweight quadcopters (a flying vehicle lifted by four rotors, one at each corner) have made them ubiquitous both as toys and as tools for carrying cameras and other instrumentation into difficult terrain. There are small ones that are sold assembled, more or less intended to be used as toys. The Makershed (www.makershed.com) and Amazon.com sell many varieties. Playing with a toy quad, perhaps indoors in a gym or some other controlled environment, is a way to get familiar with the technology and break a cheap system before you let yourself loose on a more expensive one.

If you want to go a step beyond the toy level and play with programming the quad, you can look at a Crazyflie, an open source programmable quadcopter (www.bitcraze.se). More sophisticated quads might carry a GoPro or even a higher-quality video camera. However, when and where it is legal to fly a quadcopter, particularly when it is operating a camera, are very much in flux. Figure 4-4 shows our foreword author Coco building a typical programmable quadcopter, for which the frame comes as a kit and the user needs to add a controller circuit board and other components.

*Figure 4-4.* *A programmable DIY quadcopter being made from parts. Photo courtesy of Mosa Kaleel*

■ **Note** If you are in the United States, the Federal Aviation Administration (FAA) regulates your airspace. Having many hobbyists without either traditional pilot's licenses or much aviation experience flying drones poses some real risks to the airspace. Early in 2015, the FAA released draft rules, particularly for commercial use. But areas around airports and other sensitive areas do not allow hobbyist flying, for obvious reasons. The hobbyist draft rules can be found at the FAA site at www.faa.gov/uas/model_aircraft/. If you are in another country, you should look at the equivalent agency's rules for guidance.

■ **Caution** Even if you are flying for fun, if your quadcopter has a camera mounted on it, be careful not to film someplace that invades someone's privacy, such as inside a window or over a backyard.

# Robotics as a Competitive Sport

Some groups organize contests in which teams of students create robots that compete with each other. One of the larger competitions is FIRST Robotics (www.usfirst.org), which offers competitions at several levels. The high-school level First Robotics Challenge (FRC) has teams build hefty robots that compete in "alliances" of three robots against three other robots. Parts of the competition allow the use of autonomous robots, but most of the FIRST competition uses robots that are joysticked by human drivers.

FIRST teams are also expected to fundraise, hold community events to show off robotics, and do other activities. FIRST teams are *not* required to build the robot themselves and can get unlimited help from mentors and sponsors. This makes FIRST controversial in some educational circles, but the counterargument has been that it is also beneficial for students to see professionals build something and to hang out with them while they do. FIRST was also deliberately designed to be a sport, complete with cheering sections in the stands during championships. The intent is to make engineering cool. FIRST is hard to describe without seeing it; if there is a regional championship near you (typically in the spring), you might try to check it out as an observer.

Botball (`www.botball.org`) follows a somewhat different philosophy. The focus here is on teams developing fully autonomous robots that compete against each other. Botball teams must build the robot themselves and are encouraged to use the Botball kits or their parts in their courses during the year.

If you want to see what it takes to start a robotics team, see whether a school near you already has one. Teams often are glad to help a new school team form, or sometimes may want to join forces to create a collective team across schools. Competitive robotics takes mentors, time, and resources, so sometimes it is good to team up with other schools, at least for a while.

Another popular type of robotics competition is *robot combat.* In these events, radio-controlled robots are built with the goal of damaging or disabling one another. Some of these competitions have been turned into TV shows, such as *BattleBots* on Comedy Central and *Robotica* on TLC in the U.S., and *Robot Wars* on BBC Two in the U.K. Some of these events involve competitions like racing or a "gauntlet," in which robots must survive a series of dangerous obstacles, but the finale is a battle in which the robots compete to outlast one another in direct combat.

# What Do You Need to Know to Get Started?

Many, many robot kits and guides are available to you if you want to explore how to get started. A very good place to explore is the Instructables website (`www.instructables.com`, then search on "robots") or the aptly named Let's Make Robots (`http://letsmakerobots.com`). For a specific example, you could try making a Fuzzbot (`www.instructables.com/id/FuzzBot`), which might have the plus that it can clean your floors once it works! (We considered giving this book the subtitle, "I Told My Kid to Clean His Room and He Made a Robot to Do It.")

## Kits

If those sites look too intimidating, you might want to consider a kit. Hobby stores stock them, as well as the Makershed (`www.makershed.com`), Sparkfun (`www.sparkfun.com`), and Adafruit (`www.adafruit.com`). LEGO Mindstorms kits are available online and in many stores. Once you outgrow kits, you can increase the complexity of what you are doing by 3D printing interesting parts, finding a place to machine them, finding libraries for or writing original code for control, and of course hanging out at makerspaces (see Chapter 5) to talk to other enthusiasts.

## Safety

Robots are powered and move around on their own. Safety around robots involves anticipating that the robot may move in a way you did not plan, and making sure your eyes (and those of bystanders) are protected when you are working on your robot. Other than that, safety procedures will be based on what you are doing to make the robot and how it is powered (see the note about batteries earlier in this chapter, for example).

Briefly, though, remember that it is hard to imagine how *many* ways a robot can fly apart! Be sure to check any notes that came with your kits or components, or suggestions and cautions in online instructions. You will need to learn a bit about both the hardware and software of the robot and how they interact. The level of complexity rises very rapidly, and patience, attention to detail, and a sense of your current limits are all key.

# What Does It Cost to Get Started?

The cost of robot kits (or parts to follow an Instructable) can vary wildly. The best thing to do is to look on some of the links given previously and find a starter project that matches your technical ability, aspirations, and budget. Chapter 2 gives you an idea of what it takes to get going with learning how to use an Arduino; robotics adds another layer of complexity and the costs of motors, a chassis of some sort, and perhaps a wireless controller.

For purposes of this discussion, a quadcopter is just another type of robot. There you will need to decide whether you want a more-or-less toy to play with and crash a lot, or a more serious machine that can carry a payload and be programmed. Other than buying a toy, shopping for a kit is probably the best way to get started and to get an idea of price points in your area.

# Summary

This chapter introduced hobbyist robots and quadcopters and talked about how to get started building them yourself. We reviewed how they are controlled and what is involved in getting started just for fun on your own or as part of a team that competes against those from other schools. We ended with a discussion of what it costs to get started and to grow your skills from there.

Chapter 5 is a bit of a change of pace and talks about makerspaces and hackerspaces. Where might you get some help to learn about robots? Chapter 5 may give you some ideas.

# PART II

■ ■ ■

# Applications and Communities

Chapters 5–11 show you the breadth of the possible applications of the technologies covered in Part I, and also introduces you to the communities that have grown up around these technologies. The communities and the applications can be somewhat intertwined, so we bounce between them in this section.

In Chapter 5, you hear about makerspaces and hackerspaces, where a lot of innovative applications of Arduinos, 3D printing, and similar technologies come about. These spaces can range from large commercial endeavors to corners of school rooms. We introduce you to some of the innovators in this space and relate their views on how to create a successful community of makers or hackers.

The next three chapters focus on applications of the technologies introduced in Part I. Chapter 6 talks about "citizen science"—using readily available electronics to help real scientists solve problems. Chapter 7 explores the world of wearable tech, where low-cost microprocessors, tiny motors, sensors, and all kinds of things that light up meet the fashion sphere. Chapter 8 looks at some variations of these technologies designed to make getting started easier, particularly for kids.

Then we turn to communities that have made all this possible or have grown up based on it. In Chapter 9, you are introduced to the open source community, which creates and maintains many of the technologies in this book as a common good. Chapter 10 explores the special case of getting girls interested in making things, particularly as a career path into science. Finally, Chapter 11 is devoted to a case study of a community college using a maker philosophy both to teach its own students and to develop objects to help visually impaired learners.

After reading these chapters, we hope you will appreciate the breadth of the implications both for the applications themselves and the communities that are arising to make them.

# CHAPTER 5

■ ■ ■

# What's a Makerspace (or Hackerspace)?

We talk briefly about hackerspaces and makerspaces in Chapter 1. In this chapter, we go into more depth about what these spaces can be and how people use them. Often community spaces are set up as membership organizations (like a gym). In some cases, the space is sort of a tool co-op, in that people are essentially pooling resources to buy a suite of tools that they could not afford individually. An individual's garage or basement can be a hackerspace, but the community aspect is what makes it more than a garage.

A good makerspace is more about the community than the tools. It is shared tools, but also shared ideas. It is about the ability to learn from others and in turn teach what you know. Educational institutions, like libraries and schools, are starting to consider whether they should create makerspaces (or whether they already have them, by another name). As in Chapter 1, we use *makerspace* as the generic word, but in the case studies we use the term that the group under discussion actually uses for itself.

In this chapter, we interview founders of makerspaces and visit formal and informal learning institutions that are experimenting with maker technologies. For the most part, makerspaces are aimed at adults or kids who are at least 13 or 14. (There are a few exceptions, like LA Makerspace, which uses Los Angeles Public Library spaces for some of its family-oriented programs.) For kids younger than that, if you are a parent you will probably need to find a school, camp, or other kid-focused group that also happens to support this type of activity. Chapter 8 covers technologies that might be a bit easier to get started with at home or in a classroom if only minimal support and training are available to you at the moment.

## Types of Maker/Hackerspaces

As making things has become more visible, more and more types of physical spaces to make things have appeared. These are starting to divide into for-profit commercial spaces (often focused on classes and stocked with large, expensive equipment) and nonprofit or informally organized co-op–like shared spaces. Because of a concern about possible school board, parent, or donor allergies to the word *hacker,* some schools call their in-school spaces *studios* or *labs.* Whatever the name and the scope of activities that happen there, in this chapter we are talking about spaces that allow people to make things, either in a formal class or by watching someone else.

We devote a chapter to makerspaces for a few reasons. First, often a school receives a donation, or (worse) an unfunded mandate, to go and create a makerspace, whether or not anyone really knows what that means. This kind of effort often focuses on the architecture and purchase of the bigger tools. However, it's more important to think about what will happen there and how you want the space to feel when you are done. A laser cutter with a nice ventilation system or a 3D printer will just sit there if no thought has been given to how to use it. Sometimes we joke that we should have called our consulting practice "Now What?" because that is often the reaction after a group has purchased the "big iron" of makertech.

If you are in the position of starting a makerspace, or you just need to find a place to hang out and learn, try to visit as many of them as you can in your area. The independent nonprofit ones tend to have a bit of a counterculture vibe, and the commercial ones can be more structured and feel more like a workplace than a friend's garage. You will probably know within a few minutes of starting a tour of a place whether it is someplace you would be happy hanging out to learn and invent, but it may be hard to tell from a website or at a distance. You may be able to find makerspaces near you by looking for meetups (`www.meetup.com`), by searching on "Arduino" or "robots," or just browsing around a bit. Hackaday (`www.hackaday.com`) also hosts projects and meetups in some areas and may be a place to find locals.

We are fortunate in California to have a lot of energy in the maker community, and most of the examples in this chapter are in California or associated with MIT, since those are the communities we know. But more and more groups are springing up all the time, so do not be put off by the distribution of our examples, which are meant to be illustrative of different approaches and not an exhaustive list. Hopefully, if there is no makerspace near you, you are thinking about creating one!

This chapter mostly reflects Joan's view, as she interviewed an assortment of people involved with creating or using makerspaces for this chapter. Now and again Rich weighs in to give the hacker view of a particular point.

# Why Are Makerspaces Important?

Rich and I are developing a consulting practice that is focused on helping people figure out how to use maker technologies effectively, particularly in educational and scientific applications. As you might imagine, this can lead to meetings with schools where we are either expected to do something miraculous or are not greeted with open arms by all but are there because of the zeal of one advocate of learning-by-making. Schools are often under-resourced, and sometimes teaching maker technologies is handed to a teacher who may be overextended and who may not really have the background for it. This may not be the teacher's fault, because the administration has no idea what is actually involved to select the right person. These situations can usually be sorted out with a little training and perhaps a few enthused high school students to take some of the load of preparing materials for hands-on making.

Sometimes, though, a worldview disconnect can be even bigger. In one case, we sat down with representatives from a school district that had some promising pilots underway but that were afflicted by some of the issues just noted. I asked them what their biggest challenges were, other than their limited budget to buy anything. The response was that some parents would not be happy about children making any noise in school. The perception of these administrators was that the expectation of many parents and some teachers was to see children sitting quietly in neat rows, and that anything different implied a poorly run classroom. As someone who has taught undergraduates, I know I always felt creeping dread when the whole class *did* sit there staring at me instead of doing whatever activity I had concocted to get them to work together and try out things. Pushback from parents who want the kid to sit passively was not something I expected as a problem for hands-on making in schools. Perhaps, then, one key function of a space that is dedicated to making stuff is that it officially recognizes that making stuff is part of learning and that it's not "fooling around" time.

It is also important to be able to leave things in the space to work on for more than just one 50-minute class period. Not having room to store half-finished projects and come back to them is also a common problem reported by schools. This can be exacerbated, too, by the fact that processes like 3D printing take a while, since a machine may have to run uninterrupted while several classes surge in and out (or overnight).

Another crucial philosophical point is that "playing around" with making things allows students to try something, see what works, fix problems, and carry on. This ability to put something out there, perhaps fail in whole or in part, and then keep going is a useful life skill (and is embedded in maker and hacker culture). However, traditional academic learning is typically structured such that any failure would get a bad grade. Learning by making allows for experimentation in ways that are difficult to teach through books, lectures, papers, and quizzes.

*Fail, fail, fail, win.*—Motto of Crashspace, the first hackerspace in Los Angeles

*Demo or die.*—Nicholas Negroponte, founder of MIT Media Lab

*Deploy or die.*—Joi Ito, current head of MIT Media Lab

What about outside of school settings? One can think of the maker movement as a backlash against our increasingly virtual lives. If you are writing code, you can probably collaborate largely online. But if you are actually physically building something, you need someplace to do that, and you would probably like to have someone who has already made whatever it is sitting next to you to help you out. Physical making needs physical community—the modern barn raising or quilting bee. Community makerspaces can provide that environment.

■ **Rich's view**   Hackerspaces come in many different shapes and sizes. The nonprofit and more informal ones that I've visited have all focused on different types of tools and different styles of making. One common type is focused on digital manufacturing, with a laser cutter and a few 3D printers as their centerpieces. Others lean toward large machine tools, with lathes, band saws, and half a dozen other types of cutting tools that require two or more people (or one person driving a forklift) to move. Still others have rooms and rooms full of electronic components, with varying degrees of organization, and everything you would need to build a custom circuit board and pull it apart again. Some have rows of sewing machines, whereas others can and do accommodate taking a car apart and rebuilding it as a giant spider or a pirate ship on wheels. Many of the tools are donated by members, and some of the larger tools may be older (but still working) ones that were offered for free to anyone who was willing to haul them away. A populous area may have tiny spaces of several of these types within shouting distance of one another, whereas a less densely populated area might have a big warehouse with a broader range of these capabilities.

Commercial spaces can spend more on tools and usually try to be more comprehensive than the more ad-hoc spaces. They usually have up-to-date equipment and strict rules to ensure that you don't damage them or yourself. You may make lifelong friends or decide to go into business with someone you meet at a commercial space, but they lack the community spirit that comes from a space that grows organically to suit its membership. I drool over some of the big, heavy-duty machine tools in commercial spaces, but personally, I leave them feeling a bit "icky," as if I had seen a police mug shot of some childhood idol. It's important to find the right type of space for you, and that's more about the people than it is about the tools.

# Case Studies: Community Maker/Hackerspaces

There are many experiments going on right now in creating community maker/hackerspaces. This section reviews a few typical ones. First I talk about Crashspace, a small nonprofit hackerspace in Culver City, California that has been around for a while. Then I review Vocademy, a large for-profit makerspace in nearby Riverside, California. For some East Coast representation, I talk about Artisan's Asylum in Cambridge, Massachusetts. Finally I look at two big networks of spaces: the Fab Lab spaces that spun out of MIT and the commercial Tech Shop chain.

This area is changing very rapidly. I have not made an attempt to be all-inclusive here, since any list would probably be out of date in a few months anyway. Instead I have tried to touch on the histories and styles of some typical spaces as they exist today. You will probably recognize the types of spaces when you go out to find one to join.

## Crashspace, Culver City, California

The oldest hackerspace in the Los Angeles area is Crashspace (www.crashspace.org) in Culver City, just west of downtown L.A. Joan interviewed two of the founders, Carlyn Maw and Tod Kurt, for this book. Tod is currently chairman of Crashspace's board, and Carlyn is a board member. They are pictured in Figure 10-1 (in Chapter 10), and that chapter discusses Carlyn's views on women in hackerspaces.

Crashspace appropriately formed by people getting together, several of them having met by chance at a party. Each one had previously and independently thought about starting a hackerspace because there really was not one in the area. A philosophically similar nonprofit studio space, Machine Project (www.machineproject.org) had been around for a while, but was more art-oriented and did a lot of unusual things like making felt from wool.

Sean Bonner, an entrepreneur, found the location—a small freestanding building (about the size of a suburban house) in Culver City, which made it reasonably central in the spread-out Los Angeles basin. It was a compromise between cheap spaces far from where people live and expensive urban spaces. It was within walking distance of places to eat and had affordable heating and cooling. Crashspace opened in January 2010 with, as Carlyn says, nothing. The premise was that once the space was open, people would come and bring equipment to share. This just worked, they say—the right people brought the right tools. Currently the space has a board of nine and a two-tier membership system. The first tier of people pay a monthly fee and can use the space when a higher-ranking member—one who has a key—is there. There are no regular hours; the space is open when a key-carrying member is there. (The Crashspace website has a graphic showing whether or not it is open at any given time.)

Tod and Carlyn met for the first time when it was time to sign the lease. It was a bit scary for the founders to commit to the financial needs of the nonprofit, modest though they were. When asked how the community formed, Carlyn says that you have to "define your tribe." In Crashspace's case, she describes the tribe as consisting of "curious people." Everything has to be about attracting the people, she insists, not the tools. Tod thinks of the space a little differently. Hackerspaces, he feels, are the physical equivalent of the Internet. They are a way to learn something without needing to go to school, just as you can learn online by yourself, without an institutional structure. (Crashspace does offer classes and some meetups for like-minded people interested in things like 3D printing.)

Crashspace has been a legendary incubator of many innovative projects, including the Kickstarter-launched 3D printer company that both Rich and I have worked for in the past (Rich met the founder at Crashspace). It has also birthed many LED-laden wearables and objects of varying ambition. The house feels like the cluttered home of a very extreme science fiction fan, or perhaps an MIT dorm floor mashed up with a well-equipped garage. When asked how the space is managed, Carlyn sighed that keeping the space clean and organized with an all-volunteer unpaid crew is a perpetual problem. They have kept the space running on a volunteer basis since the beginning with a few simple rules. Carlyn says her primary rule has been: Don't do something that makes us make a rule.

## Vocademy: The Makerspace, Riverside, California

Vocademy: The Makerspace (www.vocademy.com) is in many ways the opposite extreme of the low-key Crashspace. Gene Sherman, Vocademy's founder (shown in Figure 5-1), who has the intensity of a televangelist, says he thought about founding a space like this for more than a decade. With over 15,000 square feet and a lot of massive equipment, it operates on a much larger and more formal scale, with paid staff. (Vocademy is also discussed in Chapter 10, and a photo of a class there can be seen in Figure 10-5.)

***Figure 5-1.*** *Gene Sherman, Vocademy's founder*

Whereas Crashspace firmly calls itself a hackerspace, Sherman says, "I love the term *makerspace* and hope it becomes as common as *restaurant*." He notes that there are many kinds of restaurant, and that he feels that makerspaces will also evolve in various definable directions. He says that he wants to "define what a makerspace is." He also wants to be education-focused, not teaching theory but rather concentrating on the practicalities of making, from sewing to welding.

Sherman feels having formal procedures in place is essential to be sure the operation is safe. He requires everyone to take a class about each piece of equipment before they touch it at Vocademy, even if they are experts already. He says that his main goal is to bring back shop class for middle and high school students, and has been encouraging an allied nonprofit with that goal. (In Los Angeles and surrounding counties, shop has been discontinued most places.)

He says that Vocademy exists to help people find their path and that making is in our DNA. He notes that 50 years ago, if a button came off a shirt you did not go buy another one. We have lost our focus on tactile learning and fixing things. Sherman observes that if you put a bunch of kids in a room with crayons, Legos, and books, they will self-select and sort themselves into three groups, each of which will play with one of those. But, he says, now the only choice is to pick up a book.

Sherman's goal is to have hundreds of facilities to give people access to and training in making things themselves. Vocademy also has some office space available for entrepreneurs to rent in close proximity to the equipment. Vocademy is unabashedly for-profit, with a feel and a scale more along the lines of a factory than a garage. However, cosplay (Chapter 7) props and costume pieces decorate the walls. Sherman says that they are making their own furniture and other fittings, so the hacker and DIY feel is not lost.

## Artisan's Asylum, Somerville, Massachusetts

From the previous two examples, you might think that a nonprofit community space could not get very large. Artisan's Asylum (http://artisansasylum.com), near MIT in Somerville, calls itself a "nonprofit community craft studio." It occupies a 40,000 square-foot old envelope factory, which attracts so much interest that it offers two tours a day. Artisan's Asylum is run by a mix of paid staff and volunteers.

The website says that in February 2015, Artisan's Asylum had around 550 members and hosted 170 studios. The space is broken into many small cubicle-like studio workspaces from 50 to 100 square feet each, with a wild mix of projects resident in the various spaces (and a four- to six-month waiting list for spaces opening up for new residents). For many people, it is their "day job" workspace, with others who use it for labors of love making up the balance.

## Fab Labs, Worldwide

Many makerspaces are one-off affairs arranged by a group of friends who want to share tools and/or space. However, there are now several networks of hackerspaces. One of the oldest is the Fab Lab network (`www.fablabs.io`), the educational outreach program for MIT's Center for Bits and Atoms. In early 2015 there were about 450 Fab Labs in 65 countries, according to the site of its governing foundation (`www.fabfoundation.org/about-us`). Fab Labs are often tied to academic institutions and have several requirements to use the name. They have to be open some of the time to the public and have a basic set of capabilities to enable users to do rapid prototyping, estimated as an investment of around $60,000. Fab Academy (`www.fabacademy.org`) offers various certificates at some of the sites and may eventually offer a bachelor's degree.

## TechShop

TechShop (`www.techshop.ws`), which opened its first location in 2006, is a chain of large for-profit hackerspaces or prototyping studios, with eight locations currently and two more (Los Angeles and St. Louis) listed as of this writing as "in planning." Three current ones are in Silicon Valley and the San Francisco Bay area. TechShop also has a membership business model and offers classes to learn to use equipment and then access to that equipment (laser cutters, machine shop, welding, and textiles and electronics).

## Equipment Considerations

In this book, we are mostly talking about how to use smaller equipment, like 3D printers, Arduinos, and sensors. However, these technologies do have their limitations. 3D printing is slow, for example, and if you have a class of 30 students, having each of them print out something is impractical. Another piece of equipment often found in a makerspace is a *laser cutter* – a computer-controlled machine that uses a powerful laser to cut shapes out of any flat material, like plastic sheets, or plywood, or even fabric. Laser cutters are a larger investment, but can print out large numbers of items quickly. The output of a laser cutter is "2D" in that it has to be flat and cannot have structure in the third dimension (a laser cutter can etch something, but cannot carve out 3D shapes like a metalworking machine can). You can cut substantial parts out of a sheet of acrylic or plywood, but they are just cutouts.

On the minus side, laser cutters are expensive and noisy. They either need to be vented to the outside to dissipate fumes from whatever is being cut (since the laser essentially burns through the material) or used with a sophisticated air cleaner. There is a risk of fire if they are not used correctly and toxic fumes if you try to cut the wrong material. At the moment, laser cutters are definitely not a home workshop tool. If you are planning on routinely working with large classes that all need to work on something, you might look into training on using a laser cutter.

I will not address machine tools here except to note that machine tools—particularly tools that generate a lot of sawdust or metal shavings or plaster dust—should not cohabit with 3D printers. The small nozzles on 3D printers clog with dust very easily. Provide as clean an environment as possible for them.

# Biohacking

There have also been some hackerspaces focused on open source biology lab equipment and experimentation. If you search "biohackerspace" or "DIY biology," you will find some examples. Just as a makerspace or hackerspace usually has 3D printers and machine tools, a biohackerspace will have equipment normally found in a "wet lab" biology environment. Biohackerspaces are for people who are interested in learning more or perhaps doing research which they cannot afford to do otherwise because the equipment or facilities are too expensive. Some, like LA Biohackers (`www.biohackers.la`), offer lectures and workshops of general interest.

Some biohackerspaces participate in citizen science projects (see Chapter 6) by making equipment available or by providing training and publicity for the public to effectively participate in an observational research project. A project to track the spread of an invasive beetle in Los Angeles, for example, has been the subject of a training class at LA Biohackers. The intent is to demystify the technology and encourage learning and participation in significant biotechnology, ecological, or other biology-centric problems. Neil Gershenfeld at MIT's Center For Bits and Atoms has become interested biology as well and is developing a course called "How to Grow (almost) Anything," in a follow-on to his existing How to Make (almost) Anything class (`http://fab.cba.mit.edu/classes/863.14/`). The idea is to use Fab Labs (described earlier in this chapter) to make biology labs that would then be used to teach biotechnology.

# Makerspaces at Museums, Schools, and Libraries

There is currently a trend for schools, libraries, and museums to add makerspaces to their offerings. What the word *makerspace* means in this context depends a great deal on what the institution is trying to teach or display. Typically it means a place where students or visitors can either learn a hands-on skill by using a tool or craft kit of some kind or learn about math or physics or art through learning a skill. This distinction is very important both in how the space is used and in how it is staffed.

With the demise of shop class in many places, the first type of learning (hands-on skill) is largely gone in formal educational settings. This means that people are not used to learning how to do a physical skill in an educational setting (except, possibly, in labs for science classes). Thus makerspaces have a certain novelty factor but also have to overcome some psychological barriers to moving much beyond craft-type making (glue guns, paper, cloth, and so on). 3D printers somewhat bridge the gap between non-physical, creative endeavors, like programming and computer graphics design/animation, and bending metal—and may be the focus of a lot of spaces in these community learning environments for this reason.

## Museums and Libraries

Museums often have hands-on exhibits or show how something in the museum was made. But how far can a museum walk over into actually being a place for a visitor to experience making something? The Tech Museum of Innovation (`www.thetech.org`) in San Jose has installed what it calls the Tech Studio. It is stocked with 3D printers, CNC machines, laser cutters, and associated tools. The Tech Studio is used by staff to create exhibits, but most of it is visible so that visitors can see the process, too, and participate in some programs and activities.

The Exploratorium in San Francisco has a Tinkering Studio (`http://tinkering.exploratorium.edu`), which features exhibits of makertech for its own sake and maker-inspired art, as well as an area for, well, tinkering. The museum has an extensive set of projects on its website for the public to try out at home as well.

Even the younger set can get into the act. Kidspace Museum in Pasadena (`www.kidspacemuseum.org`) calls its space an Imagination Workshop. Kidspace is aimed at younger children, ages 4 and above. On its website it asks for donations of small wood scraps, cardboard tubes, two-liter soda bottles, and the like so that kids can assemble and dismantle various common objects.

Libraries have been considering whether they should have makerspaces and if so what sorts of tools and capabilities are compatible with their other archival and community-service capabilities. It will be interesting to see how this evolves, since the makerspace skill set is somewhat different than libraries might normally have available to them. The Los Angeles Public Library is collaborating with LA Makerspace (www.lamakerspace.com) piloting programming in 3D printing, coding, playing Minecraft, and other hands-on activities, along with using its community lab for citizen science projects (see Chapter 6).

At the moment, school makerspaces often evolve out of some other kind of space. In some of the examples to follow, the spaces are primarily used for a robotics team but are available when the team is not using the space. Or they can be thought of as specialized makerspaces that could be prototypes for a more general capability later on.

## Case study: Windward School, West Los Angeles

Rich and I are helping the Windward School in Los Angeles (www.windwardschool.org) expand its maker capabilities. I interviewed Cynthia Beals, the Director of STEAM Programs at Windward. Cynthia is also a math, science, and technology teacher and the robotics coach. Figure 5-2 shows her in the robotics lab working with one of the robotics team students.

*Figure 5-2. Cynthia Beals and a robotics student in the Windward robotics lab*

She has been working to bring what Windward calls an Exploration Studio to fruition. Currently, one classroom is used to house 3D printers and some other materials as the temporary home of the studio. In addition, Windward fields a FIRST Robotics team (see Chapter 4). The space used for the team's robot development is shown in Figure 5-3.

***Figure 5-3.*** *Students in the Windward robotics lab*

Windward wants its planned Exploration Studio, Beals says, because "Students have a hard time visualizing in the third dimension because of screen time. Some of their problem-solving skills have gone down, and fear of failure has gone up." She feels that students are reluctant to tinker and try things in the typical classroom because they associate things that do not work right away with academic failure and do not see the learning and growth that come from experimentation. Beals hopes that having the space will provide inspiration for teachers in every department to look at problem-based learning to teach not just the content of their courses but also those general skills.

Beals also thinks it is important to have more than one class's worth of students working at a time to encourage cross-pollination of ideas. If everyone is working on exactly the same project, it might be easier to guide the students, but if they are working on very different ones, they might be encouraged to cross over ideas. However, this idea brings with it the challenge that students might thrash around if they do not have enough guidance to get started. Beals says that students need "the right prompt" to get started—not too specific, but not too vague, either. "Something that will make me smile," was one suggestion.

## How Students Use Creative Space

Students also need to learn how to do a large, complex project and how to organize the work. Figure 5-4 shows the FIRST planning process at Windward. Figure 5-5 shows a similar place at Marlborough School, an all-girls school discussed at more length in Chapter 10.

***Figure 5-4.*** *The Windward robotics planning wall*

***Figure 5-5.*** *The Robotics space at Marlborough*

At Marlborough, the robotics team uses part of a big classroom after school, and students can arrange to do things there during certain free periods during the school day. Because the space is part of a larger classroom, the rest of which is set up for traditional lecture use, it has to be carefully scheduled. Early results have been promising. Chapter 10 discusses the all-girls Castelleja School's ambitious making program and how its space evolved.

## The Younger Set

How can you incorporate making things into teaching much younger children, say from preschool through sixth grade? The Center For Early Education in West Hollywood, California (`www.centerforearlyeducation.org`) is an independent school that has developed an Innovation Center for its students in those grades. According to Matt Arguello, Director of Innovation, the Center serves a few different functions: makerspace, video studio, and also a prototype for new classrooms down the road as they modernize the campus.

Because the children are young, they do a lot of Lego robotics, use the kids' programming language Scratch (`https://scratch.mit.edu`), build with recycled materials, do 3D printing, and learn about basic circuitry. Arguello says, "The space and program have been doing very well and given our students a space to really be creative and to start to bridge that gap between the virtual and the physical." The space is in its second year.

Arguello's background is teaching, computers, and math primarily. He says that teachers did not have much trouble getting started—after some professional development and activities like building a Rube Goldberg machine in the space so that they would be comfortable there.

Some 3D printing projects have included individual projects by the kids, who like to make tablet or phone stands or cases. The fourth-grade teachers developed a project to have the kids take an object from a book they had been reading and represent it digitally with Tinkercad. They developed characters from books, animals, and jewelry. Students also did independent math projects—one student developed a model of an airport that had to incorporate the "golden ratio" into the model. All the kids were under 12 years old.

Arguello says that students are used to operating in 3D environments for computer games, so once he shows them the tools, they intuit how to maneuver. He acknowledges that it's a big shift for some teachers, though. It is difficult for anyone to change practices that have been successful. He feels the best selling points are that kids have been creating and building things forever, and this is an extension that involves technologies.

Making can be powerful for kids in a bit wider age range, too. John Umekubo is the Director of Technology at St. Matthew's Parish School (`www.stmatthewsschool.com`) in Pacific Palisades, California, which offers preschool through eighth grade. Umekubo has been the zealous coordinator of the school's Project Idea & Realization Lab (PIRL), described at its own site, `www.creatorsstudio.org`.

He says that the uses of the space were thought of long before it was implemented. Umekubo says that the school had been looking for ways to bring in a more project-driven curriculum. He emphasizes that it is important to "give students time to iterate," doing things and making mistakes.

The space came about because of a confluence of things. The school implemented a program that gave every student an iPad. When that happened, the computer labs were not being used anymore, freeing up some critical space.

The space was divided into two: PIRL is what the computer lab became; it is the "clean space." There is also an outdoor "messy space" called PIRL Terrace. It is an old storage room and driveway and an area that was used to charge golf carts. This messy space with easy access to the outside has the laser cutter, a miter saw, and drill presses, so the students can saw and sand and carve. Umekubo says his two key lessons learned are that you need to build a space that is flexible so you can reshape it as needed and that you need to have enough storage.

He feels it is unfortunate that people refer to the "maker movement." He thinks it makes learning through making sound like a trend. He hopes "it is not a trend but a *shift*." He points out that innovative educators have believed for a long time that teachers need to get kids to question and be curious and seek for understanding. Technology-focused making things, he says, is the version 2.0 way of doing this.  The computer revolution allowed many things to happen on a screen that were not possible before, but now it can go to the next level and instantiate real objects *from* a computer screen. Chapters 15 and 16 revisit some of these ideas in discussions of learning by breaking things.

---

■ **Note**   It is very challenging to bring making into the school environment. Teachers need to think about how to incorporate hands-on learning, which can require a lot of planning if students have very uneven experience building things. If teachers have no experience, they may not have time to learn enough to feel comfortable with some of the longer learning curve technologies, like 3D printing and Arduinos. Growing out of a robotics program base can be one option, or finding someone (parent, student, or teacher) with some depth of knowledge who can act as a resource. We intend this book as an aid to bootstrapping, but the reality is that it makes a big difference when you find someone who has done some of this before to help frame your program.

---

# What Do You Need to Learn to Start a Makerspace?

If you are starting a makerspace, here are some things you will need to research to get started. Obviously, depending upon your ambitions, you may need to learn things in a lot more depth and talk to architects and contractors with expertise in building similar spaces. To do a good job starting a makerspace (or whatever you choose to call it), the single biggest thing to consider is what you want to have happen in it. To learn that, and to learn what might be possible that you have not thought of, visit existing spaces. Here are some questions you may want to ask yourself or your collaborators:

- What will users do in the space?
- Where will the space be?
- When will it be open?
- How much electricity will you need?
- What safety procedures, equipment, and training will you need?
- How will your space need to be ventilated?
- Will some of the tools or materials need to be kept locked away to prevent breakage or theft?
- What storage will you need, particularly if the space is used for something else part of the time?
- Who will have access to it? What training will they need to have to use it alone (or supervise others)? How will they be trained?
- Who can help you get started and train people to run it the rest of the time?
- Will you need to have both a clean space (computers, 3D printers) and a dusty space (wood or machine shop)?

- How many computers will you need, and will your host institution's firewalls (and rules) allow you to install open source software and drivers if you need to?

- Is the network adequate for what you are trying to do?

- What is your budget and how stable is it? How can you gradually build it up if the answer to the first is "very small" and the answer to the second is "not very"?

Each chapter in this book that discusses a technology (Chapters 2–4, 6–8) have a "what do you need to learn" and a "what does it cost" section at the end. You can look at those to get a feel for how you might want to start and then grow. Chapters 2–4 cover the basic components of an electronics-oriented maker experience; chapters that follow this one are more cross-cutting technology adventures. We inserted this discussion of makerspaces here in our narrative because these more interdisciplinary projects, to us at least, feel more like community endeavors that are be more likely to be successful in a group environment (versus a lone garage). Chapter 8 focuses on some of the simpler, more toy-like technologies that might be good entry-level or classroom technologies and those might be a place to start your thinking.

# What Does It Cost to Start a Makerspace?

As you can see from the discussion so far in this chapter, creating a makerspace can range in cost from almost nothing to millions of dollars in construction. Obviously, if you are at the higher end, you will need far more support than we can give you in this book. We can only reiterate that you should walk through a lot of scenarios about how the space will be used before going too far down any path, as noted in the previous section.

If you want to start cheaply, you can try to obtain donations of simple materials by recycling household materials (*upcycling* has become the fancy word for taking something you would recycle and making it into art or something of higher value). You might be able to get donations from parents or local businesses. If you start with thoughtful, simple projects, you can always work your way up to 3D printing and Arduinos later. Or you can buy just a few of the more expensive and fragile items discussed in Chapters 2–4 and make the design of how to use them into a group activity.

# Summary

This chapter discussed the things that need to be considered when you are developing a space for students or the general public to learn by making things. We gave examples of different approaches to these creative spaces, whatever they may be called. Some are commercial endeavors, and some are communal nonprofits. Some are mostly about sharing tools; others are about learning specific skills in fairly traditional classes. Each one serves a different need in its community, and the chapter closed with some ideas about what someone getting ready to start a space might want to consider.

The next chapters are about the type of activities that might take place in a makerspace: citizen science (Chapter 6) and wearable tech and cosplay (Chapter 7). From there we move to the special case of classroom-friendly, entry-level making (Makey Makey, "toy" making) and finally into the philosophy that underlies this and other educational hands-on activities. Because the next chapters are focused on activities that are often done in groups, we felt it best to introduce group spaces and their dynamics first so that you can envision what it is like to work on these more complex projects.

# CHAPTER 6

▪▪▪

# Citizen Science and Open Source Labs

The technologies we have talked about in this book so far can be used for many things. One of the most exciting possibilities of the combination of low-cost custom fabrication and ubiquitous electronics may be the rise of *citizen science.* This chapter uses the term broadly, to mean participation by nonscientists in the solution of difficult scientific problems. The public may be recruited to analyze data by donating time on their computers when the computers are idle, or they may help analyze big pools of data that for some reason are difficult to work with in a fully automated way. They may go out and get data in the field to allow an investigator to have far more reach than he may have been able to get by walking around on his own. In this chapter, we primarily talk about science that includes participation by a professional scientist in some way.

These falling costs also mean that scientists can also make their research dollars go farther and be more flexible in their own work. Scientific equipment is often very expensive and rather inflexible, and often researchers have to compromise their experiments to work around the limitations of the machine. In other cases, it can be hard to analyze data in the field by bringing out traditional large pieces of analytical equipment. However, in those cases, with low-cost sensors, there might be ways to do at least some screening of data or situations in the field, even if the in-the-field analysis is not as good as a lab will be able to do ultimately for a subset of the field-collected situations.

In this chapter, Joan takes you through some of the types of projects that have been successfully developed with this type of format. Then Rich takes over and talks you through some of the nitty-gritty involved in making low-cost instruments to measure things yourself in the field. Finally, we come together and talk about the challenges inherent in citizen science and some concepts the professional lab might consider adopting.

## Types of Citizen Science Projects

There are various models of citizen science projects. Astronomy has benefited from amateur observations for a very long time, starting with basic observations over millennia and more recently by observations of asteroids, variable stars, and other objects that require a lot of eyes making observations on a lot of relatively bright objects. The objects have to be relatively bright to be visible with small amateur telescopes. Speaking of telescopes, amateurs often build or modify their own, so amateur astronomy and similar field observation–oriented sciences have involved some of the first "maker" citizen scientists.

## Amateurs Analyze Professionally Generated Data

Some of the oldest data-oriented projects use personal computer processing power to analyze a lot of data cheaply. Each participant's computer has a program that runs on it (often as a screensaver) that processes a small piece of a very large dataset when the computer would otherwise be idle. This also has the bonus of publicizing the scientist's research effort and creating a community of interested people who feel they have some stake in the outcome. Researchers involved with the Search for Extraterrestrial Intelligence (SETI) in 1999 produced one of the first in this category, SETI@Home (http://setiathome.berkeley.edu). The SETI project took signals from many big radio telescopes (those big dish antennas that are a staple of science-fiction movies) and used home computers to analyze chunks of signals for possible signs of intelligent life elsewhere. Civilization on earth has been putting out a lot of signals (TV, radio, radar, microwave ovens, and so on) for the last century or so, and the premise of SETI is that if anyone else out there is doing the same thing, there will be certain characteristics of an intelligent signal that we should be able to find. This kind of search works best if you have a lot of data and a lot of eyes looking at it. No signals from extraterrestrials have been found yet, but SETI researchers by necessity have to take a long view—the project is still ongoing if you want to try it out.

There are other models of participation that use the processing power between someone's ears rather than on their computer. People are very good at image recognition, but computers are not (yet). Astronomy again was an early adopter of this. A big "sky survey" was done (the Sloan Sky Survey), which by 2007 had resulted in a huge amount of data. The scientists realized it would take years to get through looking at all of it and thought about how they could get some help from interested amateurs.

The researchers really wanted to find and categorize certain types of galaxies, which requires looking at an image of a piece of the sky and deciding what you are seeing. They had a million galaxy images in their database at the time and needed to find a new way of doing business. In 2007 they started the Galaxy Zoo project (www.galaxyzoo.org), which asks its users to do a short training exercise and then has them classify images of sky objects into several categories. As of this writing the researchers have received nearly 50 million classifications by 150,000 people. The Galaxy Zoo crowdsourced data analysis concept has since been generalized in the Zooniverse website (www.zooniverse.org) with a variety of different science projects to choose from, although still heavily weighted towards astronomy.

One of the Zooniverse projects has a somewhat different spin—the Old Weather project (www.oldweather.org). This project asks participants to look at scanned-in old ships' logs to extract weather observations made by United States ships since the mid-18th century. Historians are interested in this data, of course, but it is also critical to climate modelers. Having a long and pretty accurate set of data stretching as far back as possible helps significantly when you are trying to figure out how to predict weather in the future.

## Amateurs Take Data, Scientists Analyze It

All of the projects we have talked about so far assume that a scientist is taking the data and the public is analyzing it. Another model is for the public to take the data, at the request of scientists who cannot realistically gather as much data as they need for, say, environmental studies. One project along these lines has been running in one form or another since 1900. The *Christmas Bird Count* project (www.audubon.org/conservation/science/christmas-bird-count) originally started as an attempt to encourage people to go out and count birds on Christmas Day rather than shoot them. Over time, however, it has become a very valuable long-term, detailed record of bird populations in many areas. Cornell University Ornithology Lab (www.birds.cornell.edu) now runs many other studies along similar lines, including the Great Backyard Bird Count and Celebrate Urban Birds.

## Amateurs Take And Analyze Data

What about the even more do-it-yourself (DIY) option—to come up with a scientific study that you (or your students, or neighborhood) find interesting, and see what data you can take and analyze? These projects may arise as adjuncts to existing scientific projects, as classroom group projects, for a science fair, or just because someone was curious. In the past, a class or an individual perhaps could go somewhere and record bird or snail or toad distributions, and perhaps file their report up the chain to bigger organizations. Field instruments for amateurs were limited to bug nets, binoculars, and similar items.

Now the Internet (and social media) makes it easy to collaborate either with people you already know or people who might find you online if they are trying to study a similar problem. The availability of 3D printing and very low cost processors and sensors allows just about anyone to make cheap, distributable instrumentation. This creates opportunities for student or community groups to actually take data to answer questions of interest, which can even include designing and deploying instruments. A neighborhood or school group can answer questions that are perhaps too local to be of interest to anyone else. For example, you may want to know how well the sprinkler system distributes water on your school grounds. Or you might take part in a local contribution to addressing a bigger problem, such as characterizing how much a newly introduced bug has gotten itself established in your immediate area. In the next section, we talk through some citizen science projects that have emerged in the Los Angeles area.

# Citizen Science Case Study: Invasive Species

It is now very easy to travel between continents. According to the Port of Los Angeles's website (www.portoflosangeles.org/about/facts.asp) 176.4 million metric tons of cargo worth $290.2 billion passed through the port in fiscal year 2014, including 117,602 automobiles and 578,668 cruise ship passengers. It is pretty easy for a few tiny bugs less than 0.1 inches long to hitchhike their way in among all that. To make matters more interesting, sometimes a bug or a plant seed transplanted to a new area with a favorable, frost-free climate like Los Angeles will arrive without the predators or diseases that kept it in check back home. Add in some drought in California to stress the native plants and make them more vulnerable to infection, and the Los Angeles basin can seem a nearly ideal area for an invasive species to move in and make itself at home.

If you are not familiar with Los Angeles, pull up an online map and take a look at the region. Mountains as high as the 10,833-foot (3,302 m) San Jacinto Peak surround the city to the north and east, with the sea on the west and south, and other smaller mountain ranges popping up courtesy of the network of earthquake faults that runs under the region. The mountains may be forested, bare granite, or covered with chaparral (and, more and more often, houses) and interspersed with dense urban development as well as agricultural land. Thus there are many microclimates and ecosystems for a bug blown about the region to find and occupy.

## PSHB

The polyphagous shot hole borer (PSHB) is a small member of the ambrosia beetle family, about 0.07 to 0.1 inches long. According to the University of California at Riverside's (UCR) Entomology Department page (http://ucanr.edu/sites/socaloakpests/Polyphagous_Shot_Hole_Borer/), the beetle is native to Southeast Asia, possibly Vietnam. *Poly* means *many,* and *phagous* means *eat,* and that pretty much sums up the *modus operandi* of this bug. A pregnant female will drill into a tree, create a *gallery* (a series of tunnels), deep into the tree, and lay her eggs. The bug also plants a fungus, *Fusarium euwallacea,* in the galleries, which serves as food for the larvae when they hatch. The males and females of the brood mate with each other when they are mature, and the pregnant females crawl out and spread through the tree or they can fly or be blown to another tree to spread the infection. Figure 6-1, taken in Pasadena, shows what this looks like from the outside on a tree where the bug may have extensively taken up residence. (Figures in this chapter are photos of trees that I, a nonexpert, have contributed as possible PSHB victims to the citizen science effort and are awaiting confirmation as of this writing. They give you an idea of the challenges, though!)

*Figure 6-1.* *A Western Sycamore with a likely PSHB infestation*

As you can imagine, it is very challenging to get at these bugs when they are deep inside the tree, and very difficult to interfere with their breeding cycle. Because the hole they make when they enter the tree is tiny, they can be hard to spot early on. Over time, thousands of galleries carved by spreading daughters of the first invader can riddle the tree with so many holes that it can no longer transport around the water and nutrients it needs, and the tree dies back first from branch tips and eventually altogether. So, it is spreading… and spreading… and spreading.

Chapter 17 talks about how one UCR lab studying these beetles started using maker technologies in its own work. This chapter describes some of the citizen science efforts that are starting to pop up in the attempt to first characterize the bug and figure out where it lives.

# iNaturalist.org

A first effort has been to develop an Internet-enabled citizen science project to track the spread of the beetle. The iNaturalist.org website is a tool that was developed to allow just such projects. Currently managed by the California Academy of Sciences, it was originally a graduate student project by a group at the University of California at Berkeley and was also based on some open source projects (Chapter 9).

Users can create a page containing a description of what sort of observations they need the public to capture. The participants in a project take a picture with their smartphones and thus capture both an image and the whereabouts of the specimen by allowing their phone to record its location. Current projects as of this writing were tracking everything from "The Insects of Texas" to road-kill tallies.

Ariel Levi Simons, who runs the citizen science interest group at LA Makerspace (see Chapter 5), put together a PSHB observation collection site at `www.inaturalist.org/projects/scarab`. Early data, mostly posted by professional scientists to help out us amateurs, showed a problem right away: the PSHB infestations look a lot like other things and also look very different on different trees. Compare Figure 6-2 (a *Koelreuteria elegans*, or Chinese Rain Tree) with Figure 6-1. When a PSHB beetle enters a *K. elegans,* the tree defends itself by coating the bug in sap and pushing it out, creating a bump of amber material. (Whether this is enough for the tree to save itself remains to be seen.) So, it is challenging to come in cold and be reasonably sure you are not contributing false positives, or that you are not missing trees because the infestation is in an early stage. Simons is working on this by developing some training for Los Angeles area volunteers, but it will never be easy.

***Figure 6-2.*** *Suspected PSHB on K. elegans (note how hard it is to see compared with Figure 6-1)*

Other projects on iNaturalist.org have been designed to avoid some of these challenges by just trying to collect data on every bird or plant or bug in an area. The site allows an observer to just post an observation labeled as "Something…" with a request for expert identification. Experts can then go in and make more accurate identifications if the photographs are good enough, or go back to the location (if the phone location tag was good enough). Obviously, none of this is perfect, but it is a very good way to get at least rough data about ecosystems and populations.

# Instrumentation

You may be wondering why all this is in a book about maker technologies. For an instrument to be useful to a scientist, first we have to pose a question and define how we will try to answer it. (Chapters 12 through 14 talk a lot about how this works at the professional level and how to frame the process to do it yourself.) For this chapter, though, I have talked about how data taken by citizen science projects is managed. This section discusses how the availability of low-cost programmable electronics can enhance citizen science projects or even just enable good classroom or science fair activities.

For example, a lot of things about invasive species (like PSHB, described in the preceding section) are poorly understood. What kinds of things encourage or discourage the pest to move on? Is it affected by any environmental variables, like temperature or humidity? How does it spread from tree to tree (if it's a bug) or through an area (if it's a plant) and how quickly? If you are interested in studying such things, there are a lot of ways to do so by combining concepts from previous chapters.

Next Rich talks about how to build a network of sensors from Arduinos, shields (Chapter 2), and possibly some 3D-printed housings or ancillary parts (Chapter 3). You also need to power the whole thing (with batteries or a solar cell, if this will be away from computers) and you need to capture data somehow (on an SD card or wirelessly). And, of course, you need to program your system to take data or copy code from someone else who has done it. At the end of this chapter, the "What You Need To Know To Get Started" section has links to existing projects that you can use as guides for your own work. But for now, we start from first principles so that you can see how this works.

## Building Your Own Sensor Networks

We think of "scientific instruments" as very expensive, fragile things that come in large boxes with lots of Styrofoam and thereafter stay in a lab. In some cases, this is true. Dropping cost and increasing miniaturization, though, allow the average person (or classroom) to create small packages containing some sort of sensor, a power source, a way to record (or transmit) data, and a processor to control it all.

Small sensors can have limitations, of course (see the comments in the "Challenges and Constraints of DIY Lab Equipment" later in this chapter, most of which apply to field equipment as well). However, either hand-carrying small equipment out to take measurements or finding a way to leave a monitoring station out on its own for a longer period can give enormous insight into the daily lives of ecosystems, microclimates, and similar ultra-local phenomena. Or you can simply instrument a classroom experiment cheaply and reasonably accurately.

---

■ **Note**   You can buy a vast array of different sensors from various providers, including Adafruit (www.adafruit.com), Sparkfun (www.sparkfun.com), and Qtechknow (www.qtechknow.com). A temperature sensor from Qtechknow is shown in Figure 6-3, and a force sensor in Figure 6-4.

---

***Figure 6-3.***  *A temperature sensor from Qtechknow.com, shown on its own and installed on an Arduino*

***Figure 6-4.*** *A force sensor from Qtechknow.com shown on its own and installed on an Arduino*

The first question you need to ask yourself is what type of data you want to collect. You can measure some aspects of the environment, like light intensity and temperature, with a special resistor (photoresistor or thermistor) that changes its resistance in response to its environment. For sensors this simple, all you need is another resistor to form a voltage divider to produce an analog voltage readable by an Arduino's ADC (analog to digital converter -- see Chapter 2). On the other end of the spectrum, GPS receivers are often used to log the location of something as it moves around. These receivers process the signals they receive internally and use a serial interface to communicate with other devices. Ironically, these more complex sensors may be easier for a beginner to use because they are likely to be available on a breakout board or shield that comes with a tutorial and an Arduino library. Sensing temperature with a thermistor, though may require digging into the datasheet for values to plug into an equation to convert ADC readings into temperatures.

## Storing Data

A robot may only need to store its sensor data long enough to act on it, but a data logger needs to collect data over a longer time and keep it even if the device loses power. An Arduino has two types of non-volatile storage (storage that persists without power, unlike RAM memory): flash memory and EEPROM. EEPROM (Electrically-Erasable Programmable Read-Only Memory) is designed to be read frequently, but written only once or a few times. It is also usually less than a kilobyte. Flash memory is a similar technology optimized for larger storage and more write cycles. Flash is the type of storage found in smartphones, memory cards, USB drives, and the solid-state drives that are replacing hard drives in modern PCs. An Arduino's flash memory is used only for storing the program, and the EEPROM isn't big enough to log significant amounts of data, so you'll need somewhere else to store it.

For larger amounts of data, the most convenient storage medium is a Secure Digital (SD) memory card. Although an Arduino's on-board storage is limited to much less than a megabyte, modern SD cards are available in capacities starting around 1 gigabyte and ranging up to hundreds of gigabytes. For use with a microcontroller, the smaller cards are usually a better choice, but a gigabyte or two should be more than enough for a datalogger anyway. Sites like Adafruit (`www.adafruit.com`) and Sparkfun (`www.sparkfun.com`) have breakout boards and shields for adapting an SD card to an Arduino, as well as information about how to use them.

## Centralized Data Collection

It's also possible to use a network to collect data from multiple devices in a central location. The communication protocols built into the Arduino are not ideal for long distances (for these protocols intended for communication between chips on the same circuit board, something a foot or two away could be considered "long distance"), but they can be used to communicate with devices that are designed for a longer range. There are shields and modules to add wifi and Ethernet connectivity to an Arduino—although these are more advanced techniques, and you'll want to read the tutorials for the product first to ensure that they make sense to you and that they're able to be used the way you expect. Even the USB connection that is built into most Arduinos can be extended out to 5 meters, or further by using a repeater (look for "active extension" cables) to relay the signal.

## Weather Considerations

You'll also need to consider the environmental hazards to your device. If you're leaving your sensor outside to log changes to some aspect of its environment like temperature or humidity, you'll need to ensure that it can survive in that environment. Electronic circuits don't like to get wet, and lack of weather-proofing can destroy your equipment and cause your experiment to fail. The solution may not be as simple as sealing your device in an airtight container, though. A humidity sensor that is sealed in a container won't be able to measure the air outside it, and a temperature sensor will not respond rapidly to temperature changes with the air inside the container insulating from the external environment, so you may need to find a way to let your sensors stick out of a protective enclosure. If you have a 3D printer, you may want to print a custom enclosure, but in some cases you may be able to make something just as effective out of an upcycled food container (though if you don't clean it thoroughly, you may get wildlife interfering with your experiment). Think through the challenges and try to deduce what might go wrong, and then get creative and find ways to prevent those problems!

# Open Source Labs

Suppose you do not want to launch any particular project, but you do want to have a lab at your school that does more while costing less. Or perhaps you want to develop a science fair project, but the equipment to do what you want to do is too expensive. Or maybe you are a professional scientist and you are tired of adapting your experiments to the one-size-fits-all equipment that is out there.

Several groups have been curating equipment (particularly for classroom optics experiments), and they may be a good place to start—they are listed in the "What You Need To Know To Get Started" section at the end of this chapter. Note that many of these are *open source* projects. As you will see in Chapter 9, that means that the presumption is that other people put out materials that you can use, but you are encouraged to add to the repository if you build on it or create improvements. Open source repositories often have associated wikis or forums that are good places to ask for advice.

# Challenges and Constraints of DIY Lab Equipment

Science equipment has traditionally been expensive both because it was a small market segment (and thus did not benefit from economies of scale) but also because often the capabilities were pushing the available technologies of the time. In some cases, this may still be true. Here are some things to think about:

- Be sure to think through what you are trying to do and whether the $5 sensor you are buying actually can detect what you have in mind. Very low cost sensors, like the ones we talk about in this chapter, may have either inadequate *sensitivity* (the ability to detect dim objects, for instance, or low concentrations of something) or inadequate *specificity* (it may detect what you want, but it may also have a lot of "false alarms")—or it may not work the way the well-meaning amateur poster thinks it does. Read any available data sheets if you are using very low cost equipment for anything beyond a classroom exploration.

- If you are trying to use simple robotics to automate a very repetitive task, be sure that you are actually automating the task you think you are. Sometimes people do additional small things (wiping off a tip between samples, squeezing something down a particular way) that do not transfer well to automation. Watch any candidate for automation in exquisite detail before trying to create something that seems like it should be a very simple device until you get into it.

- If you are taking video data, remember that video files get big very fast. An Arduino will probably not be able to do any real-time video processing. You will need to go up to more powerful processors for that. Similarly, remember that an Arduino is not all that powerful a processor generally. Think through how often you have to sample something or how frequently something has to move.

- If you are growing or mixing something, determine first whether there is a possibility of a toxic byproduct or outcome, and if so, find a trained collaborator with adequate safety equipment. Be sure that whatever materials you are making your equipment out of are compatible with other things you anticipate encountering.

- If you are doing an ecological study, do not move samples of invasive plants or bug-infested materials around because you might inadvertently make matters worse. Catalog or otherwise study them where they are. (Moving around firewood is a prime suspect in the spread of many invasive bugs, including PSHB.)

- Be sure wherever you put the sensor is representative—not next to a ventilation duct or someplace where it will get run over or even eaten by the local fauna.

If you are designing a project yourself and you are out of your area of expertise, be sure you know what the risks might be before you get started. Talk to an expert in the field before embarking; biohacking spaces often make experts available (see Chapter 5), or you can call a local university department and ask for someone to talk to. You might find someone who will want your data! And, as always, use eye protection and other safety precautions appropriate to your situation.

# What Do You Need to Know to Get Started?

This chapter integrates some of the materials from Chapters 2 and 3, and we will not repeat that material here. 3D printing objects to use in your lab obviously is less complex than building yourself an entire set of field-deployable sensors. As with all things in the hacker universe, it is good to look at what others have done and build on that. This section is not an exhaustive list of every project out there, but a sampling to give you an idea of what sorts of things people are doing and how you might get involved. Most of them are community-contributed sites, so always think through claimed data accuracy and overall design before using them for mission-critical research or municipal policymaking.

## Websites

The sites that sell sensors intended to be interfaced with an Arduino typically have tutorials or at least some suggestions on how the sensor is intended to be wired up (for example, www.adafruit.com, www.sparkfun.com, and www.qtechknow.com).

The Instructables website (www.instructables.com) has many relevant projects. Within Instructables, you can search on:

- "weather stations" (www.instructables.com/howto/weather+stations/) or

- "sensors" (www.instructables.com/howto/sensors/)

and find projects of varying plausibility. Remember that these are community-donated projects, so some may work beautifully and some not so much. But you can at least use them as starting points for your own explorations.

## University Labs

Tekla Labs is a project at University of California at Berkeley (www.teklalabs.org) to develop open source science equipment. They ran a contest called "Build My Lab" on Instructables (www.instructables.com/contest/buildmylab/). This project asked for submissions for common lab equipment that could be built out of low-cost or repurposed parts. The Tekla Labs group also surveyed scientists in low-resource areas to see what kind of equipment they would like to be able to make in this way (and felt they would be willing to make). As of this writing, the guides and other materials were rather incomplete, but the Instructables from the contest are available.

Michigan Tech Open Sustainability Technology Lab is one of the bigger resources in this space. Joshua Pearce wrote the 2013 book *Open Source Lab*, published by Elsevier. If you are interested in optics lab equipment, the group has a website (www.appropedia.org/Open_source_optics) and paper in the open access journal *PLOS ONE* about making your own optics equipment. The paper is by Chenlong Zhang, Nicholas C. Anzalone, Rodrigo P. Faria, and Joshua M. Pearce: "Open-Source 3D-Printable Optics Equipment" (27 March, 2013) *PLOS ONE*, DOI: 10.1371/journal.pone.0059840 (http://journals.plos.org/plosone/article?id=10.1371/journal.pone.0059840).

## Other Sources

Public Lab (www.publiclab.org) has put together a few projects that build equipment and open source software. A sort of hybrid of some of the citizen science project types described earlier in the chapter, the group defines initiatives and host designs of open source hardware and software projects to make relevant measurements (of air quality, for example).

Charles Bell's book *Beginning Sensor Networks with Arduino and Raspberry Pi* (Apress, 2013) describes creating a network of sensors with wireless connections and then storing the resulting data with a Raspberry Pi computer (see Chapter 2). This is a more complex situation but may be appropriate if collecting data from SD cards would be impractical.

# What Does It Cost to Get Started?

Here again it depends to a degree on what you are trying to do. If you own a 3D printer and you are printing a small object to hold something during an experiment, the answer is probably less than a dollar. If you are going out and buying an Arduino, some sensors, and ancillary materials like wire and resistors and some means of storing data, you are probably about in the $50–150 range, depending on the sensor(s) involved and which Arduino or compatible you are using.

In earlier chapters in this book, we adopt something of a "hack first and ask questions later" mentality. However, here it is more important to think through your system, or how what you are building answers a science question or contributes data to a larger effort. With a little thought about the big picture, you may be able to make your little backyard detector simpler by considering where you might have people intervene, when a cell phone and its instrumentation might be the best choice, whether just taking samples and having a central lab process them might make more sense, and similar considerations about ways to move complexity away from your little Arduino (or Raspberry Pi) command post. In this case, the point is the use of the devices you are making rather than the device itself, so this is more of a maker than hacker situation (a distinction drawn in Chapter 1).

# Summary

This chapter covered different ways of doing citizen science projects and ways to develop your own projects as well. You learned that you can use an Arduino to take data from a low-cost sensor and store that data on an SD card. Finally, we reviewed how a professional lab might use some of these technologies and offered a few cautions about things to think about when developing systems like this.

Chapter 7 moves on to a different set of applications of sensors, Arduinos, and 3D printing for projects that can be worn as clothing or costumes. The technologies and challenges have some overlaps, albeit in very different contexts!

# CHAPTER 7

■ ■ ■

# Cosplay, Wearable Tech, and the Internet of Things

Most of what we have talked about so far in this book are projects and applications that fit traditional definitions of "electronics," and you could imagine buying the parts in a store that sold soldering irons. What happens when you cross these types of capabilities with clothing or at least things made (mostly) out of fabric? This chapter goes over the technologies that can create clothing which react to anything a small Arduino-type sensor (see Chapters 2 and 6) can detect. Very frequently, people create clothing that can light up with arrays of LEDs when something happens.

A common application of these technologies is in *cosplay,* a mashup of "costuming" and "play" that refers to creating and wearing costumes that make the wearer into a fictional character (often from movies, comics, or video games) or sometimes a character of the creator's own design. Cosplay does not have to include electronics or lights or animation, but obviously those features can make a costume way cooler. Anecdotally, we are hearing that cosplay can be an entry point for girls into other maker technologies. People enter it from the fashion and sewing side or the electronics side and then migrate across the divide as they need the opposite skill. In this chapter, we also talk about traditional costuming (with limited use of electronics) as an interesting way to learn math and mechanical design.

*Wearables* is a rapidly developing area, and the terminology is used somewhat sloppily. Fundamentally there are two types of wearable electronics: *wearable computing* and *e-textiles*. Both types are more commonly referred to as wearable electronics, wearable technology, or simply wearables, but the technical distinction is that *wearable computing* typically refers to technologies like Google Glass—sophisticated computers that happen to be intended to be worn. E-textiles, on the other hand, usually have less computing power (the equivalent of an Arduino or less), and are wearable first, and electronics second (unlike wearable computing devices, which are electronics first and wearable second).

This chapter is a blend of both our expertise, and so we will just say "we" here as we pass the ball back and forth except when one of us has a specific thing to note. We start off with an introduction to the Arduino-compatible wearable technologies and move on to talk about *fashiontech,* where couture meets electronics. Then we take you through some cosplay case studies—using electronics or in some cases just using traditional sewing materials, although applied in unusual ways. We close by talking about the Internet of Things (IoT), an area frequently conflated with the sorts of things in this chapter, but which we feel is really a distinct space.

# Basics of Arduino-type Wearables

Chapter 2 talks about Arduinos, which are microprocessors that are good for controlling real-world objects; Chapter 6 shows how Arduinos manage taking data from sensors. Wearables take this sensor capability in a different direction by allowing you to create clothing or other textile-based objects that can react to their environment by moving or lighting up LEDs or performing some other simple activities.

You can connect any Arduino-compatible board to a garment if you are resourceful enough, but few are designed specifically for that purpose. The first of these was the LilyPad, first sold by Sparkfun. This was a minimal Arduino circuit board that required a separate USB adapter for programming. These boards have their pins routed to large pads around the edge of a circular board, with holes intended for use with a needle and thread rather than a wire and a soldering iron. Conductive thread, usually made from stainless steel fibers, allows you to create sewn circuits or cloth "ribbon" cables, which can make more complex connections—both are shown in Figure 7-1. These boards are also designed for 3.3V operation, for use with a small Lipo battery, and most include a battery connector and switch to conveniently power your wearable electronics.

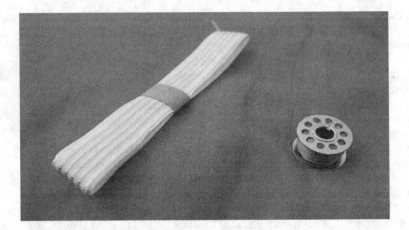

***Figure 7-1.** Ribbon cable and conductive thread*

This first LilyPad was followed by a simplified version that added the battery connector and switch, as well as a similar design that used a USB-capable chip to avoid the need for an external adapter. These versions made fewer pins available, but left more space between them. This additional space helps in avoiding a short circuit, which is a particular concern when you are making circuits with uninsulated conductive thread. Along with the main LilyPad boards, several smaller companion boards are designed to be sewn onto different parts of the same garment and controlled by the LilyPad. These share the LilyPad's large sewable pads and other aspects of its design aesthetic, including its circular shape and distinctive purple color.

Adafruit has its own line of wearable tech products based loosely on the LilyPad design. Adafruit's Flora board has a similar design and feature set to the LilyPad USB. A Flora is shown in Figure 7-2 (along with a NeoPixel, described next). Adafruit's Gemma board is smaller and particularly inexpensive (about $8 as of this writing) and thus cost-effective for projects that do not require as many I/O signals. Like the LilyPad boards, Adafruit has a series of sewable companion boards. These two sets of add-ons are electrically compatible with one another, but may be aesthetically incompatible, as Adafruit's versions of these products are all black instead of purple.

*Figure 7-2. Flora and a NeoPixel*

What can you connect to these sewable circuits? You can get sewable boards with things like accelerometers, vibration motors, buzzers, and of course several types of LEDs. Though it's now uncommon, older wearables tutorials may also show you how to curl the leads of a standard LED intended for through-hole soldering to make it sewable as well. More common now are RGB (red, blue, and green, the three primary colors required to make any other color of light) LEDs that include a driver chip allowing many of them to be controlled from a single microcontroller pin, such as the NeoPixel shown in Figure 7-2. These devices give the appearance of a single LED that can cycle through the rainbow, to spectacular effect. Actual buttons and switches are uncommon in wearables, but things like metal snaps and conductive Velcro can be used to integrate these functions more seamlessly into a garment. The LilyPad accessories include sewable protoboards with a grid of solderable holes that you can solder your own components to if you want to use something that isn't already available in that form.

---

■ **Note** Because the shape of these boards has been optimized for sewing, they lack the traditional Arduino shape and pin layout. This means that Arduino shields (see Chapter 2) cannot be used with them in any practical way. It's still possible to solder to the pads around the edges of these boards, but if you want to use something that's not intended for sewing, you'll need to figure out whether you want to try to sew it, mix sewn and soldered connections, or use something like the LilyPad Protoboard to bridge the gap more tidily.

---

# Fashiontech

These electronics, along with 3D printing, are starting to be incorporated into fashion, both at the *haute couture* and at the DIY hobbyist levels. Exemplifying the high end is fashiontech designer Anouk Wipprecht (www.anoukwipprecht.nl). Wipprecht's creations include the Spider Dress (a dress with 3D-printed robotic mandibles that click menacingly if someone gets too close to the wearer) and the Particle Dress. The Particle Dress was an open source project which requested that contributors create a 3D-printed "particle" (based on a template 62 mm across) which was then assembled into a whole. See www.instructables.com/id/JOIN-OUR-OPEN-SOURCE-ELEMENT-DRESS/ for details.

On the more playful and DIY side are Becky Stern (check out www.beckystern.com and her Adafruit tutorials page at http://learn.adafruit.com) and Limor "Lady Ada" Fried, the founder of Adafruit (www.adafruit.com/about). Both of them have many projects and tutorials online. One of Joan's personal favorites is the Sparkle Skirt (https://learn.adafruit.com/sparkle-skirt), which uses a Flora to control lights that twinkle when an accelerometer detects that the wearer is moving. Take a look at the videos at the links to get a feel for what is possible; static pictures often do not do wearables justice!

Having said that, we wanted to give you an example of a hobbyist-level project here with some photos. Our friend Metalnat "Metal" Hayes (shown in Figure 7-3 contemplating his next "#testcase," as he likes to say in his posts) recently used a Teensy 2.0, a development board with similar capabilities to an Arduino Leonardo, to control a pair of NeoPixel rings made into goggles.

***Figure 7-3.*** *Metal contemplating his next #testcase*

To do this, he 3D printed the goggles and a small pack to clip to his belt (Figure 7-4). The pack contained the Teensy and a battery, and because the LED rings only needed three wires (power, ground, and a control signal), he came up with the idea to use an audio patch cable with 1/8- inch stereo plugs (the kind usually used for headphones) on each end to connect it to the goggles. He initially had some trouble sourcing stereo audio jacks to plug them into, but once he found ones he liked, he was really pleased with the solution. Figure 7-5 shows the NeoPixel ring, Figure 7-6 shows the mostly complete goggles, and Figure 7-7 gives you an idea of what they look like on Metal.

*Figure 7-4. Goggle frames, just printed. Photo courtesy of Metalnat Hayes*

*Figure 7-5. NeoPixel ring up close. Photo courtesy of Metalnat Hayes*

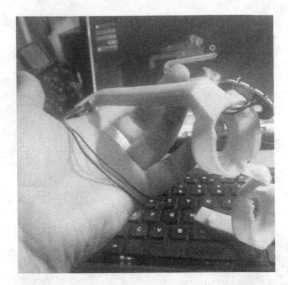

*Figure 7-6.* *Mostly complete goggles. Photo courtesy of Metalnat Hayes*

*Figure 7-7.* *Metal wearing the finished goggles*

There are similar designs that use these LED rings mounted inside of costume goggles, but they are generally designed to be worn on top of the head rather than over the eyes, with the wires, battery, and microcontroller blocking the eye holes (hidden behind tinted lenses). Adafruit sells a kit for this style of goggles and has a detailed tutorial for building them at `https://learn.adafruit.com/kaleidoscope-eyes-neopixel-led-goggles-trinket-gemma/`.

# Cosplay

As mentioned earlier, one activity that often uses wearable tech these days is cosplay, or more broadly just hobbyist costuming in general. Technology can be an enabler for interesting costume effects (or apparent superhero powers), but just traditional sewing fits the definition of "making," too. Laser cutters can be used to cut fabric, but so can scissors.

Joan's friend Bridget Landry has a day job as a rocket scientist, but when she is not doing that she likes to say that she is one of the few costume creators who has a protractor and is not afraid to use it. She is well known in science fiction and historical costuming circles for her humor, creativity, and attention to detail. Figure 7-8 is a period-piece "computer pirate" costume she developed with 1980s era computer hardware and circuit boards. It was wired up (this was before sewable circuits!) with small lights.

***Figure 7-8.*** *Computer pirate costume design by Bridget Landry*

As Landry likes to point out, costume designs require an ability to visualize and a deep knowledge of load-bearing geometries. She noted that designing patterns for complex costumes is just as difficult as designing any mechanical structure. In fact, it may be harder than designing a metal structure, because the materials are soft, and the dynamic loads can be unpredictable. We include this section in this chapter to help you think about unconventional ways to start teaching mechanical design and geometry through costume design for those for whom it might be more familiar and accessible than other beginner "making" might be.

# Georgian Gown Structural Analysis

One example Landry gave of a project requiring complex structural analysis was a Georgian-era (1714–1830) gown. She is wearing the gown in Figure 7-9. The pink fabric is a drapery fabric that she had to line with cotton so that it was the proper weight and stiffness. The middle of the bodice and the underskirt are made of a brocade fabric (Chinese silk with gold thread woven into it). Because it is expensive, brocade is only used on the areas of the dress that are most visible. She had to cut all the pieces out of the brocade and cotton and use them together, a process called flat-lining. In other words, this is a structure made of out several materials with different properties that all had to come together to make the design work for the user.

**Figure 7-9.** *Georgian-era gown. Design by Bridget Landry. Photo courtesy of Mary Alice Pearce*

Skirts like the one in Figure 7-9 have support structure that gives them whatever shape was popular at the time. In the case of a gown of this era, there was impressively complex infrastructure under the skirt. *Panniers*, made out of cotton fabric with hooping to stiffen it, supported the skirt (see Figure 7-10). There were quite large pockets so the lady could carry around whatever she might need during the day. (Joan thinks of panniers as saddlebags on touring bicycles, but Landry confidently said the gowns had come first!)

**Figure 7-10.** *Panniers detail, designed to be worn under the dress in Figure 7-9. (Pannier courtesy of Bridget Landry.)*

The hooping (the stiff part of the pannier) is made of two 1/4-inch spring steel bands wrapped in buckram. *Buckram* is fabric stiffened with, basically, white glue. Hooping is also used (oddly enough) to make hoops worn under hoop skirts of various eras. Landry's closet (Figure 7-11) shows examples of many different styles of costumes she has made for various events where she or others have worn them as parts of competitions or sometimes just for fun.

**Figure 7-11.** *The closet of cosplay expert Bridget Landry*

## From Knitting to Programmable Textiles

Knitters need to visualize complex geometries, but "math" is not normally the first word that comes to mind when we talk about traditional crafts. Yet why not? Knitting can be a very good way to learn to visualize geometry. In fact, some people create knitted visualizations of sophisticated mathematical objects per se—for example, the Klein bottles at `www.toroidalsnark.net/mathknit.html#smmk`—but here we were thinking of teaching simpler math.

Landry points out that the design of the piece shown in Figure 7-12, which is being *blocked*, or stretched into a final shape while wet, required her to do some complex 3D thinking. The piece is created in a scrunched-up form, with the knitter needing to think ahead about how the blocking process will alter the wet yarn and work with the natural dynamics of the material to create the desired end result. This process may seem somewhat humble and medieval, but it is fundamentally not very different from work being done at MIT in *programmable textiles*. These materials are made by starting with stretched textiles and then 3D printing another material onto them to make amazing structures (`www.selfassemblylab.net/ProgrammableMaterials.php`). Who knows what sort of new materials will be developed by someone who becomes an expert knitter and then crosses over into engineering?

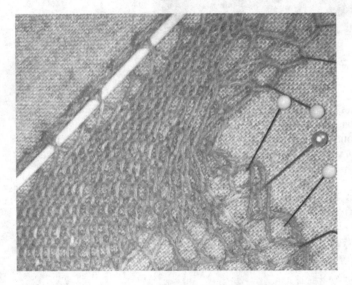

*Figure 7-12. Knitted piece being blocked (detail from a photo by Bridget Landry)*

---

■ **Tip**   Joan had heard anecdotally that a good way to interest girls in math and science who are not naturally self-driven is to come at it through fashion and jewelry design. Although it makes us both cringe to be stereotypical about it, we have heard suggestions that starting with the more traditional craft end of making and moving into laser cutting and 3D printing can be a way to step from the familiar into the more "techie" exotic. We mentioned this in the context of Vocademy's philosophy about using laser cutters for sewing projects in Chapter 10. With forethought, one can perhaps work in learning some programming and more confidence in trying new things along the way.

---

# The Internet of Things

The IoT probably has as many definitions as there are people talking about it. We think of it as the universe of things other than traditional computers and phones that can connect to the Internet. Typically these other objects (such as refrigerators or door locks) are not normally thought of as "smart," but have a processor and some communications capability added for a particular functionality—for example, a refrigerator monitoring its contents for automatic reordering.

The GlowCap (www.vitality.net) is a cap that attaches to a standard prescription bottle and glows when it's time for the user should take the medicine. It communicates through the cellular network with caregivers and pharmacies to manage medication, placing refill orders and allowing caregivers and doctors to monitor compliance.

---

■ **Tip**    MIT Media Lab researcher David Rose's book *Enchanted Objects* (Scribner, 2014) is a popular introduction to IoT applications, including the GlowCap. Check out his website at http://enchantedobjects.com.

---

If we add wireless connectivity to some of the devices discussed in this chapter, one can imagine sensors and actuators that could be worn and remotely monitored. At the moment, most of the devices that work this way are either special-purpose, with an embedded processor that the user cannot program or alter (like the many fitness trackers that synchronize daily workout results with a central server), or are more substantial monitoring stations than could be driven by an Arduino or a Flora. But the DIY Internet of Things is definitely in the process of arriving, bringing with it both privacy concerns and some interesting possibilities.

The privacy (and hackability) concern is a serious one when devices can be quite small and addressable from anywhere. Even when the device is not hidden, if it is perceived to invade privacy, there will be social pressures or even regulations against its use. For example, Google Glass, Google's experimental head-mounted viewer and camera, unnerved people who felt they might be being filmed by the wearer. Thus it did not catch on and was banned from some places, notably some bars. The etiquette and laws about Internet-connected devices are evolving, but it is probably safe to say that it is not a good idea to monitor others' refrigerator contents, prescriptions, or activities without their permission.

# What Do You Need to Know to Get Started?

Like Chapter 6, this chapter integrates material from earlier chapters (primarily Chapters 2, 3, and 6), so we will not repeat the suggestions from those chapters here. If you are interested in ideas from these traditional crafts as a starting point, some good websites for ideas and patterns are Ravelry (www.ravelry.com) and the amateur costuming website (www.costume.org). As noted earlier in this chapter, there are many excellent tutorials in using Flora or other boards at the Adafruit site (www.adafruit.com).

You do not need to be an expert tailor to create something wearable, but it certainly helps to confer with someone who knows something about creating clothing. A local cosplay or theater group might be a good place to find a friend if you are not competent in this yourself. Or, the first time out, use an existing article of clothing and add lights or sensors to it as a starting point.

# What Does It Cost to Get Started?

Costs to create a wearable project can vary widely, depending on the processor, fabric, and thread costs, plus ancillary items such as conductive thread and any materials needed to sew or glue or otherwise create the fabric part of the item. Flora boards are $19.95 in small quantities as of this writing, and then it depends on what you are doing. For example, the parts for the Sparkle Skirt mentioned earlier cost $63.65, not counting the skirt per se, according to a bill of materials on the Adafruit project site for it (a set of needles, conductive thread, a Flora, a Flora accelerometer/compass, a pack of four NeoPixels, a battery, and a charger for the battery). So you should probably budget around $100–150 to allow for making mistakes, breaking a few things, and buying some cheap fabric or maybe secondhand clothing or a hat to wire up on a first outing.

# Summary

In this chapter we talked about wearable technology, which includes Arduino-compatible circuit boards in a different format that can be sewn into clothing and "wired up" with conductive thread or other materials. We also talked about traditional sewing, costuming, and knitting, and how with a little creativity these activities might be a good bridge into teaching sewable circuit design and then ultimately programming and more complex soldered circuits. Designing cool clothing and accessories that can sense and react to the wearer's environment might just be a perfectly adequate goal in and of itself. In the next chapter we introduce some even more unusual ways to interface with circuitry and computers, as well as some circuit design toys intended for children too young to work with the technologies we have talked about so far.

# CHAPTER 8

■ ■ ■

# Circuits and Programming for Kids

How young is too young to make things? Obviously, little kids have always made things, and probably everyone's parents have some strange dried-out thing in a drawer as a memento of past artistic endeavors. Where is the line between "playing" and "making"? Or is there a line, and does it matter?

In this chapter, Joan talks about some of the maker technologies that are aimed at this younger group, or at least at those who have not yet had a class in circuits. For the most part, the official age of entry into electronics, from a manufacturer's point of view, is 13. That said, we know an entrepreneur who had his own branded line of circuit boards when he was 12. In the United States at least, there are a lot of laws and liability issues when dealing with kids much before high school, and so you will probably find that most U.S. programs require that anyone in them be at least 13 or 14.

The last few years have seen many new definitions of what *making* is, or what it "should" be. Is an art studio with traditional kids' project materials in it a makerspace, in the sense of our discussion in Chapter 5? Going farther, is creating a picture with dry macaroni and glue "making"? As a trained engineer who is used to working with things that are visibly technological, Joan's intuition says no, but it is hard to clearly define why not. This chapter talks about this ambivalence, and you can decide for your own particular situation what level of sophistication makes sense for any young maker in your life. Rich weighs in at a few points with his take on the virtues and problems of starting off at these toy-like entry points into making.

It is worth noting that our experience with the devices we will talk about in this chapter is limited since our focus has been on the Arduino ecosystem and 3D printing. However, we felt we would be remiss if we did not at least acknowledge these devices and give a quick tour. Bear in mind that various entry-level electronics packages are coming on the market all the time now, and this chapter is not exhaustive. We point out a few examples of devices we have heard a lot of excitement about so that you can take a look and evaluate them and similar devices. Don't take these as final recommendations, but rather as a broad sweep showing the sorts of things that are available. We give you an idea of some options (including some interesting ones that got their start on Kickstarter), and you can go from there.

## Crowdfunded Inventions

A lot of the technologies for the younger set that I talk about in this chapter got their start in academic labs. The Lifelong Kindergarten Group at the MIT Media Lab (https://llk.media.mit.edu) launched the Scratch programming environment. MaKey MaKey by Jay Silver and Eric Rosenbaum got its start in the Lifelong Kindergarten Group.

Many learn-electronics sets also have passed through Kickstarter (www.kickstarter.com) as crowdfunding projects. Table 8-1 gives some of the statistics for projects that began on Kickstarter and are discussed in this chapter. LightUp—magnetically-connectable circuit components plus a training application—started as a project in the Transformative Learning Technologies Lab at Stanford (https://tltl.stanford.edu). Founders Josh Chan and Tarun Pondicherry took it from there with a successful Kickstarter. The Hummingbird robot controller board comes from Bird Brain Technologies (www.birdbraintechnologies.com), which has a team with its roots in the CREATE (Community Robotics, Education And Technology Empowerment) lab at Carnegie Mellon University (www.cmucreatelab.org). The Hummingbird Duo was a recent Kickstarter to integrate a regular Arduino-compatible controller into the company's robot controller, the idea being that students could gradually use more functionality.

Circuit Scribe's (www.electroninks.com) Kickstarter sold a pen that dispenses conductive silver ink, intended to allow people to just draw circuits (although not aimed at young makers per se). Some young maker toys or kits have just been developed by engineers who did not like what was already in toy stores, including the Goldieblox, another Kickstarter discussed in Chapter 10, and the KitHub (http://kithub.cc) series of kits from engineers Tara Tiger Brown and Luz Rivas.

*Table 8-1.* *Some Crowdfunded (Kickstarter) Projects Discussed in This Chapter*

| Project | Number of Backers | Amount Raised ($) |
| --- | --- | --- |
| MaKey MaKey | 11,124 | 568,106 |
| Hummingbird Duo | 255 | 42,074 |
| LightUp | 1,034 | 120,469 |
| Circuit Scribe | 12,277 | 674,425 |
| Goldieblox | 5,519 | 285,881 |

If you are interested in what sorts of new things people are coming up with, you can always cruise the crowdfunding platforms like Kickstarter or Indiegogo (www.indiegogo.com). Just be aware that backing a Kickstarter project is *not* ordering a product. It is pledging money to a group that hopes to be able to reward you for backing them. So you need to read their pitch carefully and decide how likely they are to deliver. Kickstarter does not give people any money if they do not raise their minimum. Indiegogo has some options for their project leaders. Be sure to read the project descriptions and what their plans are for various levels of money raised before pledging any of your money. Note, too, that most Kickstarter campaigns are run by people who have not done anything similar before, so the delivery date may be woefully optimistic, too.

# Learning Programming

I learned the programming language BASIC in high school (a precursor of several modern languages, or an oversimplified backwater, depending on whom you ask), but the world has changed a lot since then. The Scratch programming language and community came out of a project started in 2003, and according to the project website (http://scratch.mit.edu), there are about 8.7 million projects built in the environment so far. Scratch allows children (they suggest ages 8 to 16) to create interactive stories and games by dragging around tiles with actions for a character to perform. Scratch is free and open source (see Chapter 9). It is a good way to learn how to break down actions into small code-able fragments without exposing children to the frustrations of coding (which can involve very picky formatting and spelling requirements).

Once a kid has mastered Scratch, what is a natural next step? It depends on what the next activity is going to be. Good bets would be using an Arduino (see Chapter 2) or other processors in that family and learning a programming language like C, Python, or Java (all similar and closely related — C is the actual language used by Arduinos). Arduino is a big step from Scratch, however, and if that is too much, just taking example Arduino programs and altering them methodically might be a way to learn by doing, perhaps with a reference book about C if you need it. There are graphical interfaces available, but they limit the functionality of the Arduino, as Rich describes later in the chapter.

# Learning About Hardware

As noted in Chapter 2, getting started with Arduino can be challenging, because you have to learn about hardware and coding more or less in parallel. If that seems like it will be too much at the outset, there are several "learn about circuits" kits out there that are well below an Arduino in user complexity (although the hardware that hides the complexity from the user may need to be a lot more complicated to accomplish that). In Chapter 7, you saw how to create circuits by sewing them. This section talks about creating circuits using other means to connect them. Some of these have very limited applicability in terms of the types of problems that can be solved, but they have interesting niche applications.

## MaKey MaKey

It is hard to describe a MaKey MaKey (www.makeymakey.com) if you have not seen one. Fundamentally, it is an add-on partial keyboard for your computer that talks over a USB port and emulates certain keys on the keyboard. But that is not the point. What it lets you do is interface anything conductive—a banana, a piece of celery, a heavily drawn pencil line, a line drawn with water—to your computer in place of a few keys (up-down/left-right arrows, spacebar, and mouse click). When coupled with a program that expects inputs from those keys, like, for instance, a six-key piano coded in Scratch, available at www.makeymakey.com/piano, you can make a celery piano. Hence the name MaKey, since you are making other things into keys for your computer keyboard.

Figure 8-1 shows a MaKey Makey as it is attached to a computer through a USB cable. The computer recognizes it as a keyboard with just six keys (you can daisy chain them for more options, but we will not get into that here). The next step is that you need to provide the ground for the MaKey MaKey (Figure 8-2). I like to do this by attaching the ground connector to some metal object that is easy to hold. (In this case, I used a metal spoon.)

*Figure 8-1.* *MaKey MaKey and alligator clips*

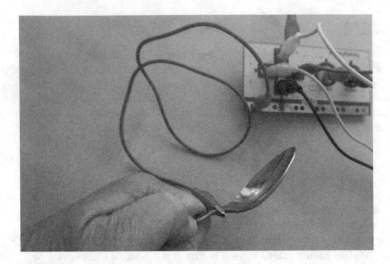

***Figure 8-2.*** *Grounding a MaKey MaKey user*

Next, connect the remaining alligator clips to six conductive objects that will correspond to the up, down, right, and left arrow keys, spacebar, and a mouse click. Keep the MaKey MaKey grounded (by holding on to the spoon, in this case) and touch one of the conductors. The version in Figure 8-3 used damp celery. You will hear a sound, or whatever the programmer assigned to that key. You don't have to use celery. Anything reasonably conductive will do, including people—if you have six friends hold the MaKey MaKey alligator clips, you can high-five them to play a tune. Be sure *you* keep the MaKey MaKey grounded, though, by hanging on to the grounding object with one hand and touching your friends with the other. Otherwise you are not completing a circuit, and it will not work.

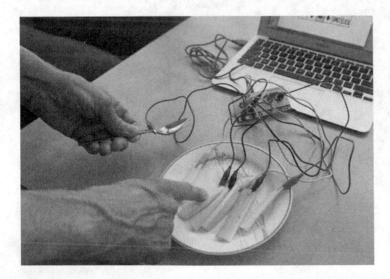

***Figure 8-3.*** *The celery piano*

■ **Tip** There are various other ways to play around with circuits by using whatever conductive material is at hand. Whether you play with it in conjunction with a MaKey MaKey or not, you can also make circuits yourself out of various kinds of conductive and nonconductive dough. These so-called *squishy circuits* use two different dough recipes, one conductive, one not, to develop electrical connections (or resistive components). Squishy circuits were popularized by AnnMarie Thomas, now at University of St. Thomas; see http://courseweb. stthomas.edu/apthomas/SquishyCircuits/.

## Drawing Circuits

If building circuits out of dough or playing pianos made out of food does not sound like your thing, you could try drawing circuits with conductive-ink pens and attaching components with magnets. Several groups have been working to come up with a quick-drying conductive ink, and after a successful Kickstarter, ElectronInks (www.electroninks.com) is now selling a pen and magnetic conductor components. The pen, called the Circuit Scribe, allows you to draw the circuit interconnections (with conductive ink) that you would normally need to use wire to make. The way it works is that you have a metal sheet and magnetic components. You lay down the metal sheet, then a piece of paper, and then your components. Lastly, you draw your circuit on the paper between the components. The pen and a couple of magnetic components are shown in Figure 8-4; I backed the Kickstarter and have been trying to find time to seriously play with my purchases!

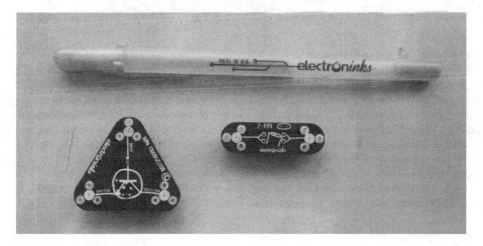

***Figure 8-4.*** *Circuit Scribe pen and magnetic components*

## Magnetic-Connector Circuits

LittleBits (www.littlebits.cc) was one of the first companies to create circuit components that snapped together with magnetic connectors, thus removing the need to wire up a circuit at all. However, this requires that you purchase modules that have these connectors, and depending on how the modules were designed, your flexibility may be limited. LittleBits is an open source standard, and it maintains a public collaboration forum, Bitlab (http://littlebits.cc/bitlab) to encourage invention.

An extension of the concept is LightUp (www.lightup.io), which adds a magnetic-connector Arduino-based board (Figure 8-5) to its set of component modules that include things like a buzzer, temperature sensor, or switch. Libraries have been added to make programming activities with the LightUp board and the available components a bit simpler than the standard Arduino would be.

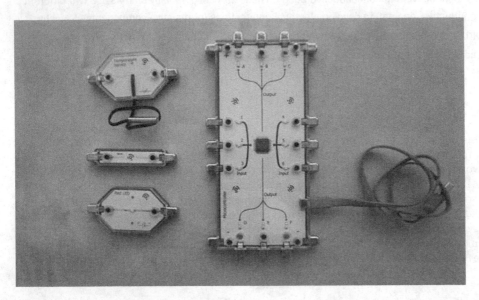

***Figure 8-5.*** *Some LightUp components: a temperature sensor, "wire," an LED, and the programmable board*

A twist that LightUp adds is a machine-readable icon on each module. The user takes a picture of a circuit made with LightUp modules. If the circuit is put together in a way that will not allow current to flow, the LightUp phone app circles where the problem is and allows the user to fix it. If the circuit is put together correctly, it shows how electricity is flowing. In some ways, this feels like a best of several worlds, because it simplifies the hardware part without overly constraining the software. However, the system is relatively expensive compared to a standard Arduino and components, and you are limited to the components that LightUp has made available. Using LightUp also involves downloading software for the board (on a laptop or desktop) and installing a smartphone app for the circuit-debugging capability.

Figure 8-6 is a comparison of some of the different approaches to components discussed so far, two magnetic connector LEDs (ElectronInks and LightUp), and peel-and-stick LEDs from Chibitronics, called Circuit Stickers (www.chibitronics.com). Expect to see a lot more variety as more and more people get into making!

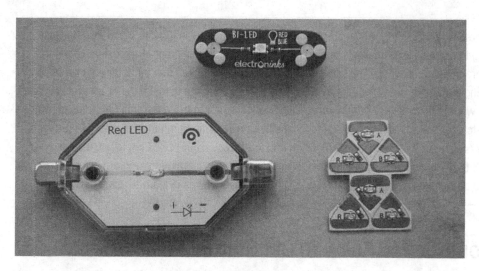

*Figure 8-6.* *Different approaches: LEDs from LightUp (bottom left), ElectronInks (top), and Chibitronics (bottom right)*

## Robot Kits with Programmable Microprocessor Boards

The granddaddy of kits in the robotics sphere is LEGO Mindstorms (www.lego.com/en-us/mindstorms/), which has an entire ecosystem of its own with big competitions (such as FIRST Lego League, www.usfirst. org/roboticsprograms/fll). This chapter focuses more on paths toward Arduino and wearable-tech style "making," which are a bit different from kit-oriented projects that use LEGO's proprietary processor. But if you are looking for robot kits to explore, Mindstorms is definitely another (though rather pricey) area to look into. Chapter 4 discusses other robotics projects at a more sophisticated level, so you can look there for ideas as well if you are interested in robotics.

Many (relatively) easy-to-program microprocessors are available for student projects in addition to Arduinos, although many of them are actually Arduinos with some sort of twist, as we just saw with LightUp. Another such board is the Hummingbird (www.hummingbirdkit.com), which is an attempt to simplify the Arduino toolchain for children. It comes pre-programmed with a simple program that allows the user to use a graphical, mouse-based interface to make programs that run on a computer and use the attached microcontroller board for input and output functions. In doing so, it limits what you can do, with specific pins confined to certain functions and minus their inherent versatility. It does this by simply translating signals for the USB connection with its default program, though this program can be replaced for more autonomous functionality (it is, after all, built around an Arduino-compatible design).

The Hummingbird can be programmed using normal Arduino tools, but using it that way just makes it just an expensive Arduino board. The Software page for the Hummingbird lists a number of choices (possibly too many) for programming it, but unless you really love the Hummingbird's CMU CREATE Lab software, there's nothing there that can't be used with any other Arduino-compatible board. On the plus side, Hummingbirds are intended to be used in simple robotics applications and are sold with kits of parts for robots and some software intended to ease the learning curve.

■ **Rich's view**    Personally, I think that visual programming interfaces for beginners are a bad idea because they require learning to use a strange interface that you will never need for real programming, in addition to learning actual programming techniques. The same goes for languages like Logo that jump through hoops to try to make programming statements look like English sentences but only manage to make the exact syntax easier to get wrong. If you want to try graphical programming, it's probably better to make Scratch programs on your computer first. Scratch can be extended to provide functionality similar to the Hummingbird with S4A (Scratch For Arduino, `http://s4a.cat/`), or you can try Ardublock (`http://blog.ardublock.com`) to use a similar interface to program the Arduino itself. But I think that anyone interested in learning to program will outgrow these interfaces and be ready to move on to real code in less time than it takes to learn to use them.

# What Do You Need to Know to Get Started?

One common criticism (from the technologist side of the fence) is that things like MaKey MaKey do not actually teach anything other than that a computer is not intimidating, which presumably most people under the age of 18 know anyway. One could suspect that these technologies are perhaps made more to bridge teachers and parents into making than students. Is it a good idea to take flexible, powerful technologies and remove almost all the functionality (and raise the cost in the process)? That is a question you will need to ponder if you are thinking about using one of these systems.

Concerns about physically handling materials and soldering are valid ones when students are very young, but by and large we imagine that most kids will be 13 or so before they have the focus to write significant code anyway (the writer of our Foreword being the exception that perhaps weakens this rule).

Magnetic-connector systems have obvious advantages for younger children or environments (such as museums or school programs) where an Arduino and a breadboard just would not survive very long, but these systems tend to be relatively expensive. Drawing circuits to connect components on stickers is an interesting idea for quick prototyping, as long as the components you want are available on stickers. Making dough circuits is a bit messy and qualitative, but it is very cheap.

In short, you can do some qualitative experiments with some of these to get a feel for how things work, but if you want to lay the groundwork for something more sophisticated, you might be better served by taking the plunge into Arduinos when students are old enough rather than linger in the younger-set technologies. A lot of it comes down to what you are trying to teach or accomplish. If you have thought through a project that works with one of these simpler systems, then that might be adequate for experimentation. But think about where you are going and consider that the shortest path to the top might have an initial steep bit of trail.

The systems described in this chapter range from one-off systems (like MaKey MaKey), which pretty much just requires you to read the instructions, to systems that start off more or less as playing with blocks and build to Arduino programming (LightUp). Given that, read the instructions (typically on a website or, increasingly often, a smartphone app) and go from there.

■ **Tip**    In general, it is never a waste to take a software package through "Hello world" (or in the case of an Arduino, through "blink")—the standard first step in coding. It can be frustrating to take the next steps. If you feel a bit trapped between the world of the simplified interfaces in this chapter and the technologies discussed in earlier chapters, take a look at our discussion in Chapter 15 about learning incrementally.

# What Does It Cost to Get Started?

Basically the farther you get from buying a bare Arduino and finding parts for a project on your own, the more it costs. In Chapter 2, we gave some prices for base Arduinos, and in Chapters 6 and 7 for sensor-using and wearable projects. Here you are paying for someone to package these technologies for you in one way or another. If the packaged version takes you where you want to go and allows you to go places you might not have had the time to get to yourself, then it may be worth it for you.

However, if you want to learn a bit more deeply, and if your participants are old enough to handle it, you will probably save money and learn more by taking the paths in Chapters 6 and 7. Sparkfun (www.sparkfun. com), Adafruit (www.adafruit.com), and the Makershed (www.makershed.com) all sell kits that might be a middle ground between buying component by component and buying kits that are closer to toys.

As a few data points, MakeyMakey kits currently sell at $69.95. LightUp has two kits: the Edison, with just the magnetic blocks ($49.99), and the Tesla ($99.99), which also includes the "Arduino-based" board. Hummingbird robotics kits ($159) are intended to be used to control simple robots and come as kits along with parts to make a robot.

If you are a school administrator who is looking at paying for teacher training, of course, the tradeoffs may be different. As noted in the beginning of the chapter, new things pop up in this sphere every day, and our picks were somewhat arbitrary based on items that had caught our eye on Kickstarter or that we had been asked about often enough that we thought we should investigate. We have not played extensively with the items in this chapter, because, as we note elsewhere, our focus is on the steeper-curve, but (we feel) ultimately more rewarding, Arduino path.

# Summary

This chapter talked about some of the types of products that are aimed at learning how to make circuits and associated software. Most of these products are focused on circuit basics, or robotics. We talked about the MaKey MaKey, which is a way to interface a computer with almost any conductive physical object. We reviewed the tradeoff you make with these systems, which usually involves a shallower learning curve and potentially higher costs. The simpler systems also usually require you to learn an intermediary interface before jumping to the types of projects we have seen in the chapters up till now.

This is the last chapter that describes different types of technologies. The next two chapters talk about the open source community that underlies a lot of the developments we have seen so far. Then Chapter 10 looks at ways people are trying to interest girls in making. The balance of the book explores what scientists do and then ties together the world of the maker and hacker that you have seen so far with that of the scientist and engineer.

# CHAPTER 9

## Open Source Mindset and Community

We have been talking a lot about open source technologies in this book so far and have shown you a lot of examples. But what does open source really mean? Why does Rich believe in it so strongly? What technologies have enabled open source development and/or benefited from it? This chapter takes you through Rich's point of view on the open source movement in general and how it applies to the technologies we are discussing in this book in particular. A lot of software you use at home or work – say, to do your taxes or play computer games – is typically not open source. It is software one company owns. You pay to use it and the company does not let you look under the hood. Free and open source is becoming more common, though, and we will describe both what it is and the benefits in what follows.

## What Is Open Source?

When programmers work on a program, what they write is called code. *Code* is a set of instructions for the machine, and can refer to either machine code or source code. *Machine code* is an impenetrable string of binary ones and zeroes that make up a list of low-level instructions that tell a processor to do simple things like compare or add one number to another, or store a value at a certain location in memory. *Source code* does the same thing, but uses human-readable names for variables, functions (pieces of code that may be used repeatedly), and more complicated data structures like lists of numbers or letters. Source code also usually has comments that explain why the code is doing what it is doing. A compiler uses these names and then throws them away, along with the comments, to turn source code into machine code, so it is a one-way process.

Most software, especially commercial software, is distributed only as a binary file of machine code, along with any images and other data used by that code. If you just want to run the program, this is fine, but if you want to modify the way it works, it is virtually impossible to do so without the source code. Some developers make the source code of their programs available for free, and this sharing ethose is called *open source*.

Many modern computer programs are too big and complicated for one person to write alone. In a software company, a number of developers will share source code among themselves to work together to build a program that they can sell. In an open source project, one or several developers will share the source code publicly so that anyone with the knowledge and the interest can help develop it, submitting their changes back to the maintainer of the project for inclusion in it. Anyone can start an open source project, although you do have to know what you are doing if you expect people to join you.

## The Early Days of Open Source

Open source software has existed in some form since the early days of computing, when source code had to be printed out and re-typed by the user. (Joan notes that when she started using computers in the mid-1970s, she used paper tape, which could be loaned to others and laboriously copied by a machine, as long as you didn't drop the spool.) In those days, computers tended to be centered at large national laboratories and universities, and so a lot of software was open source because most of it was academic (solving large scientific problems, for example) to start with. Cheaper storage (8-inch floppy disks giving way to 5.25-inch and then to 3.5-inch) and faster connections started to make collaboration possible for people who were not at major research centers. Easy collaboration became really plausible when the Internet came along and increasing connection speeds enabled sharing files without prohibitive wait times.

---

■ **Tip**   If you are interested in the early days of open source development, Walter Isaacson's book *The Innovators* (Simon and Schuster, 2014) is a great overview of the personalities and technologies of that early era of software and hardware development, and how the two alternately pushed each other forward and sometimes held one another back.

---

## Perspectives on Collaboration

Developing sophisticated software or hardware collaboratively isn't easy. It requires a shared attention to detail and in many ways a group agreement about how to think about a problem. Joan was around for some of the earlier attempts at this, some of it literally before Rich was born.

---

■ **Joan's perspective**   I first used a computer in about 1975 to learn to program in the BASIC computer language. There was a Teletype machine at my high school—considered very advanced at the time—that used paper tape or a keyboard as input and communicated over a phone line with a central computer who-knows-where. (If you want to see what they looked like, an example can be found at: www.quickiwiki.com/en/Teletype_Corporation). The big project to do if you were really cool was to get something to print out in banner letters on the paper scrolling out of the machine.

Looking back on the 40 years of development since, how we collaborate to build software has changed in many ways. It really does not feel like there were any real inflection points. Hardware, software, and connectivity all became incrementally better, with the occasional jump. In the process of writing this chapter, we have been comparing perspectives on how change occurred.

To me, it feels like software development morphed from something that only scientists and engineers did to something that a hobbyist could do. The earliest hobbyist computers did very little, and from my perspective the single biggest innovation was probably the 1984 introduction of the Macintosh, because interacting with it was so profoundly different than the one-command-at-time green text on a black screen that preceded the Mac. (Ironically, though, the Mac was set up so that you really could *not* program it.) But it took a long time for connectivity and software-development tools to catch up so that people who were not in the same building (or at least connected by dedicated lines between their big institutions) could work seamlessly.

In some ways, the current open source movement feels like a return to the early days of computing, when most of it was academic and developed for scientific purposes or just to see what would work. Hackerspaces I have visited feel a lot like the MIT student computer lab in the late 1970s and early 1980s.

## The Internet and the Open Source Hacker Learning Style

Joan experienced the evolution of online networks from its early beginnings as a primarily academic and national laboratory resource to something any consumer could use. By the time the consumer Internet came along, she was already used to using early versions of some of the tools, although many innovations (such as easy-to-read web pages and search engines) came later. Her experience does not reflect the democratizing effect that the Internet represented for people like me. When I hear stories of what it was like in those days, all the things that my generation takes for granted sound almost insurmountably difficult, even for those with the most access.

Joan says that she learned about things being done at a distance by reading journal articles and ordering reports through a major university library. The time one had to wait to receive these orders would have been measured in days or weeks. You would have had to plan ahead of time to figure out what information you wanted and what was essential, since you could not order absolutely everything. Once something did show up, Joan or her secretary would have had to copy the important bits and put them in a file or three-ring binder for future reference.

When I learned, the wait time was measured in milliseconds, and I didn't need to be a part of a prestigious organization to get that access. These changes didn't happen overnight, but I think they do constitute a qualitative difference in how I was able to learn versus the options available before about 1990. I could not learn the way I do with a latency of days. My learning style has been enabled by the existence of the Internet. When I'm researching a topic, I can (and frequently do) spawn dozens, sometimes more than a hundred browser tabs in a matter of minutes, each prompted by what I read in the previous ones. Doing the same with the methods Joan describes would take months or years. This low-latency access to information is part of the reason I often see it as no longer necessary or useful to learn a subject (as someone else has chosen to define it) thoroughly, all at once, and in a linear fashion.

My ability to learn and think this way builds on many open source innovations (beginning with the Internet itself) and is at the core of why I feel it is so crucial to keep building open tools so that progress can keep getting faster and faster.

# Open Hardware

Source code for software is all digital information, and the only thing you need in order to use it, aside from the computer, is more software. Figuring out how to create open source hardware, such as an Arduino board (Chapter 2) or a 3D printer (Chapter 3), posed more difficult problems because you could not turn digital zeroes and ones into physical objects—at least, not until recently.

Digital manufacturing devices such as 3D printers, laser cutters, and CNC mills use files similar to a program's source code to create physical things. This means that people can share designs for physical things that don't take a master craftsman to reproduce on the other end. It's still not as easy as just pushing a button (see Chapter 3 on 3D printing), but it's accessible enough for a global open source community of hardware developers to have formed.

Another crucial innovation was software for designing physical objects. Computer-aided design (CAD) software has been around since the 70s and has been used for virtually all mechanical, product, and architectural design for years, but these programs traditionally cost hundreds or thousands of dollars. In recent years, a plethora of free CAD programs have become available, many of them open source software. My personal favorite is OpenSCAD (`www.openscad.org`), which actually uses source code that looks very much like software code to describe objects.

Recently, the design of open source physical objects has become popular in two major categories. First, there is the design of Arduinos, 3D printers, and the other platforms we have talked about in this book already. Secondly, there are the designs of things meant to be made by using 3D printers and other digitally controlled manufacturing machines. But figuring out who has the right to make what can get pretty complicated, as I will get into next.

# Free Speech vs. Free Beer

The term *free* is used a lot with open source software. This leads to some uncertainty, because *free* has multiple meanings in English. Sometimes, the Spanish *gratis* (no cost) and *libre* (referring to freedom) are used to distinguish between these meanings. Other times, the distinction is explained by referring to the difference between *free speech* and *free beer*. A lot of software is *free as in beer*, meaning that users can download and use it without paying money, but the source code is not available. Other software is *free as in speech,* meaning that the source code is available and users are free to use it as they want.

Sometimes source code is released under license terms that restrict what you are allowed to do with it. The software may be free, with source available, but the license may disallow commercial uses of the code. This type of license is often criticized as not being truly free (*libre*), and not in the spirit of open source.

Hardware works a little differently. Information can be copied freely, but physical things cannot. For this reason, open source hardware is frequently *free as in speech*, with the design files available and unrestricted, but not *free as in beer* because the parts, materials, and time needed to produce them are expensive. If you have the tools and materials, you can produce your own copy, but it still (usually) costs something to acquire them if you don't.

The first *RepRap* (self-REPlicating RAPid prototyper) 3D printer was built using plastic parts that cost thousands of dollars to produce on a commercial 3D printer. Once it was built, it was able to reproduce those parts much less expensively. Probably inspired by the free beer concept, in the early days, these sets of printed parts were often described as costing "about the price of a case of beer," and some early sets were either traded for a case of beer or sold for an equivalent price to cover the cost of materials.

The intention of the RepRap project, started by Professor Adrian Bowyer at the University of Bath in the U.K., was to distribute these parts virtually for free, with each new "child" printer becoming the "parent" of several more printers, resulting in exponential growth. Instead, capitalism reared its ugly head, and by the time I started trying to acquire a set of these plastic parts, they were selling on Internet auction sites for around $1000—for just the printed plastic components. At the time, it often cost this much again for all of the electronics (which were also open source), motors, linear motion components. Some printers now ship assembled for less than $500, and "print-it-forward" programs have started popping up again, with kits being sent out for free on the condition that the machine must be used to produce one or more kits to be sent out under the same terms.

I developed one of the early RepRap printers, the Wallace (shown in Figure 9-1), described at `www.reprap.org/wiki/Wallace`. It was tradition in the RepRap community to name printer designs after biologists, starting with Darwin, since the printers were seen as evolving themselves from one model to the next (with a little human help, of course). You can find an attempt at an evolutionary tree at `http://reprap.org/wiki/RepRap_Family_Tree`, but the number of designs quickly outstripped the ability to maintain such a list.

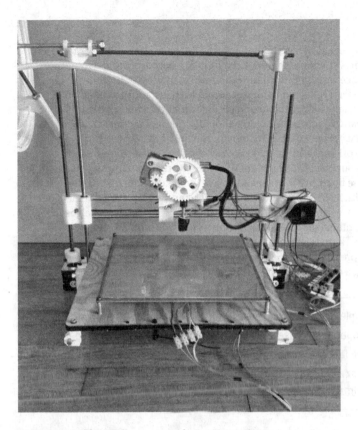

***Figure 9-1.*** *The Wallace, an early RepRap printer*

The Wallace's place in the evolutionary line went like this:

- The original RepRap printer was built in England in 2006 (Darwin).

- The Mendel became the new standard in 2009, with a simpler and more reliable design.

- In 2010, the Prusa Mendel was produced as essentially the same design, but with massively simplified components.

- The Printrbot (late 2011) was derived indirectly from the Prusa Mendel.

- Reprap Wallace (also late 2011) was inspired by early pre-release pictures of the Printrbot.

- The Printrbot evolved into the printers now sold by Printrbot, Inc.

- The Wallace had as a direct descendant the Alu RepRap (early 2012) and indirectly affected the Deezmaker Bukobot (2013) and Bukito (2014).

An even more extreme case is the various *RepStrap* (combining "Reprap" and "bootstrap") printers. In these cases, builders do not have access to some of the materials needed to make a RepRap printer and instead cobble together a first printer from what they can get their hands on. This limited printer is used to make parts that are a bit closer to the mark, and this process is used until the result is adequate for the purpose. Developing-world 3D printers can come about in this way.

# Share Alike

A variety of existing licenses are available to use to release an open source project. These licenses tell users what they have permission to do with the files you have shared. Commercial use is one thing that authors may or may not allow. Authors may also place restrictions on how their works may be redistributed. Open source software sometimes uses GNU licenses. (*GNU* is a recursive acronym that stands for *GNU's Not Unix.*) On the other hand, hardware and designs for printable objects are sometimes released under a *Creative Commons* license, though the Creative Commons organization discourages using its licenses for software rather than licenses like GNU's that are specifically written for that purpose.

Most licenses require attribution to the original author, so you're not allowed to distribute something that someone else wrote or designed and call it your own. This includes *derivative* works— when you have modified or used parts of something that someone else has written, you need to give them fair credit for what they did. Some licenses even disallow derivative works. Such a restriction is not really compatible with the idea of open source but is more common when these licenses are used for things like books or music that are released for free distribution but the author wants to maintain control. An open source license is more likely to have a "share-alike" clause that allows derivative works to be distributed but requires them to be distributed using the same license terms as the original. This prevents someone from, for instance, taking a work that allows derivatives and commercial use and making a derivative with a non-commercial, no-derivatives license.

---

■ **Note**  If you would like to see some sample open source licenses, you can check out some that have been community developed and posted for shared use. GNU licenses and samples are available from `www.gnu.org/licenses/license-recommendations.html`. Creative Commons license samples are available at `http://creativecommons.org/licenses/`. As always, you should consult a legal professional for the implications of using a particular licensing strategy, especially for commercial projects.

---

You've probably noticed the use of the term *author* in this section. This is because these licenses deal with copyright. Copyright can be applied to code just as it can to music or a novel, but the situation is less clear for hardware. Open source hardware is often released using the same licenses used for open source software, but for functional hardware, copyright is almost certainly not applicable. These devices are covered instead by patent law, and patents are much harder to get and shorter-lived than copyrights. There are just beginning to be efforts to develop "open source hardware licenses" per se, but the Creative Commons and GNU ones discussed to this point can be useful for the designers of mechanisms and machines to express how they want their work to be used, and these license terms are generally respected in the open source community even if they are not enforceable.

Outside the open source community, these licenses may not be respected. The open source community develops new technologies, usually with no expectation of financial benefit. When I invent something, I do it because I want to advance the state of the technology. Making a technology better creates the proverbial rising tide that lifts all boats, but a patent can lock up a particular advancement for nearly two decades, preventing others from building upon it. I like to say that every new patent issued extends the Dark Ages by 20 years. By contrast, open source development allows for the most rapid development. People around the world can collaborate and build upon each other's work, sharing both the burden and the benefit.

Obtaining a patent also costs time and money. A patent prevents others from using a technology, but often a more important function is to prevent another from patenting the same invention and keeping it from you. Open source may achieve this goal too, because public disclosure of an invention can also be used to block anyone else from obtaining a patent on it. In this way, releasing a new innovation as open source can be a more economical way for a small company to avoid being blocked by a larger one. (Joan notes here, though, that this area can be complex, and if you are living it you should obtain some actual legal advice. There are some notable cases of a company apparently trying to patent something put out open source, and how that sort of case will play out is uncertain.)

# What Does a Beginning Open Source User Need to Know?

It can be intimidating to jump in to an ongoing open source community and try to figure out how everything works. If you use open source hardware or software, you are not under any obligation to modify it or contribute to its development. (If it's a non-commercial license, you may not be able to use it to make money though—be sure to check that and see the discussion about types of licenses in the previous section.) If you do want to contribute, this section will give you some suggestions.

---

■ **Joan's perspective**    It can also be hard to get going in an open source environment if you do not actually *want* to know how everything works in detail, since that is an underlying assumption. If you are like me and want to read a high-level overview first to see how things work, then you might first check to see whether anyone has written a book or, failing that, a web page discussing at least the high-level philosophy about how the system works. In this book, we have tried to give references like that for the technologies we have discussed. (In part, this book is intended to provide some of that big picture, too.) Failing all that, open source communities are usually good about giving a starting point if you can find a forum or wiki related to what you are doing.

---

## Contributing to Open Source Yourself

Most open source projects use revision control systems to allow people to participate. These systems allow users to create a local copy of the code, modify it, run the code to test their changes, and then make those changes available to other users. The procedure for this varies with different revision control systems. Older programs like Concurrent Versions System (CVS) and Subversion (SVN) use a client/server model in which a user must check out the code (or some subset of it). As with a book from a library, a checked-out piece of code is not available for someone else to check out at the same time, which prevents conflicts but can limit the rate of development.

Distributed systems like Git are becoming more common. In Git, every user has a complete copy not only of the code, but of the entire revision history, while another master copy usually sits on a central server. Each user can make their own changes and then copy only the changes back to the central repository or directly to one another. Git has sophisticated utilities for merging changes made concurrently by different people, so even if the central version has changed in the time you were working on your modifications, it's likely to be able to integrate your changes automatically.

It is possible to break things with incompatible changes, or just through insufficient testing of your changes. A project generally has one or more maintainers who control which changes are and are not allowed into the central repository. On github.com, a popular website for storing online Git repositories, users generally submit a pull request when they have changes that they want to submit for inclusion in the repository. A *pull request* consists of one or more *commits*, which are changes to the code with a title and description so that the history of changes can be tracked and specific changes can be located later. A pull request should always leave the code in a working state (it shouldn't break existing functionality without fixing it, and should not introduce new code that does not yet work). Each individual commit should preferably do the same, though it is not uncommon to see one commit that is simply a fix for a bug introduced by another.

When something does break, the commit history makes it possible to look back and find where the code was broken, undo those changes (even if more changes have been made to other parts of the code since then), and to blame the person who introduced the error and discuss with them how to fix it. Github also includes an issue tracker that can be used to discuss possible changes, or for non-coders to report bugs so that those participating in the development can try to fix them.

For users of these open source projects, there are usually no requirements to contribute, though contribution is encouraged. If you have the skills, submitting improvements and bug fixes is almost always welcome. Just be sure to check coding standards or style guides (for instance, there are strong, differing opinions about the formatting of some types of code, particularly the use of brackets in C-like languages) and make sure that your commit message and comments are helpful. If you're not a coder, that's OK too.

If you encounter a bug in the program, be sure to check the issue tracker to see if it has been reported yet. If the issue has been reported, look at the report and see if you can add any helpful information, but don't make a new one. Redundant bug reports waste time, and developers who get a lot of them have the understandable tendency to get crabby about it. If the issue hasn't been reported, check for any guidelines for bug reporting and try to give as much information as possible about how to reproduce the problem. A bug report that includes whatever settings and files you were using (or better yet, the simplest version that still causes the error to occur) and a description of what you were trying to do when you encountered the problem is much more useful and will be better received than one that simply states that a problem occurred. Basically, the more you do to help the developer find and fix the problem more quickly and easily, the more it will be appreciated.

If the program works, but lacks an ability you would like to have, you can submit a feature request. Some projects are more amenable to feature requests than others, and, as with bug reports, redundant requests are never good. If you have a simple fix that will significantly improve things, some developers will be grateful for the idea, but keep in mind that what seems simple to the user may not be simple for the developer. Offer your idea clearly and don't be demanding or make it difficult to understand what you're suggesting. Remember, also, that very often the person maintaining an open source project may be a volunteer or merely doing the work as a small part of a larger academic job.

## Hackathons

Software is becoming more of a service than something you buy in a box, and perhaps given that, joining a hackathon to develop some open source code to solve a problem is the newest way to volunteer for your community. The big difference now is that you do not need to happen to live in Cambridge, Pasadena, or Palo Alto to be able to contribute. You can search for a combination of your city name and a phrase like "civic hacks" or "civic hackathon" to see what is going on, or look at the national site http://hackforchange.org.

# The Challenges of Open Source

To this point, we have heard mostly from Rich about the benefits of open source and a bit of history. Now to close with a bit of a counterpoint, we will hear from Joan about some of the practical issues that still need a little work. She has the perspective of someone who has been around some form of open source coding since before it was really called that, but who has now re-entered it and is looking to get some specific tasks done.

---

■ **Joan's perspective**   Chapter 1 discusses Rich's learning style, which he very evocatively compares to crystals forming in all directions. The virtue and problem of a lot of open source materials is that they evolve in a pretty similar way. Someone seeds a project and then it becomes the hub of interesting things that branch in many directions. As people develop this material, they document what they add.

This means that, unless the originator of the whole thing gave some background about the big-picture view, there may not be an introduction to the big picture of the field available anywhere. New users have to just sort of dive in the middle and flail for a while, asking questions on community forums or trying out stuff on their own, to figure out what is going on. When a community gets big and lots of people are starting to do the same thing, the result is usually not very efficient.

When I started learning 3D printing, this is how things were. There was a big ball of interconnected string, and, in principle, you could get to any point on the ball somehow. But starting in the middle of the ball made it hard to see the big picture or why things were as they were. That is why I wrote *Mastering 3D Printing* and, now, it is why we are writing this book—to help create some bigger-picture context and some entry points into the ball of string.

This "ball of string" documentation style works well if you learn things the way that Rich does, from the middle outwards. However, if you are traditionally educated as I am and like learning with some structure and hierarchy around your materials, you may be frustrated. If you are dropped into learning something this way and it is not your thing, try progressively harder test projects so that you can grow yourself some scaffolding around the information.

The other challenge in using open source is that programs and hardware are continuously changing. This incremental improvement is a good thing in early-stage development and can move a new idea ahead quickly. However, if you are writing a class that requires the use of open source software, for example, the constant change makes it hard to use screen shots or detailed explanations. If you are using open source materials in a traditional class that is supposed to have materials fixed for several years, some creativity is required. (Universities, and more so K–12 schools, typically develop curriculum tied to a textbook that will be used for several years. Whether these practical limitations will be overcome when textbooks are electronic is an interesting question.)

It's also important to keep up in the community, since "everyone knows" that you should use version 4.1.17 for application X but 3.2.9 for everything else. For those immersed in it, these are familiar streets in their hometowns, but for immigrants just trying to get something done, they can be frustrating. If you have read straight through the book so far, you will have seen how some standards are emerging in some of these primarily open source hardware and software technologies, and you probably already have a sense of how far there still is to go in many areas.

# Summary

This chapter covered a bit about the open source communities that have developed and that support the fundamental work that underlies many of the technologies discussed in earlier chapters. We also talked about the rules of the road for collaborating in an open source environment and about the different types of open source licenses you might see when you start digging into these areas in more depth. Chapter 10 moves on to the topic of how to encourage more participation in these open technologies by women and girls.

# CHAPTER 10

■■■
•

# Creating Female Makers

Engineering and science have historically been mostly male—overwhelmingly so, until very recently. When Joan arrived at MIT, the percentage of women students was about 16%, and it had risen to about 20% by the time she graduated. This chapter starts with Joan's viewpoint of how this disparity has played out, talks about some statistics, and discusses some projects that are attempting to attract more female makers. There are probably as many hypotheses about why women turn away from math, science, and engineering as there are female technologists. Joan will explore a few of her hypotheses in the next section.

## The Engineering Life

I have always disliked the label "female engineer." As far as I was concerned, I had a degree from MIT and I was an engineer, no modifier required. MIT was very much a meritocracy, and pretty much you got the grades you worked for. I always felt that if someone pointed out your gender, they might be implying you had gotten a pass on the standards because of it, so I tended to avoid women in technology groups and the like until I was very established in my career. When I was a young engineer, women in tech groups also tended to be all about how to manage having children, which I was not concerned with at the time. I just wanted to get to build cool spacecraft and discover new things about other planets.

I have several hypotheses about why some girls and women find it hard to get into and stay in tech, based on both my own experiences and observing others. These are necessarily very anecdotal and biased by my experiences. The next section gives you some objective numbers and then talks about programs that are trying to change things. But, for what it is worth, here are some things that I believe make it tough unless a girl has the right combination of traits.

### Quiet, Please

Many male techies of my acquaintance are very shy, at least in person (online can sometimes be a different story). An introspective personality and ability to focus help a lot in learning math and science. Thus one would expect the pool of prospective scientists and engineers to be skewed quite a bit toward quiet introverts. However, girls interested in science and math are unusual and therefore visible and remarked-upon. Unlike a quiet male who might be left alone to pursue making things in the garage and who would not have to explain an A in math, a girl has a harder time being left alone to do this. A girl who wants to be left in peace might do something less unusual than becoming a scientist or engineer so that she does not have to continually defend her choices.

As an extrovert, I enjoy flaunting expectations. Early in my career, everyone around knew who I was, what my research areas were, and so on. Even for me, it was disconcerting that people would stop me in the hall and offer opinions on my work when I had no idea who they were. I realized that it was good for visibility and capitalized on it, but it would have been very hard if I had been like some of the quieter guys I have known. Thinking about it, I can only remember a handful of introverted female engineers and scientists my age. Perhaps as the world goes more virtual it will be easier for introverts, male and female.

## Stupid Girl

If I am in a virtually all-male professional situation, I think pretty hard about asking a question that might make me look stupid. I always feel the difference between "that was a dumb question" and "dumb girl." The reality is that in a technical discipline, no one knows everything, and asking your colleagues questions about their areas of expertise is critical. I think this really hurt me in graduate school, where I was frequently the only woman in classes and I hesitated to ask a question if I thought everyone else knew the answer already. I have no such compunctions now, but it took a long time to get past my reticence.

---

■ **Tip**    There is a marvelous story told by Martha Beck in her short piece, "You're a good man, Dr Smurf"—available at www.salon.com/1999/02/16/feature_378/—about the day that she realized (as a Harvard graduate student) that senior male professors sometimes fake it if they do not know something.

---

## About Bias

People are people, and everyone brings some bias to the table when they meet another person. Women are usually shorter than men (I am five-foot two) and have higher-pitched voices. This means that I disappear at meetings where everyone is standing up, and a colleague with hearing loss might literally not hear me. I am conscious of this and have to allow for it, either by bouncing around a bit to draw people's eyes, wearing bright colors, towing along a tall colleague, or otherwise being visible.

Once I have someone's attention, I still have to validate myself. I rely heavily on my formal academic credentials for this. It is unfortunate but true that sometimes people just simply do not believe a female engineer can be competent. The only thing I have found that works is to be frequently and assertively right about things, which causes some of the problems noted in the previous section. It does not take a lot of imagination to foresee some scenarios in which these tactics do not go down well. That said, most of the time I have gone into professional situations assuming I would be taken seriously and just acted accordingly. Usually, this works. When it does not, sometimes the only thing to do is to cut losses and move on.

Sometimes, though, being female can make me an ambassador to non-technologists of both genders who, for whatever reason, have not followed a technical career path but who want to learn a specific skill (like using a 3D printer) from someone who they perceive will treat them as an equal. This has brought me into a lot of unusual, interdisciplinary projects.

## Purposeful Making

I have never really been able to get into a tool for its own sake, at least, not for very long. For example, in the case of 3D printing, I find the technology intriguing, but the application of it far more so. I have always been more interested in how different technologies might work together rather than the in-depth detail of how any one thing works. I can learn that detail when I need to. Typically, though, I need a problem to solve before I dive into something too deeply. This gives me a direction which allows me to structure what I learn. Although there are certainly exceptions, I have found that on average this style is more common among women engineers than among men. In Chapter 1, Rich talks about the difference between a maker and a hacker in his section on the hacker path. If we are both on the right track, it means women tend more toward making and men more toward hacking, which would fit at least the authors of this book!

# Getting More Girls Into Tech

Assuming you are trying hard not to be biased and to involve more girls into making and, ultimately, into technology-focused careers, what should you do? The rest of this chapter shares some formal research into this area. Before delving into that, though, the following are some things that I do not hear mentioned often that I would like to add to the mix for those of you creating spaces at school or at home for a young female maker and perhaps her buddies:

- Chapter 5 talks about the importance of allowing for experimentation and failure in makerspaces. A perceived need to appear competent at all times fights against this and should be something you think about if you are designing a makerspace to attract both genders. Some of the programs discussed later in this chapter try different tactics to encourage girls to play with things in less structured ways or, alternatively, to give a sense of some structure.

- If you have a quiet daughter or female student who loves math and science, try to find ways to celebrate that while respecting introversion and perhaps her desire not to have too much drama. A good resource might be Susan Cain's book *Quiet: The Power of Introverts in a World That Can't Stop Talking* (Broadway Books, 2013). The author has a TED talk and other more abbreviated versions of her work online as well.

- If your daughter or student has a mix of maker interests and traditional female interests, do not comment on how weird this is. I took a ballet class at night and was heavily involved in figure skating for years just because it was nice not to stand out some of the time. But when people discovered my "other identity," I would get commentary on how "strange" this was.

- Many makerspaces have training programs and resources that are primarily focused on tools or skills. If you are the one developing programming for a makerspace, consider more project-focused classes and meetups rather than ones that are primarily about particular technologies. In other words, serve the maker as well as the hacker, to use our Chapter 1 distinction. The projects do not have to be stereotypically female, but perhaps can have a civic or scientific purpose beyond learning to use a 3D printer or CNC machine for its own sake.

- Consider the physicality of the space and tools. Can someone short get at and use tools safely without having to climb on stools? Do you have to move things that weigh 50 pounds around to get at the screwdrivers? Do not go out and buy pink tools or floral toolboxes, but consider whether your setup will be overwhelming for someone with small hands or shorter arms. In general, think about whether someone who is not the size of an average adult male will be put in awkward positions when they are using equipment.

- Avoid using terminology as a barrier. As you will see in Chapter 12, I had a lot of exposure to soldering and electrical work as a child, but pretty much zero exposure to anything mechanical, because we lived in a small apartment. I did not see a machine tool until well into my MIT education and distinctly remember, over 30 years later, how it felt to raise my hand and ask what "tapping" meant in a room with a couple of other women and a few dozen guys. Define your terms and use analogy without being condescending. If there is one woman in a class, and she does not understand the basic terminology, she might leave rather than ask what seem to be dumb questions. I use cooking metaphors a lot, even for mixed-gender audiences.

119

Chapters 12 through 14 contain more stories about becoming a scientist and daily life in the profession. These anecdotes reflect my perspective and that of other scientists and engineers of both genders. Getting into a technical career is a lot of work for anyone, and wisdom that helps girls in particular might well help your young male makers, too.

---

■ **Note**   I have not talked about the harder situation faced by girls living in cultures with higher barriers that hold them back from getting into making, much less into math, science, and engineering careers. If you are on the other side of a cultural divide, consider how to be supportive of all parts of the girl's life and personality. There are no easy answers or one-size-fits-all solutions, but I have found that encouraging the girl to ask for help and advice usually will at least open a door and give you ideas.

---

## One View: Why Are There So Few Women at Hackerspaces?

I asked Carlyn Maw, one of the cofounders of Crashspace (the first hackerspace in Los Angeles, www.crashspace.org), why there were so few women in hackerspaces. Figure 10-1 shows her with one of her cofounders, Tod Kurt. Carlyn wrote back with her thoughts (slightly edited for this book).

*Figure 10-1.* Carlyn Maw and Tod Kurt, two of the founders of Crashspace

■ **Carlyn's view**    I am a forest person, and this always seems like a tree question to me. The bigger question is "How does any space or profession become gendered?" I think Vi Hart and Nicky Case did an excellent job with their Parable of the Polygon (http://ncase.me/polygons/). That piece demonstrates visually how basic math predicts that even a slight preference to be with people similar to you leads to segregated neighborhoods.

So once we get comfortable with the idea that it isn't really the nasty guys causing the problem, it becomes the more insidious, harder thing to address, of nice people being even slightly more able to relax around people of their own gender, that just might be the primary creator of gendered professions.

My Dad gave me a now hard-to-find Barnes & Noble audiobook: *He Said, She Said: Exploring the Different Ways Men and Women Communicate* by linguist Deborah Tannen. He gave it to me when he saw me struggling in male-dominated workplaces, I guess over a decade ago now. I didn't listen to it at first because I hate books that just go wallow in stereotypes. But he gently pestered, and I did listen, and it blew my mind. I've since had the chance to meet her, and she's just a lovely, reasonable person who avoids hyperbole and tries to give voice to the data the best she can.

What I took away from her work is that *statistically speaking* (and that is an important phrase), when you are talking to a guy he is trying to establish hierarchy, and if you are talking to a woman she is *statistically likely* to try to establish that you are just like her. And this is completely independent of what the conversation is nominally about. So it isn't just that you are having a different conversation in the moment, it's that the basic rules behind interacting with another person come from completely different motivations. That's huge! Also, she shows, there are enormous consequences if you don't conform to your gender's stereotype.

So if *statistically speaking* men and women are using language itself for different purposes, you can sort of see why being with the people who play by the same rules as you is kind of more comfortable, at least in the short term. Long term it means you live in an echo chamber that ratchets up the crazy. So we've got to work on that.

What does knowing about the different language patterns buy us? Well, it makes life as a freak possible for me. Because let's be clear, when you ask a woman who is involved with something why everyone else like her isn't at that same party, you are calling her a freak. Maybe nicely and with admiration, but freak nonetheless. So for myself, I think I pop in and out of the two language styles unconsciously. I'd be better off if I could be more conscious about it, for sure. But knowing that the different language patterns exist has helped me reframe certain situations and kept them "not about me" in a way that makes my life more comfortable.

For the rest of the world, the short-term answer is to have lots and lots and lots of hackerspaces that enthusiastically let their own freak-flag fly, because there are lots and lots and lots of different kinds of people. Everyone deserves a home that validates them and their experience. More. Let's just have more. More. More. More.

Do girls learn making differently? Study after study after study shows that we conform to the expectations of those around us. Girls (and boys) are going to act out what is expected of them. The biggest favor you can do for any girl in your life is to expect curiosity. Expect bravery. Expect awesome. She will not disappoint.

# Why Focus on Female Makers?

The discussions to this point have not talked about why it is important to help girls and women become a bigger part of the maker community. Basic fairness and letting everyone have the career they want is a basic reason, of course. However, there are also social costs if a lot of people who otherwise might have become technologists do not. The world needs more people who can objectively analyze the world, no matter what profession they ultimately choose. More people trained as engineers, scientists, and mathematicians may mean that all the jobs that could really use technical training probably will actually have someone appropriately trained in them, which might not be the case otherwise. Many baby-boomer engineers are starting to retire, and some farsighted tech companies are beginning to worry that not enough young people are entering tech fields to replace them. The following section gives some statistics. All the sources noted in what follows are gathered into one note at the end of the section to make things a little easier to read.

## The Numbers

Every ten years the U.S. Census tallies up the professions of Americans. The last census was taken in 2010. As reported by the National Science Foundation, engineering occupations in 2010 employed 1,569,000 people, of whom 200,000 were women (13%). In 2010, there were 91,000 employed aeronautical engineers (Joan's background), of which 10,000 were female (11%). At the master's degree level, it drops to 34,000 and 5,000, respectively—so in 2010, I was personally 0.02% of the population of female aeronautical engineers in the United States. There are also a lot of women who move into other things rather than stay in a strictly engineering role. I wonder what I would be counted as now, for example.

The Anita Borg Institute's Why Women Leave report found that women leave technology companies at twice the rate of men, with the leading reasons being lack of advancement, too many hours, and low salary. An intriguing article published in the January 2015 issue of *Science* by Sarah-Jane Leslie et al (see upcoming note) showed that fewer women get PhDs in professions where it is perceived that innate talent is required for success. The authors suggest that practitioners in technical fields stress the hard work to succeed, rather than implying that everyone is brilliant to start with! Of the fields the researchers looked at, philosophy, math, and physics had the highest perceived need for brilliance, and education and psychology the lowest—with the various scientific and engineering disciplines scattered between.

## The Problem

According to the NCWIT report cited in the note that follows, there will be 1.2 million computing-related job openings expected in the United States by 2022. If nothing changes by then, only 39% of these jobs will be filled by U.S. computing undergraduates. According to the same report, 57% of 2012 undergraduate degree recipients were women; 18% of computer and information science undergraduate degree recipients were women (which falls to 12% at major research universities). This is a *drop* from 37% in 1985. There has been a *64 percent decline* in the number of first-year undergraduate women interested in majoring in computer science between 2000 and 2012.

The news is not any better in the workforce. The computing workforce was 26 percent female in 2013. The Intel MakeHers report (full reference in Note that follows) discusses cultural and social discouragements for girls and women in maker activities, particularly cultural biases, a lack of mentorship, and a feeling that makerspaces are not safe for them. Teachers also may underestimate girls' math and science ability relative to boys, as reported by Claire Cain Miller in *The New York Times*.

So the bottom line is this: there will not be enough computing professionals in the years to come, and half the population has declining interest in filling them or perhaps perceives they cannot fill them.

■ **Note**   Data on women in engineering and other technology professions is available from several sources that are cited in this section or referred to in the rest of the chapter. I have gathered them in one place here to make them easier to find.

National Science Foundation, National Center for Science and Engineering Statistics, Scientists and Engineers Statistical Data System (SESTAT), 2010, available from `www.nsf.gov/statistics/wmpd/2013/tables.cfm`.

Society of Women Engineers (SWE) reports statistics on the status of women in the professions at `http://societyofwomenengineers.swe.org/index.php/trends-stats#activePanels`.

The Laurel School in Ohio has a Center for Research on Girls. Their Girls In STEM: Tinkering can be retrieved from `https://www.laurelschool.org/page.cfm?p=625`.

The National Center for Women and Information Technology (on the web at `www.ncwit.org` and @ncwit on Twitter) is a strategic partnership of the National Science Foundation, Microsoft, and Bank of America, with other corporations listed as investment partners. This chapter notes its data as NCWIT.

The Anita Borg Institute sponsors various activities to help women, particularly women in computing. Its Why Women Leave infographic can be found at `http://anitaborg.org/insights-tools/why-women-leave/`.

An article in the 16 January 2015 issue of *Science* (Leslie, S-J., Cimpian, A., Meyer, M., and Freeland, E., "Expectations of brilliance underlie gender distributions across academic disciplines," 347(6291), pp. 262–265, doi 10.1126/science.1261375) discusses how fewer women enter professions whose practitioners think raw talent, as opposed to training, is the critical factor for success.

Intel released a report in November, 2014 called MakeHers about the issues of falling numbers of women in STEM careers. You can download it in full or executive summary or infographic form at `http://www.intel.com/content/www/us/en/technology-in-education/making-her-future.html`.

Toy companies are beginning to perceive that there may be a market for maker-oriented toys aimed at girls, as described in a *Los Angeles Times* article (and as discussed later in this chapter in a section about the Goldieblox case study). You can access the article here: `www.latimes.com/business/la-fi-girls-toys-20141214-story.html`.

*The New York Times'* Claire Cain Miller reported in January 2015 on a study showing that teachers graded boys' math and science exams higher than girls' exams if they knew the students, compared to graders who did not know the identities of the students. This effect was not seen in English or Hebrew classes (this was in Israel). The article is available online at `www.nytimes.com/2015/02/07/upshot/how-elementary-school-teachers-biases-can-discourage-girls-from-math-and-science.html`.

# Case Studies

All this might just be pretty depressing, and it is tempting just to throw up your hands and think that maybe the stereotypes are true. But fortunately, there are a lot of people trying various things in school and community settings. Many of these are at this point experimental, and it is not yet clear where they will go. Out of these experiments, there will doubtless come many new ways of learning. Not all of them are complicated; they can be as simple as repurposing part of a classroom or taking on an intern—or as complicated as launching a 50,000 square-foot makerspace.

## Marlborough School: Robots, Visual Arts, and More

The Marlborough School, an all-girls, 7th–12th grade independent school located in the Hancock Park area of Los Angeles (www.marlborough.org), is experimenting with various new maker technologies at the school, mostly focused for the moment on its visual arts program and on its FIRST Tech Challenge robotics team (see Chapter 4).

Visual Arts teacher Kathy Rea was an early adopter of classroom 3D printing and had her architecture students design models for an urban village in Tinkercad and produce them using a 3D printer (Figure 10-2). In her new 3D product design class, students are first taking apart existing objects (rain gutters, heating vents, stove parts, etc.) then repurposing or "upcycling" them for new applications, such as lighting devices. Later, students will have the opportunity to design a new product to solve a problem they have defined, or to redesign an existing object to make it more aesthetically pleasing or to improve its usefulness. The prototypes for this project will be designed in CAD and printed on a 3D printer.

*Figure 10-2. Architectural models by students at Marlborough School*

Meanwhile, the school fields a FIRST Tech Challenge team and has arranged a space that the girls can use to work on their robot. The space was featured in Chapter 5, and the girls working on the robot are shown in Figure 10-3.

***Figure 10-3.*** *Marlborough School students working on their FIRST Tech Challenge robot*

Darren Kessner teaches math and computer science. He has been developing a new computer science class that uses the Processing language (described in Chapter 2) controlled by Makey Makey interfaces (Chapter 8). He finds that the Makey Makey part is a good entry point for students who are not so into coding, and that the programming part is substantive enough that the enthused girls can really have substantive projects.

Science teacher Andy Witman, who advises the robotics team, won a FIRST's Compass award for his outstanding mentorship. The girls have a video online nominating him for it in which they talk about how much they appreciate his faith in them. The group talks about Witman's motto—"Fail Forward!"—and that it means a lot to them to have his support on the team. The team recruits members through a club fair at the beginning of the year and builds awareness by showcasing 3D-printed objects at a trade fair during the year.

The teachers hope to develop a more substantial makerspace and program at Marlborough and to build on the current enthusiasm and word of mouth among the students to get more girls onto lifelong math and science trajectories. The teachers also hope to incorporate some collaborative STEAM-based projects into their curriculum in order to encourage and support creativity, imagination, and innovative thinking across disciplines.

## Castilleja School

The Castilleja School in Palo Alto, California is an independent all-girls school for grades 6–12 with 444 students in the 2014–15 academic year. The school has a makerspace it calls the Bourn Idea Lab. Angi Chau is the lab's director. In an interview for this book, Chau said that the reason for starting the lab was for their FIRST robotics team to have a place to work. Robotics, however, was an after-school activity, so then they began to think about how to use the lab during the school day.

The Bourn Idea Lab is linked from the school's home page (www.castilleja.org) and includes many links to descriptions and photos of projects for various grade levels (including building a microscope and replicas of Leonardo da Vinci's machines). The students are using Tinkercad for design projects and OpenSCAD for geometrical ones. They are trying a Teachers Fellow program to get more involvement. In this program, Castilleja teachers commit to spending some time in the lab and get one-on-one coaching in ways to get their students making things.

Chau feels that it is important to have some things in the Lab that are familiar to girls already so that they feel like they have an entry point. To that end, she stocks some traditional craft supplies in the lab and tries to avoid having it feel too much like a man's garage or having it be too cluttered and messy (while recognizing that making is not tidy, either). As she says, "Softer circuits [as in wearable tech, Chapter 7] teach the same thing as robotics."

Many maker toys are aimed at making monsters, but it does not have to be that way. She has an all-girls environment to start with, but she says that coed schools have had a lot of success with some girl-only times in their makerspaces after school. Otherwise, she says, boys will appear to know how to use tools (even if they do not) and will tend to intimidate a girl who has not yet seen some of the tools in use.

## Bridgette Mongeon

Bridgette Mongeon (shown in Figure 10-4 with some of her 3D-printed art) is a Houston-based sculptor who has been an early adopter of 3D printing. She is also a passionate advocate of teaching students that an art education can lead to many different careers other than being a studio artist. She visits schools and then takes on interns at her studio to work with individually. Mongeon encourages girls to get interested in the technology behind the art and to get past the idea of 3D computer-generated art as being nothing but monsters. Her book *3D Technology in Fine Art and Craft: Exploring 3D Printing, Scanning, Sculpting and Milling* is coming from Focal Press in September 2015, and her blog is available at http://creativesculpture.com/blog/. Because she feels that a lot of 3D modeling is focused on monsters and more masculine examples, she tries to show that a different style is possible, too.

***Figure 10-4.*** *Bridgette Mongeon and 3D-printed friends*

## Vocademy: The Makerspace

Vocademy is a 15,000+ square-foot makerspace in the Los Angeles suburb of Riverside, California. Chapter 5 discusses it in general, but it is worth another look here because Vocademy's community is 40% female. When asked how he did it, Vocademy's founder, Gene Sherman says simply, "Cosplay." Cosplay (see Chapter 7 for more) involves dressing up as a character from a game or a movie; it can be close to traditional costuming or can incorporate a variety of wearable technologies.

Sherman says that for each subject taught at Vocademy, there is a free introductory class. More than half of the examples are gender-neutral or lean toward the stereotypically female, like shoes or jewelry. The intent is that girls and women will be drawn in by the familiar and then will have the confidence to go forward into areas that might otherwise be too big a leap. Sherman says, "Half the world is female. Why aren't half the world's products designed by females?"

Machines do not care about gender or ethnicity, he says, and he encourages people to think in terms of designing solutions for problems. Vocademy has a huge 4×3 foot laser cutter, because he wanted to enable using a laser cutter to cut patterns for sewing. Figure 10-5 shows a mostly female thermoplastics class at Vocademy—so it looks like his plan is working out well!

*Figure 10-5.* *A thermoplastics class at Vocademy – The Makerspace. Photo by Neeley Fluke*

## Construction Toys for Girls

Another way for girls to get into making is through toys. Traditional builder toys (like LEGOs) are at least in principle gender-neutral, and some LEGO kits have been developed that are intended to appeal to girls (but see the note after this section for some issues that this raises). Two companies founded by women engineers have developed builder toys intended in particular to appeal to girls.

One builder toy aimed at girls is Roominate (`www.roominatetoy.com`), which encourages building wired dollhouses. This company was founded by Alice Brooks and Bettina Chen, who met in the master's engineering program at Stanford (and who hold, respectively, undergrad degrees from MIT and Caltech). The wired dollhouses make me very nostalgic, since my electrician dad was always helping me wire up a dollhouse—but the components were a lot bigger then, in the pre-LED days.

Kickstarter-funded Goldieblox (`www.goldieblox.com`) combines stories about Goldie, a girl inventor, with construction toys. The company launched on Kickstarter in the fall of 2012, aiming to raise $150,000, but raised nearly twice that from 5,000 supporters. The toys are now sold on the mass market.

This effort was helped immensely by the company winning a contest to advertise during the 2015 Super Bowl. The company's founder, Debbie Sterling, herself a Stanford-trained engineer, wants to change girls' toys away from the stereotypical pink boxes and princesses. Figure 10-6 shows one of their products, "Goldieblox and the Builder's Survival Kit," which includes a storybook, three character figurines, and 190 construction pieces intended to teach mechanical engineering.

**Figure 10-6.** *Goldieblox and the Builder's Survival Kit. Image courtesy of Goldieblox*

■ **Rich's view** Upon seeing these toys, I was struck by the apparent need to reinforce gender stereotypes with these construction sets specifically *for girls*. LEGOs were my favorite toy as a child, but I never saw them as a toy *for boys* in the same way that dolls were *for girls*. Together, Joan and I looked through some of the current LEGO sets available, and although some of the sets seemed more geared specifically toward boys than what I remembered from the early 90s, we also found sets that were very obviously aimed exclusively at girls, while a significant contingent still reflected my perception of a toy that was not strongly gendered.

I find this separation worrying in that it seems to promote the idea that some toys, and thus some subjects, are off-limits to one gender or the other. While the sets geared towards boys may include monsters or big machines, it seems like there is less of a barrier to girls liking these things than there is to boys playing with the pink-and-purple-princess sets intended for girls, in the same way that a little girl in pants won't draw attention, but a little boy in a dress will.

Joan, on the other hand, thinks this reflects the reality that girls are just not exposed enough to building things and that "boy toys" have to be "sweetened" first for many girls to feel comfortable playing with them. Whether this is true or not in a particular child's case is something for the reader to consider when making birthday present purchases.

## One Girl at a Time

Any educational endeavor really is about helping out one girl at a time. Coco Kaleel and her parents tell their story in the Foreword to this book. Somehow it just happened that the authors sort of adopted her technical interests, and she has absorbed everything we could give her. She is shown in Figure 10-7 hard at work. If you are into making things, the easiest thing to do is to help out just one girl now and then. You never know what you might create!

*Figure 10-7.* Coco at work. Photo courtesy of Mosa Kaleel

# What Do You Need to Learn To Get Started?

What you need to know depends on which technologies you decide to start with. If you are a parent, it could be as simple as buying an age-appropriate construction toy or one of the beginner's kits discussed in some of the earlier chapters. If you are a school administrator trying to design a makerspace that will draw in girls, consider finding some female engineers or makers in the community to help think of fun ideas. (See also Chapter 5's discussions of experiences with these spaces.) The most key point is not be so worried about what the users will learn that you suck all the fun out of it. Experiment! Fail! And figure out what went wrong for next time.

There are many groups and events aimed at teaching girls and women how to get started with writing code, building hardware, or combining both. In the case of learning how to code, type "girls learn to code" into an Internet search engine and you will find many options. You can narrow this down into online or in-person opportunities, camps, free events, expensive events, and pretty much anything else you can think of. Some groups, of course, are more reputable than others. As you would with any camp or after-school program, diligence the group and try to find out what they are about from places other than the group's website.

In the case of learning hardware, you can check your local makerspace for classes. There are some interesting programs at some schools, too. Luz Rivas is an MIT-educated electrical engineer who grew up in the Los Angeles suburb of Pacioma. After a career as an engineer and working at a nonprofit, she decided to start a program at elementary and middle schools to encourage Latina girls in particular to enter science and math careers. The organization DIY Girls (www.diygirls.org) has been ramping up its program and as of this writing have served nearly 400 girls and created a meetup group of 700 women.

# What Does It Cost to Start a "Maker Girls" Group?

As you can see from the examples already mentioned, projects can start at a variety of different levels. Consider your budget, how much space you have, and how many trained adults are available to help. The cost estimates in Chapters 2 through 8 should be helpful in determining what you can afford and what you might try first. Just as we say you should encourage experimentation and learning from failures in your makerspaces, so too should you try things out and adapt as needed.

# Summary

In this chapter we talked about the issues facing girls and women in getting started with making, and what barriers remain in later technical careers. We referenced a lot of research on girls and women in technical careers. We wound up our chapter with stories of efforts by a variety of individuals and groups to create events that will draw girls and women into making things.

■ ■ ■

# CHAPTER 11

# Making at a Community College and Beyond

Community (two-year) colleges have often been seen as having a more "vocational" focus than four-year universities. Historically, a lot of hands-on technical training has taken places at the community-college level. Community colleges have been focused on the career-oriented student (whether of traditional college age or older) who wants to get applied, employment-focused training to get started in a first career or to switch to a new one. This would seem to be a pretty good environment to create programs that involve a heavy dose of making things, and as a case study, this chapter for the most part talks about a project with the Design Tech Pathway program at Pasadena City College.

We thought this story was important to tell in a book that otherwise might seem to be focused on K–12 because it shows how a maker project can create a community where none was before. A concentration on designing and then making physical objects can spawn a lot of unanticipated positives that might never have come about if the students had been in a purely traditional classroom lecture program. As such, it might be a model for you to think about if you are considering adding a making or design element to a community-college or other adult-education program. Mixing lectures with hands-on solutions to real problems can be a powerful combination. As you will see, Joan was in the thick of this from the beginning, and Rich had a role somewhat later. Joan mostly tells the story as she saw the situation evolve, and Rich chimes in later with some observations.

## The Design Technology Pathway

Pasadena City College (PCC, www.pasadena.edu) is a large (30,000-student) public community college in Pasadena, California, with a long tradition of excellence in technical training. It helps that it is a block away from Caltech and in the thick of many established and startup technology businesses in Pasadena. However, it has developed strong programs in its own right as well, for some years in biological technology and now with a program called the Design Technology Pathway.

---

■ **Note**   "When we stop organizing ourselves to provide students with a class, topic, lecture, handout to address a deficiency and let them grow through challenges that not even we can accomplish, is when we are collectively creating the best educational system for them."

—Salomón Dávila, Dean, Career and Technical Education, Pasadena City College

---

Hands-on making is sometimes classified as Career and Technical Education (CTE) in California. At PCC, there are *Pathways* within the CTE program According to the PCC website, the Design Technology Pathway offers its students the use of "2D + 3D design software, rapid prototyping [such as] 3D scanning and 3D printing, laser and plasma cutting, vacuum forming, robotics," in addition to developmental math, English, and other courses. The program is heavily focused on tying what is being learned to the design of real things.

## The Facility

The actual hands-on part takes place in PCC's FabLab, a relatively new space outfitted with several 3D printers, a laser cutter, and computer workstations, adjacent to a traditional machine shop. The students are strongly encouraged to spend time working and studying together in the FabLab and other spaces oriented toward the students in the Pathway. This creates a mutually supportive community to encourage the students to hang in there and finish the program. Many students in the early cohort described in a minute are now in the process of applying to transfer to four-year universities as they finish up the PCC two-year degree. Dean Salomón Dávila and Design Technology Pathway Director Deborah Bird started the program in 2011 and have watched it evolve and grow. Bird likes to say that the philosophy of the program is "technology in the service of humanity."

## The Project

One of the philosophies of the Design Technology Pathway was to have community mentors for students in the program. In early summer 2014, some of the Design Technology students had just finished up some classes in Solidworks, a very powerful 3D-modeling software program aimed at engineering types of problems (precisely dimensioned modeling). I heard that the students were trying to think of a good project for the summer.

Meanwhile, the Los Angeles Unified School District's coordinator for technology for visually impaired students, Lore Schindler, was interested in the power of 3D printing to create objects for blind students to learn various subjects that were hard to teach any other way. However, the process of modeling an object so that it can be 3D printed (see Chapter 3) takes time, and she just did not have the time to do a lot of modeling. Just as the PCC students were looking for something to do, I was talking to Schindler, and she wondered aloud if perhaps I knew of someone who might have some time to create some model designs.

I did the obvious thing and put the two groups together. I volunteered some of my time to drop in at the FabLab and mentor a group of PCC students to develop models for blind students. Engineer Peter Ngo also came on board as a day-to-day mentor for the students and guided them through some of the details of the projects.

After consultation with Schindler and her colleague Michael Cheverie, we decided to develop two things initially: a tactile map to help young blind students learn how to navigate their school, and a set of models of molecules for advanced high school chemistry students. Later on, they also created a "dissectible" model of the human eye, which could be taken apart to help explain to a blind student why they were blind. The next section talks about the models themselves and the process, and then concludes with a group reflection by the students about the process and what they learned by being involved in it.

## The Tactile Models

Making tactile models is still something of an art more than it is a science. Teaching science and math tends to be a very visual process; think of all those equations and sketches on the board, and how hard it can be to type math and science homework (versus, say, an essay). Imagine the difficulty of explaining these subjects to someone who is completely blind or at least severely visually impaired. There are several projects underway to try and standardize or at least streamline the production of tactile graphics, notably the DIAGRAM (Digital Image And Graphic Resources for Accessible Materials) Center (http://diagramcenter.org), run by the nonprofit Benetech (www.benetech.org). But as we learned, these standards are still very much in development, and we really had to start with making our own. The students would particularly like to thank PCC's Stephen Alexander Marositz, Assistive Technology Specialist, and Mark Mintz, Alt Media Specialist, for their help in understanding these issues.

## The Map

One of the projects the group took on in summer 2014 was to create a tactile, 3D-printed map of an elementary school in Los Angeles Unified School District, which has both sighted and blind students. Some blind students learn to navigate there when they are 10 or 11 years old. Teachers have made tactile maps out of what was lying around, but Schindler, the coordinator for visually impaired student technology, thought it might be interesting to try 3D printing a map. Students Bryce Van Ross, Chi Yeung Chiu, Carlos Andrade, and Sandra Perez, with some help from many other students and staff, took on the map project.

There were a lot of challenges. First, there was a paper map of the school, but it was pretty confusing even for a sighted person, because one of the buildings had two floors. The first question was how much detail to show, and whether or not to label in Braille. Then, the question arose about *which* Braille conventions to use, because there are several different conventions. The most basic one takes up the most space, but was the one the users would be most likely to know, so the PCC students decided to use that. Then they decided that labeling everything in Braille would be too hard to distinguish from features on the map, so they added just a few symbolic labels and used a key with Braille.

When the students proudly gave the first prototype to users, they discovered some problems. For example, an arbitrary symbol used for "entrance to the campus" was one of the few standard tactile map symbols—the one for a ladies' restroom. Oops. The symbols for restrooms were changed to the standard circle and triangle. This iteration was also pretty complex, and it was simplified down to its bare essentials in the next round. Figure 11-1 shows the group in the PCC FabLab with some of the map prototypes (and a laser cutter in the background). Figure 11-2 shows the map open, and Figure 11-3 is a close-up of the Braille key.

*Figure 11-1. Student group with the map prototypes*

*Figure 11-2.* *The open map*

*Figure 11-3.* *Close-up of Braille key*

The next part of the design brief was that the map had to be portable for an elementary student. Ideally, it was also supposed to be fun to use and something that the sighted students at the school might feel slightly jealous about, so that they would be encouraged to interact with the blind students and the map to help with navigation while the blind students were learning. The solution was to back the 3D-printed map with some thin plywood (with holes cut out of it to make it lighter) and to make it hinged so that it would fold up. Figure 11-4 shows the folded map. The exterior was covered with a thin rubbery sheet so that it felt nice in the hand and so the users could not trap their fingers in the hinges easily. The colorfulness came about because the initial one was made from scraps left over from other things, which was, as one of the students said, a happy accident. It is so cheerful in person that people who can see it smile.

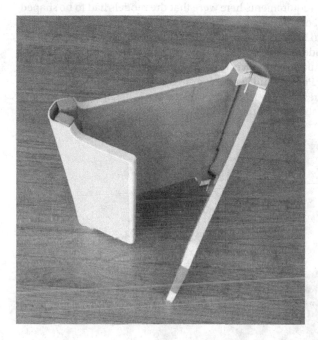

*Figure 11-4.  The earliest prototype, folded*

The students consulted frequently with both campus staff in disability services and also with whatever experts they could find. As a mentor, for the most part I reassured them that they were perfectly able to come up with solutions to the problems they were encountering, since in many cases no solutions, or at least no standard solutions, existed. For me, it was wonderful to watch them gain confidence and learn how to have technical squabbles and work them through. They also had to have a lot of empathy for their users; blind users need different things on a map than sighted ones do, like which end of a handicapped ramp is the high end, and the PCC group had to take a field trip to the elementary school and walk around some to get a feel for what would be necessary.

Several things were suggested that could not be fixed before the group ran out of time. Because some users would have some residual vision, high contrast between the map elements would have been helpful. It also turned out that it would have been easier and better to use a Braille labeler than to attempt to 3D print the Braille. That way, it would be easier to change the key if buildings started being used for other things.

# The Chemistry Models

The other model set, proposed by chemistry teacher Michael Cheverie, was to develop a set of models of the distribution of electrons in certain molecules, or *molecular orbitals.* This is a topic normally taught in Advanced Placement chemistry, so the PCC students also had to teach themselves enough chemistry to understand the problem and what was being taught. Students Free Tripp, David Harbottle, Naomi Galladande, and Brent Cano focused on the chemistry models, again with a lot of interaction with other PCC fellow students and staff.

Typically this sort of model is made up of some sort of construction toy or whatever happens to be lying around, and students rely on pictures in a textbook to go from the oversimplified 3D toy models to the more complex ideas of clouds of electronics. The design requirements here were that the models had to be shaped like the clouds of electrons; had to be able to be taken apart so that students could learn about how the molecules went together; and, of course, needed to be manageable by a blind student.

The students came up with shapes that were identifiable and tried out various ways of labeling, finally deciding that Braille labels on small pieces was counterproductive. Figure 11-5 shows the team at the Cal State Northridge (CSUN) Conference on Disabled Persons and Technology in March 2015, where they presented the work (along with their map colleagues). Figure 11-6 shows a Solidworks version of an ethylene molecule, and Figure 11-7 shows 3D-printed models of ammonia and ethylene molecules.

***Figure 11-5.*** *The students with the chemistry models*

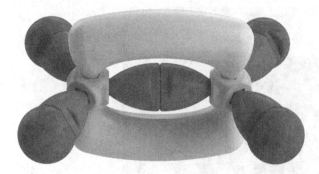

*Figure 11-6.* *Solidworks rendering of an ethylene model. Rendering courtesy of Free Tripp*

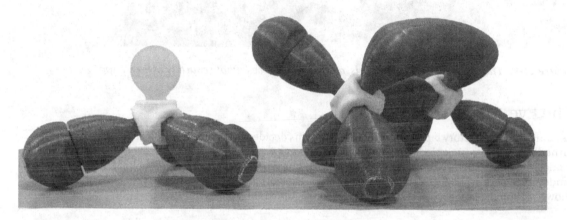

*Figure 11-7.* *3D-printed version of ammonia and ethylene molecules. Photo courtesy of Free Tripp*

The group went through many, many iterations, trying to find versions that would print easily and reliably, that would not break after being repeatedly put together and pulled apart, and that had a good feel to them. They eventually built up jars of experiments (Figure 11-8) as a visible record of how many iterations go into a good product. That jar seemed to get fuller and fuller (and turned into multiple jars) as time went on. It is also a powerful statement of how useful 3D printing is as an iterative design tool. That many versions would have been out of the question with most conventional tools.

*Figure 11-8.* *The many versions of the parts, analyzed and saved. Photo courtesy of Free Tripp*

## The Eye

As something of a victory lap, some of the PCC students decided to try one last project as summer 2014 turned into fall, also at Schindler's request. Blind students want to know why they are blind. Anatomy models are both expensive and often have features painted on them, which are not helpful. After surveying models that were available for some of the health care majors at PCC, the students came up with the design shown assembled in Figure 11-9 and "dissected" in Figure 11-10.

*Figure 11-9.* *The eye, assembled*

*Figure 11-10.* *The eye, "dissected"*

The eye muscles were pieces of weather-stripping Velcroed to the rest, so that they could be a bit floppy, like real muscles. The base was laser-cut wood; the rest was 3D printed and held together either by design of the parts or by bits of glued-on Velcro. The bumps at the back of the eyeball are rods and cones, the structures that turn light into signals the brain can process. The students were playing with different features and textures on some of the other parts to see what might work well. As of this writing, the eye was headed to a first encounter with some blind students, so we will see how that works out for all.

## Further Implications

These projects obviously benefited students who had no other options. But what about "tactile learners" in general? Not all students learn best from a lecture or a picture on a board. Tactile, or *kinesthetic,* learners may learn best by making something or doing something. It is hard for a visual learner (which I am) to come up with ways to teach math to someone who needs a mostly tactile approach. Designing an object for a blind student, though, forced all of us to think in a purely tactile way. The objects we come up with may also help tactile learners (which different sources cite as being from 5 to 10 percent of the population) learn math and science. Interestingly, students who will be the most enthused about getting into the technologies in this book may learn this way. We have suggested to several groups that they encourage students to come up with an object to teach a blind peer something hard to learn. In that way, we may get some interesting objects that will help both the students who invent them and the ones who receive them!

# The Students Reflect on the Experience

We sat down for a roundtable discussion with some of the project students (Bryce Van Ross, Naomi Galladande, Free Tripp, Sandra Perez, Carlos Andrade, Chi Yeung Chiu, and David Harbottle) to talk about what they had learned from their experiences. Here are some of their key points:

- The students felt that the hacker-style iterative design process we used had given them a lot of freedom—"artistic freedom" as they put it—to do what they wanted. They felt that they could learn from mistakes and figure out the design process for something "real and substantial" in their careers going forward.

- One student said that in a regular class if you got behind, you could ask the professor for an extension. Here, though, for the product to be delivered on time, everyone had to work together. There was no one to ask for an extension, since the team was in charge, so everyone had to keep up (and did).

- If they had it to do all over again, they said they would have liked to have more user input.

- They found the experience of starting with a lot of possible directions and then prioritizing and simplifying to be a very compelling experience.

- One student said that she had learned chemistry better by making the models than she had in a chemistry class. Another chimed in and said that if he becomes a chemistry professor someday, he will take a month, put the students into groups, let them figure out what to focus on, and have them go for it.

- One said of making things rather than sitting in a classroom listening, "I feel like you need noise to effectively demonstrate that you're actually learning something. Otherwise, it shows you are bored and not challenged to vocalize your thoughts." Others added the difference between "obnoxious noisy" and "productive noisy." Productive noisy, they said, was "narrating the game"—helping think through problems out loud. The question, then, is how to help teachers not mistake "productive noisy" for "obnoxious noisy"!

They all made it clear that it was a powerful thing to be allowed to experiment and fail and keep trying. As we have said in previous chapters, notably Chapters 1 and 5, this is the core of the hacker/maker ethos.

---

■ **Rich's perspective**  There has been an endemic absence of this learn-by-doing approach in schools that I believe is responsible for so many college graduates being unprepared for work in their respective fields. Unemployment and under-employment among college graduates is on the rise in the U.S. Meanwhile, Joan tells me that all of her rocket-scientist colleagues are getting desperate because they're all nearing retirement, with no new crop of qualified graduates to take their places. Some people blame my generation, saying that we lack attention spans or a work ethic, but maybe the blame should be laid at the feet of the school system that systematically left us unqualified to use our education for anything beyond passing standardized tests. I'm hopeful that programs like this one at PCC mark the beginning of a reversal of this trend.

---

All the students are working to finish up their PCC experience and are looking to transfer to 4-year colleges to get degrees in technical subjects. The PCC group presented the work described in this chapter at the prestigious CSUN conference mentioned earlier, and attendees in the session were amazed to discover that these students were not grad students, but undergrads at a community college between their first two years. Dean Dávila likes to use the word *empowerment,* and certainly this project was a powerful example of how a good real-world project can empower a group of students beyond anyone's expectations. We are working to find ways to take this project forward to the next level.

# Summary

This chapter described a case study of a community-college project to create models to help blind students learn math and science and how to navigate their schools. It is an example of how a combination of a real problem, some equipment and solid training in how to use it, and freedom to invent can be empowering at the community-college level. There is no reason this model would not apply in an age-appropriate way for both younger students and community-service groups looking to create change in a very tangible way.

■ ■ ■

# PART III

# How Scientists Get Started

The three chapters here introduce you to some stories of how scientists, mathematicians, and engineers actually got started (usually, by breaking something) and how they work every day.

Chapter 12 focuses on the early signs that someone is headed for a science career, usually indicated by breaking something and (sort of) fixing it. Chapter 13 focuses on how scientists think about the world. Chapter 14 ties things up with some pragmatic views about what it is like to work in these fields day to day.

In these chapters you will see how similar the scientific mindset is to the maker mindset, and how accessible the scientific process is to the average person who has some patience and a problem they feel driven to solve.

# CHAPTER 12

■ ■ ■

# Becoming a Scientist

In the first part of this book, we talked about specific technologies and how to get started using them. Then we gave you an overview of different communities that are successful at making things – the open source crowd, people running makerspaces, educators trying to interest girls and minorities in engineering, and finally traditional educators incorporating making into community college or other adult-education environments. But we have not talked much about how all this ties in to learning science, math, and other subjects.

In these next three chapters, Joan gives you a first-person tour of the experiences she has had as a traditional engineer, and shares the backgrounds of a few engineers and scientists. We have found that many of them have experienced a moment when they made something (and it worked) that they feel started them down their career path. If you are trying to encourage someone to start down a technical career path, these stories may give you ideas for creating moments that students may recount 20 or 30 or 50 years from now. Joan also tells you a little about where each person wound up, so that you can see where their path has taken them so far.

Chapters 15 through 17 tie the book together with case studies that illustrate the intersection of learning science and math and making things.

## Beginnings

In Chapter 9, Rich gives his view of the importance of the open source community in the past and future, and how it helped him become a 3D printer expert. Making things is not the only way that people can get excited about learning technical subjects. Often it involves reading science fiction – or possibly getting in trouble – instead. In this section, we talk about Joan's memories and then explore some variations on this theme. Now and then Rich chimes in with his perspective.

### Joan's Start

You can never be sure if a fuzzy memory from early childhood really happened or if you have just been told the story so many times that you fluffed it out from family legend. You might start with a vague snippet and add a detail here and there, as newer remembrances leak into and color older ones. The first seed of a lifetime passion or goal is particularly like that—a memory revisited so many times that it is rubbed to gleaming, like a genie's lamp.

Mine involves the innards of an early-1960s television: a failed television, fixable with a dab dropped just so from a soldering iron. I have a soldering iron in my seven- or eight-year-old hand front and center, framed by my blonde pigtails. Dad the electrician says in his Brooklyn accent, punctuated with a jabbing finger, "See that busted wire? That's your problem, *right there*."

With Mom worrying that my hair will catch on fire from the soldering iron, a blobby silver bit goes from solder wire to TV. The broken connection now whole, the iron goes back into its curled wire holder. The TV guts with my solder job returns to its cabinet, and *works*. In Figure 12-1, you can see the electrician and his assistant, taking some time off from their labors.

***Figure 12-1.*** *The electrician and his assistant*

■ **Rich's perspective**    My own first attempts to solder were less successful. Before the maker movement created a wealth of information on the Internet, and with the cheapest of equipment that I could save my allowance for, neither the heat nor the flux on the joint was sufficient. The solder would bead up or just fall off. It was years before I even realized that the circuit board wouldn't melt from the heat of the iron. The Internet now puts great tutorials and instructions within a few clicks' reach of anyone who knows how to use it.

Growing up in the rocket-fueled 1960s, it seemed like everyone wanted to be an astronaut. I certainly did, a short blonde kid in 6A of a New York City apartment building. My favorite show, *Star Trek,* was in its first run, and the TV had to be in top working order to keep up with Kirk and Spock. (Rich notes that, appropriately, he grew up on *Star Trek: The Next Generation.*) I did my homework suspended six floors up, maybe one-fifth as high off the ground as my heroes sitting on top of Apollo 11's Saturn V. In those days, aspiring to be a scientist or engineer (particularly a "rocket scientist") was like the call to the priesthood was in medieval Europe. You would learn the mysteries and save the populace from the evils of the world- in this case,the Russkies. It never occurred to me to wonder whether "girls" did these things—I was a scientist in my head from about age seven, and being a girl was pretty much irrelevant one way or the other. Belying the geek stereotype, I even still liked to dress up then, which will astonish people who knew me after the age of 18. I was much more worried about needing to wear glasses, since everyone knew astronauts needed perfect vision.

Becoming a scientist or engineer is hard. For six years of undergraduate and graduate school, during the term it was rare to study less than 12 to 16 hours a day, six or seven days a week. Given that, why do people become scientists? Common wisdom would say that a teacher, a mentor, or a role model drives the decision. Certainly, that can be true. Yet many of us remember an incident—a puzzle being solved, figuring out how something worked, some time when we had to creatively keep authority figures from discovering the aftermath of our first experiments. (When that propeller-driven aeronautical experiment landed in the pretty girl's hair in fourth grade or so, it was an accident. Really.) It's the chase that takes us through it, the feeling that there are greater and greater things to fix and to solve out there—if only we learn, say, one or two more ways that magnetic fields bend around wires. MIT, where I got my undergraduate degree, refers to the sensation as "drinking from the fire hose."

Nearly anyone can become turned on to science. The "a-ha!" moment can arrive in a variety of ways and at any age, and can even jump off the pages of a book or a movie screen. If there is a curious child in your life, how do you encourage the spirit without burning down the house? A science career starts with the need to try something purely to see what will happen (sometimes with unexpected, even spectacular, results).

Shortly before he passed away, my dad, then in his 90s, decided to entrust me with his electrician's toolbox. This treasure chest included some beautiful old instruments, with knobs and dials that I remember from my earliest soldering days (but was not allowed to touch back then). These instruments are probably less accurate than their modern digital equivalents, but they still work, and when I look at them I can hear him say, "That's your problem, *right there.*" They remind me that scientists learn by trying things out for themselves.

---

■ **Tip**   One symptom of nascent scientisthood is a driving need to take everything apart. Trying things with unknown outcomes implies taking occasional strategic risks. In its earliest manifestations, this results in pieces left over when the victimized home appliance is put back together. Risk taking is what makes sports exciting, and scientists similarly find out early on that they thrive on the sensation of trying something intellectually hard—and succeeding. Figuring out a bit of physics is not as visceral as nailing a double somersault in gymnastics class, but the sensation can be the same. The next section looks at some memories scientists and engineers have of their first intellectual swan dive (or splashy cannonball…).

---

## Building on Experience

"When I was four or five," says Sir Martin, "I had two baked bean cans and a piece of string, and I played with my sister down the garden." Sir Martin Sweeting is chief executive officer of Surrey Satellite Technology, Ltd. of Guildford, England, an aerospace company that does things like develop spacecraft to manage disaster relief. You can see a picture of him in Figure 12-2. Of his two cans and string, he says, "This ability to communicate at a distance fascinated me, and when I got a little older, about ten years old, we got headsets." Next, it was playing around with building radios. In those days before the Internet and cheap long distance, he loved speaking to people around the world freely on his ham radio set. Sweeting was 16 or 17 years old in the Apollo era, and the moon flights launching on the other side of the Atlantic inspired him to "go to university" and eventually obtain a PhD.

*Figure 12-2.* *Sir Martin as CEO (photo courtesy of Surrey Satellite Technology, Ltd.)*

Professor Sweeting attributes much of his science and engineering intuition to the government-surplus radio components and other parts readily available in post-World War II England. He worries that today, "a lot of children lose the concept of real safety and danger. Pick up a soldering iron, burn your finger, and you don't ever do it again. Everything is protected to such an extent that there are real dangers out there [that will be encountered by today's kids] and they'll be out of their depth." He says that human beings learn by their mistakes, and that science teaching needs to recapture that. "Kits of bits isn't enough. The key thing would be to find those really inspirational teachers to get students to do more than they think they could."

Sweeting tells the story of Geoff Perry, a physics teacher in Northern England who really excited his elementary school students in the 1960s. He got interested in Sputnik and computed the orbit of early Soviet satellites. His students would make observations of Soviet satellites as they passed overhead, know when to pick up signals, and so on, using just pencil, paper, and slide rule.

To excite kids about science, Sweeting says, you "have to expose kids when they are very young—between five and ten, since that's the point at which they are most inquisitive and don't get distracted by the pressures of the world. Somehow get them to have a practical involvement in that excitement. No matter what field it's in, it's the practicality of it. Not just have it all laid out for them, make it where they have to struggle a bit. I'm not sure that putting it all on the computer is as exciting." Today's electronic technology is so packaged that it's difficult to get inside, he worries, unlike when he could take apart government-surplus radios. "Now it's robots and things like this. Mostly they tend to get their pleasure out of computer games. I feel that it's really important that young people have a practical feeling for how you physically make something. We're losing that so fast."

Sweeting is not the only one who learned engineering by building seemingly mundane things. "One of the big events for me was my dad retired when I was in sixth grade, and we moved to a farm," says Chris Kitts, head of the Robotics Systems Lab at Santa Clara University in the heart of California's Silicon Valley. "When I was 16 or 17, we built a barn and put it into use. The notion of going through that whole process—I'll never forget that. I remember taking day-by-day photos." In his Central Pennsylvania rural neighborhood, 45% of the graduating seniors enlisted in the military. Chris did that, but stopped off at Princeton, where, emboldened by his barn-raising success, he and a buddy built an ultralight aircraft. Princeton became so worried they would kill themselves flying it that they were supervised cutting the craft in half.

These days, Kitts runs a university lab in which undergraduate and graduate students work together to make robots. Among other things, these creations explore the bottom of Lake Tahoe and are launched into space. He says of the ability of his students to try out really building robots, "Hands-on experience lets them go through hypothesis testing. They go off on their own tangents. The next step is matching it up with the real engineering analysis. The practical tinkering stuff you can do better if you inform it with engineering analysis."

I always wonder: If I had grown up in the computer chip age (before Arduinos were available) and not in the era of vacuum-tube TVs, would I have learned as much about how things are put together? Today when I analyze a problem in my head or on paper, I still find myself hanging the problem on mental scaffolding that looks a lot like the guts of a 1960s TV. Sweeting has it right: the only way to learn to build the frames of great ideas in your head is to take apart a lot of things and see how far you get putting them back together.

---

■ **Rich's perspective** I have trouble relating to the idea that it's beneficial to have learned with an obsolete technology. Yes, there are things that you will learn out of necessity when using vacuum tubes rather than semiconductors, but are those things any more germane than if you first had to learn to blow the glass for those vacuum tubes, or to mine and refine chalcopyrite to get the copper for the wires? You must at some point consider a component to be a black box and trust that it will work the way the math says it will. Learning how to count in binary may be useful when you're developing a smartphone app, but knowledge of semiconductor doping used to make the transistors in the processor probably won't, because the chip is a black box to the programmer. It can certainly be fun to peek inside one of these black boxes to see how it works on a lower level, but making use of higher-level black boxes allows you to do higher-level things. Whether your black box is a smartphone, vacuum tube, or subatomic particle, you can disassemble whatever is built on top of it and learn how to build with it, but disassembling it further will be of limited use toward that goal.

---

## The Equation

I learned how things worked at an electrician's knee, so it's not too surprising that my earliest memories involve the practical. Engineers and scientists, though, go beyond the electrician's how-to-fix-physical-things to understand theories about why things work the way they do. Often, rules about why things are the way they are can be captured in equations—abstract mathematical relationships. Equations may come from combining and analyzing other equations, or be based on observations. In any case, they allow prediction of how the world behaves.

The science experience can start just as easily with equations as soldering irons. Some years ago in New Jersey, a five- or six-year-old George Musser demanded of his chemical engineer father: "Tell me an equation, Daddy." Obligingly, Daddy presented the gift of the Ideal Gas Equation, discovered about 300 years earlier by Robert Boyle. This equation says that if the temperature of a gas (like air) goes up, so will its pressure. The two pulled out one of the first programmable calculators and figured out how the pressure of the air around them might change as it got colder or hotter.

"My primordial equation," sighs Musser, contributing editor at *Scientific American* magazine and author of *The Complete Idiot's Guide to String Theory* (Penguin/Alpha, 2008) and *Spooky Action at a Distance* (FSG, 2015). "I get a frisson of excitement thinking about it." But the equation was not the end of it. Later excursions at age eight using a telescope to see Comet Kohoutek solidified a desire to observe and measure things, further encouraged by his third- and fourth-grade teachers. (Meanwhile, Rich notes that his first foray onto the Internet, in third grade, was to learn more about another comet—Shoemaker-Levy 9.)

Musser rewinds his memory to his teacher, Mr. Edgerton, guiding fourth-graders to build a simple calculator from potentiometers—devices that change the turn of a dial into electrical resistances. Seeing the machine they had built actually work was a powerful thing. "I did define myself as a science-oriented person as far back as I can remember," he recalls, reading science books (even during recess ) far back into his past. Becoming a scientist, he says, is a process of winnowing, not sieving. "Kids start with a remarkably broad series of interests," and the tragedy is that often an adult will turn off an interest inadvertently. He recalls that he had a teacher who wanted to squash her students' love of art. He wonders what other interests he might enjoy today if those interests had not been pruned as early as they were.

## The Spark

Like my own soldering iron adventures, many scientists perform an early experiment involving a closer-up view of hazardous household items than a parent would prefer. Microbiologist Barry Chess, now professor of natural sciences at Pasadena City College, shakes his head and smiles at the image he has of a metal fork in his five-year-old hand. What would happen, he had wondered, if he pushed it just so into a particular electrical socket? The spectacular results of this science experiment—a suddenly blacked-out California home—still spread a wide grin across his face. He is amazed by how little trouble he got into at the time. "Very shortly thereafter, I found myself in a class about how things work for pre-kindergartners."

This risk taking might make parents of young talent bite their nails a bit, like the parents of a gymnast who might look away during certain moves. Also, like parents of young athletes, they need to find a good coach so that Junior learns without injury. "I was always cutting things open," remembers Chess, who now encourages his own students to take things apart. He describes his job teaching community college biology as "trying to teach people to think."

As a faculty member training students who will go on to be medical technicians, dental assistants, or radiologists, Chess works to help the students in his lab classes understand the need to be careful observers. "The only thing you can measure is how different something is from a control. For example, how do you know you're sick?" He urges his students to find ways of making the subjective measurable. "You can take your temperature," for example, rather than depend on vague feelings of the blahs. He says that too many people just can't "connect the dots" between cause and effect—and, worse, might not even be trying very hard to figure out why it's important to connect them.

Chess is acutely aware of how crucial a faculty mentor can be. He began grad school under the mentorship of a well-known biologist. Partway through his PhD, Chess returned home from a long overseas trip and opened a newspaper to discover that his advisor had committed suicide. Science is a game in which every individual is precious and has a unique contribution; Chess's advisor was really the only one working in his field. Because the department had no one else who really could guide Chess in his work, his mentor's death ended his formal education. That was a long time ago. Now, in the midst of cheery chaos, glassware, and books (Figure 12-3), he tries to generate a spark in his own students—or, at least, to make them think.

*Figure 12-3. Barry Chess in one of his teaching lab classrooms*

## Cowboys, Spaceships, and Baker Street

Not every scientist-to-be starts out with activities that involve getting into trouble. Not everyone has exposure to someone who fixes televisions or writes equations. For the rest, sometimes the first adventures and role models live on the pages of a book. I certainly tried to read as many books as I could during the summer the New York City Public Library featured its moon program. Every book you read earned a dot that you could put on a map of the moon; I could not wait to finish another book so that I could go to another spot on the moon.

A few years before I was staying up late on summer nights to earn my self-adhesive colored dots in New York, second-grader Charlie Mobbs was making his weekly search of the San Antonio, Texas bookmobile. The bookmobile traveled around to schools, like his, with limited or no libraries. He was hunting for his favorite reading material—books about cowboys or dogs. Sadly, they were all checked out. But what was this? A picture book: *Sun, Moon, and Stars*.

"It captured my imagination. I loved that book," says Charles Mobbs, now professor of neuroscience and geriatrics at Mt. Sinai Medical School in Manhattan. "Then I discovered the shelf in the bookmobile called Science Fiction." Soon, Robert Heinlein was keeping him company at home, followed quickly by just about every other science fiction writer. After that, his undergraduate future at MIT and graduate work at USC were foregone conclusions. "To know what you want to do your whole life is a great gift," he says softly, just the smallest Texas twang left from the streets of San Antonio.

Mobbs is not the only one to enter the profession through the printed page. Chris Rapley (Figure 12-4), former director of the British Antarctic Survey (BAS), spent a lot of his career working the puzzles involved in maintaining Britain's scientific presence at the bottom of the world. In the mid-2000s, Rapley was in charge of about 420 people, bases with names like Halley V (named after the Astronomer Royal who discovered Halley's comet—they keep renumbering it as the ice melts and they have to relocate farther inland), and the ships *RSS Ernest Shackleton* and *James Clark Ross*. Thus, he could hardly be unaware of Britain's scientific history and heritage.

*Figure 12-4.* Chris Rapley (courtesy of Linda Capper)

However, Rapley was drawn into science from another bit of British tradition altogether. "The irony is that my English teacher at the age of 11 got me into science by giving me Sherlock Holmes," he laughs. He says that Holmes was a "horizontal thinker," teaching him to carefully gather evidence to spell out what had actually happened, deduced from a whole range of clues. The best part, of course, was when Holmes figured out the case. "That kind of eureka moment—when I started doing science, I discovered that was exactly what science was about," he enthuses now, "when suddenly everything falls into place, whether through a bit of math or modeling."

Asked whether Holmes was his only inspiration, he notes that he was blessed with good teachers. To make the point that any given inspiration might lead various places, he says, "I actually had a good chemistry teacher, and that's why I did physics." In any case, he lives now in the spotlight that polar science occupies as the ice at the poles shows signs of dramatic melting, with implications for shorelines everywhere. How does he handle the complex, interdisciplinary, controversial work? His explanation could have been worked out at 221B Baker Street: "The real world, not the world that you might imagine, is all about finding the truth."

Rapley needed that perspective when he later became director of BAS, which put him squarely in the middle of controversies over how climate is changing. The current climate debate centers on how much human actions affect Earth's climate. The best tools scientists have now to develop long-range climate predictions are adaptations of computer programs developed to predict weather, paired with observations of how the world is changing (and thereby validating, or not, the predictions made by these computer programs). The polar regions' growing or shrinking ice coverage shows the effects of climate change more dramatically than temperate climes. Thus polar researchers act as a sort of early warning system.

Rapley says that what really separates science from anything else is that a scientist is able to make predictions based on known facts. This, he says, is where the extraordinary power of mathematical science emerges: modern computer power allows us to build entire virtual worlds in a computer, using real data as the starting point. However, any computer model has assumptions buried in it, and so even when these reflect the best scientific consensus at the time, often holes are picked in the results based on the weakest assumption.

"In a way," he says, "examples where numerical models have got it wrong have provided a sort of Achilles' heel" for those who want to dispute predictions of climate crises. This is ironic, as these discrepancies reveal the limits of our current knowledge, allowing us to focus and prioritize our efforts to know and understand the system better. However, he notes, as often as not the problems appearing in the Antarctic are apparent even with calculations scribbled on the back of the proverbial envelope. How does a scientist like Rapley evaluate evidence of climate change? The best evidence is to be found in the layers of snow that fall year after year on the polar regions. In the coldest places, this snow persists year-round and builds into ice sheets kilometers thick. The layers left behind vary in thickness from year to year, with the isotopic compositions of the ice (and the composition of the air trapped in bubbles in the ice at the time of its formation) depending on worldwide conditions at the time. This thick blanket of snow builds up over millennia, with layers visible if a section is lifted up out of the ice.

In a technique known as *coring*, a machine drills down into the ice, and scientists carefully cut out a long, thin cylinder of ice called a core. By keeping careful track of which core segments came from which depths, a great deal of information about the Earth's climate for thousands or millions of years can be read from these records. The bubbles of air dating back to those long-ago winters can also be analyzed to see how the air differed then from its current makeup. Over time, other records—in the layers built up at the bottom of the oceans, for example—can be cross-checked with the polar cores, and, after a while, a preponderance of evidence begins to be obvious.

Rapley shows people of various stripes ice core data so that they can draw their own conclusions. He says, "We start to show them ice core evidence. About half an hour into this, one of them will stop us and ask us, 'You guys really believe in this, don't you?'" Rapley finds their wording very frustrating, since he sees cores as hard evidence, which does not require a leap of faith. However, since some background is needed to understand that evidence, it can sometimes appear to be based on a belief system to those without the requisite years of training. Rapley sighs at how hard it is to get the public to take up a call to action. "The message at the end of the season is that climate change is serious and potentially dangerous, and climate change is now. What do you do about it? That's where it gets difficult. What we're missing are the instruments for global collective action. People have known for long enough now that smoking is bad for you, but still smoke."

He explains that if you stick your finger in a fire, you know you are hurting yourself immediately, but smoking appears at the time to be a net booster of mood, and the negative effects lie far in the future. It is important, Rapley says, that the general public see science as accessible, and for scientists to contribute to that accessibility. "Stick to your science, communicate it clearly, and it is fundamentally powerful. Truth will out."

## Finding Proto-Scientists

How do we find budding scientists? Sometimes it takes someone who just decides to go out beating the bushes, like Gil Moore. Gil Moore was born in 1928 and, when asked how he got into science, says that he mostly remembers trying to stay alive in the post-Depression economy of the time. He did, however, arrive at New Mexico State University in 1945, just as the German V2 rockets captured at the end of World War II began to be analyzed and flown at nearby White Sands Missile Range. "The real fire in my belly came from watching those vapor trails over the Organ Mountains," he remembers. In 1946, the Army brought over a V2 and put it in a parade; Moore has a picture of himself next to it. In 1947, he was offered "grunt work" at White Sands at a then-princely salary of 65 cents an hour—a huge raise from his 35-cent-an-hour job in a chemistry lab.

Moore went on to a career that spanned the entire space program; after his first attempt at retirement in 1987, his wife asked him, "What do you want to do when you grow up?" He decided to travel the country and try to do what he could to excite kids about science. He started taking a rocket into classrooms. He fired it at the start of class and told the students that if they did not go to sleep or talk among themselves, he would fire it again at the end of class. Attention was rapt. He developed a list of home phone numbers of physics teachers; he called them at home and asked if he could come speak to their classes. No one ever said no, and typically he gave about six lectures a day. Figure 12-5 shows him recently.

**Figure 12-5.** *Gil Moore (photo courtesy of Rex Ridenoure)*

Moore says, "Once I was in Idaho Falls and lectured at a third-grade class and then lectured to a junior high class and then to a high school class." All were from the same economic stratum. With the third-grade kids, "you'd start to talk and *zing*—up the hands would go." Pretty dang smart questions would be asked, he says, and kids would be bubbling over with ideas. Then he got to the junior high class and got a lot of questions—more intelligent and better-grounded ones than from the smaller kids. When he got to the high school, three students were asleep in the front row, and there were practically no questions. Based on that, he decided to come up with a project to capture kids' imaginations during the key years of junior high.

To apply Moore's philosophy of "hands-on, brains-on science," students created parts of an actual spacecraft, named Starshine. This spacecraft allowed students to measure how far Earth's atmosphere was extending into space on any given day. The atmosphere expands and contracts a bit depending on a variety of things. If it were bigger and puffier than usual, then spacecraft around the Earth would go overhead at a different time than if the atmosphere were smaller. When a lot of students measured the times when Starshine went overhead for a few months, their data could be put together to get an overall picture. To make it easy to see from the ground, Starshine resembled a high-tech disco ball: a sphere covered with small mirrors. Students were sent kits to grind and polish these mirrors. For the first one, Moore's house became a kit factory. His wife Phyllis built most of the kits, working 12 or 15 hours a day, seven days a week, for about four months, periodically hauling a huge bag to the post office. Gradually they got some help, first from Jackson State University in Alabama and then from various schools and corporations, and Starshine remained an all-volunteer project.

"We've had such wonderful messages from teachers," Moore says. Teachers say: "This is the first time that our kids have been interested in anything to do with math and science." Project Starshine sent three unpolished mirrors to a class in a given school. Each mirror occupied about ten kids, who competed with each other to do the best job. It takes a couple hours or so to grind a mirror by hand; students would get tired, and pass it around. "Grind and grind and grind, polish and polish and polish," as Moore cheerfully describes the process, with excitement building once the students could begin to see themselves reflected. They'd send Moore the best two mirrors and keep one for the school trophy case. The very best would be attached to the spacecraft and go to space. Various engineering organizations donated services for final preparation of the mirrors and assembly of the spacecraft.

By 2007, three Starshines had been flown (one launched in 1999, two in 2001), and all generated excellent data on the atmosphere. Eventually, all Starshine spacecraft fall into the Earth's atmosphere and burn up; Starshine 3 reentered on January 21, 2003, so there has been a gap in the program since due to a lack of funding to launch more of them. Starshine 4 and 5 languished in storage for years and never flew.

Moore says, "You can't turn science on and off," and waits, frustrated, for student spacecraft launch to become a national priority again. Meanwhile, Moore (who is fond of pointing out that he has 60 years of experience in aerospace) has become a passionate advocate for his brand of hands-on, brains-on science, in which a young student can say, "Hey, I did that. That's mine." He emphasizes: let students get involved in science and do not have students simply be observers of a professional science elite. If you do, there might be no elite left 20 years hence.

# How Do We Imagine Scientists and Science?

If I were to say, "He is a typical scientist," that would trigger a certain image in your mind. How do we develop the image of a "typical scientist?" (Or, for that matter, a typical anything?) Whether we admit it or not, we all operate with stereotypes of professions, often enhanced and reinforced by images in television and film. As someone who is female, five foot two, and blonde, I have the advantage that everyone remembers me, because normally I'm one of the few people fitting that description in my particular specialty of aerospace engineering. Not looking like a "typical engineer" has the disadvantage that although everyone might know my name, I still have to squint up at name badges. I usually wear a bright-colored jacket, too, and then I know that being the "short lady in the yellow jacket" will let people find me in a crowded room at an engineering or science meeting.

You may have noticed that we talk about both scientists and engineers in this book. I'm a bit of each, which would make me an applied scientist to some people and a research and development engineer to others. My particular case aside, though, scientists discover new knowledge that engineers then apply to solve real-world problems. There are more similarities than differences for the purposes of this book; we explore the distinction between scientists and engineers in depth in Chapter 15. Accepting that I'm not the stereotype of the "typical rocket scientist," who is? Even just lumping together all "scientists" loses the distinction between a laboratory chemist and a theoretical physicist, or even the broad array of jobs encompassed by science, engineering, and mathematics. In the popular imagination, all typical scientists are male, frumpy dressers, and wearers of horn-rimmed glasses with tape on the bridge.

Once I needed to find science consultants for a student film about the perceived evils of cloning. For help, I called a professor whose research interests were in plant genetics. Plant cloning has been around for centuries with no controversy, but somehow recent cloning advances have drawn comparisons to Dr. Frankenstein, with nothing in between: a sea of hype threatening to drown out some nice, near-term, and practical applications. At any rate, the professor asked a few of his biology graduate students to stick around one Friday to show the lab to the film graduate students. With clear trepidation on both sides, the two groups of graduate students hung out together for an afternoon. The film students discovered to their disappointment how routine and harmless the work was (and how closely a key piece of equipment resembled a toaster). The film was not made, and everyone went on to other things. Was this a good outcome? On the one hand, it avoided adding to the pile of "evil scientist" imagery out there. On the other, a story about science was not told, and an opportunity for a positive story was missed.

As an engineer, I like to read science fiction because I can learn something in an entertaining way. Often when I read a story, I end up searching the Internet to see whether the author's premise indeed reflects current science (or is made up of whole cloth). Although I can't think of any instance where I directly solved an engineering problem because of an analogous fictional solution, the energy I put into solving problems in a science fiction story along with the characters is certainly good practice. As we have mentioned, science is in many ways like a sport, in terms of discipline and the need to get in there and try things yourself to really learn. For me, reading science fiction and trying to keep up with the characters is like a good pick-up game for a basketball player—it keeps me in practice and lets me know the talent on the street.

Sometimes the public gets a little fuzzy on what scientific capabilities we actually have now, versus those that exist only in science fiction television. When I worked at the Jet Propulsion Laboratory (JPL), the NASA center that runs planetary exploration, I gave public talks. More often than you might think, someone would ask me why we were wasting money sending probes to planets using rockets. After all, everyone has seen instantaneous ways to send probes (and people) to their otherworldly destinations on their favorite TV shows. I never did find a good way to politely explain the difference between fantasy and reality, and usually asked why, if the technology existed, airlines didn't offer that means of transport from Los Angeles to Denver. This would generally trigger comments about "the government" keeping the technology secret (except, presumably, from science fiction writers). Government cover-ups of key technologies is an unfortunate theme that makes for good storytelling, but can frustrate scientists whose discoveries fall into areas the public wants to believe "the government" is working on and keeping from them.

## Science Reality Meets Science Fiction

Donna Shirley is uniquely qualified to discuss how science fiction and science fact feed each other. She spent many years at JPL, where her last engagement before she retired was directing the Mars Exploration Program. Later, though, she was the founding director of the Science Fiction Museum and Hall of Fame in Seattle. I asked her: what are some trends in science fiction, and do they in some way predict trends in real science?

Shirley offers the opinion that interest in hard science fiction is decreasing, and the appetite for fantasy is increasing. "When I was a kid," she says, "escapism was science fiction." The problem is that spacecraft are now science fact, and to compensate, space-oriented science fiction has outstripped reality so far that they've become fantasy. "The thing is," Shirley says, "you get back to swords and sorcery." Fiction can still fire the imagination, whereas many aspects of real science are just not presented in a way that excites people and draws them into the detective story of science.

The fast pace of science itself creates challenges for writers. Shirley notes that as science gains more knowledge of alien places (like the surface of Mars), the people who write science fiction have to be scientists or engineers themselves, or at least consult with them. Edgar Rice Burroughs could write Martian fantasies in the 1910s and '20s because no one knew what the surface of Mars looked like. Now, if a writer is going to write about Mars, he's got to take off from the current groundwork, like Kim Stanley Robinson did in his *Mars* trilogy or Andy Weir in his book *The Martian*. (Figure 12-6 shows what fiction has to compete with these days.) Compared to the research required to write about a trip to Mars, Shirley notes that it's a lot easier to postulate a universe with dragons that fly and talk, at least in terms of needing to interview scientists for background.

**Figure 12-6.** *Wdowiak Ridge on Mars. Image constructed from a series of images taken September 17, 2014.*
NASA/JPL-Caltech/Cornell University/Arizona State University

Why does fiction sell better than fact? Some of it is storytelling—if a work of fiction has clearly identified Good Guys and Bad Guys, we can identify with the characters without much effort. No background research is required before reading the novel. However, if a storyteller elects to pick and choose what information to present (or to misquote a source), without background, you'll never know. Scientists themselves feel excitement in the discovery inherent in their work, but that excitement is hard to convey effectively to the armchair observer. Without actually studying a field yourself, it is harder to feel the "a-ha" moment when all the pieces fall together, unless an expert has laid out all those pieces for you. A reader has to work harder to learn about something relatively abstract, which includes full discussion of many uncertainties instead of asserting one right answer. I often have people pointing out cool "new" discoveries to me—often these are things I read about in science journals (or even textbooks) years before. But I never discourage them, particularly if they seem excited about learning something new.

In the other direction, sometimes real exploration suffers by comparison to science fiction. The public is so used to seeing feature-film "footage" of space battles that real footage of Mars or space launches seems ho-hum. Even if people intellectually know that science fiction is not real, human nature does sometimes invite the comparison between real and imagined spacecraft. On the other hand, science fiction that shows a far future world with evil applications of a particular technology might block an important piece of real-life research. Readers might assume that one early step necessarily leads down the pictured dark path—even if everyone acknowledges that the path is fictional.

The great irony of the limited choices in "true science" entertainment is that science is a giant detective story, inherently richer in twists and turns than any invented world could be. How are the mysteries solved, and how does one area of science build on the next? What are the non-stereotypical scientists like anyway? The next two chapters let you try the discovery process out for yourself and then meet some different types of scientists, without a pair of taped-up glasses in sight.

■ **Note**  Why does it matter what image people have of scientists? If you are a student looking for a role model, it matters a lot. Many technologists know from early on what they want to do—but by no means is that the case for everyone. If it appears that "normal people" can be scientists too, then maybe there will both be more scientists and more trust in their advice.

# Summary

This chapter reviewed some stories of childhood epiphanies by people who went on to be scientists or engineers. We saw how often that involved making something, or breaking something and then learning how to put it back the way it was (or better). We also talked about how scientists' image can be distorted in the public's mind, and why this matters. Chapter 13 talks more about how scientists and engineers think about the world and how that thought process can be honed by what Rich instantly recognized as classic hacking.

■ ■ ■

# How Do Scientists Think?

You have lost your keys again. You just had them, and you needed to be out the door five minutes ago. The first thing you do is try to remember where you saw them last. Next to the door? You go to the door and then to the kitchen counter, but no luck. Pockets in the last coat you remember wearing? Nope. No one is home but you; they have to be somewhere.

Finally, you retrace your steps all the way out to the garage and find them sitting right where you left them: up on the roof of the car. You must have put them there when you got the last package from the back seat! If you are short, you might never have found them until someone taller came into the garage and asked what your keys were doing on the car roof.

A scientist is someone who looks at the facts and behavior of the world in an orderly way, then uses that knowledge to solve a problem or to predict something. (There are nicetics here about what part of this is science versus engineering, but more on that later.) In the lost keys example, you are taking a scientific approach. You have a list in your head of the places you normally put your keys. You also have a set of assumptions and knowledge about the world that you rarely have to spell out for yourself or anyone else—until a problem arises. Then you slow down and start to recite your assumptions and habits: "I know I opened the door, so I had them then. I put down the groceries, and I had on the green coat." You decided to check those places and, when there was no success, concluded that because keys do not move on their own, if you were to revisit all the places you had been since you last saw your keys, you would find them.

Scientists call this process the *scientific method*. First, you collect data. Here the data would be all the times you've observed yourself, without thinking about it, putting your keys somewhere when you come into the house. Next, you develop a *hypothesis*—a best prediction given the data you have (my keys are missing but are probably by the door). Finally, you test the hypothesis (by looking at the door) and reject it (because the keys aren't there) and continue to develop new hypotheses until such time as the facts fit the new hypothesis (you find your keys). Once a hypothesis proves to a reasonable degree to fit the way the world works, it becomes a *theory*. We could develop any hypothesis we wanted to about where our keys have gotten to. Testing our hypothesis, though, and elevating it to a theory, requires observing how the world actually works. For example, you presumably have never dug a hole in the yard, dropped your keys in, and covered them up. Thus, there is no need to look in the yard (but there might be, if you share your space with intrepid small children who just discovered the concept of buried treasure).

Most of us stick to a tightly controlled, rational approach when we need an answer quickly, but rarely analyze this process of developing a theory. So, if we are all scientists, why does science seem so alien to most of us? Part of it is because scientists need to know about a lot of specialized stuff. In other words, to make progress, scientists have to learn what others have discovered already about how certain parts of the world work. If you do not know about existing antibiotics and the best theories about how they kill bacteria, it's hard to figure out how to search for a new one. If you do not know the physics of how an airplane works, you have to recreate more than 100 years of experiments on your own.

Another alien thing is the language. Often scientists invent new words for things to simplify the way they talk to others in their field. We all do it every day. Ten years ago, many of the items we are looking at in this book did not exist (and even now take some explanation—think about how many things you complain about every day, such as pop-up ads and home movie streaming speeds, that would have been mumbo-jumbo to you a few years ago).

Scientists have this problem in spades. Their fields change rapidly, and so most fields develop a whole language to describe ideas and help organize facts to make them easier to remember and understand. The trouble, too, is that if instead of referring to Twitter by its name, you said, "That web service with 140 characters where people send each other what they had for lunch," you would be terminally uncool. Scientists, being people, also do not like looking uncool to their peers. Therefore, they learn to use their field's jargon, and it's hard for them to turn it off when they talk to nonscientists. Imagine how it would be for you if someone from 1945 landed in your living room and you had to explain the Internet or, even worse, Internet cloud services to him or her. It would be frustrating not to use any of the normal names for things, wouldn't it? More fundamentally, though, in daily life we cannot question our assumptions as much as a scientist must. For instance, we get up in the morning, walk across the room presuming that gravity will keep us on the floor, and so on. Most of us do not spend our days in games of "what if" but pretty much believe what we see. We do not ask: What if gravity stopped working for five minutes? What would happen? What new things could I learn while the gravity was off? We believe what we see, and for many purposes this serves us well.

In this chapter, we give some examples of how scientists go about trying to observe and understand the universe. You will recognize many of the same skills you probably have been using to get the projects described in earlier chapters to work. Joan will be the tour guide through most of this chapter about how scientists think, but a lot of it is the same process hackers use to learn—with some twists. Later on, Rich weighs in on that part.

# We See Only What We Believe

Often, we see only what we believe, a trait that scientists have to work to suppress. Try the following experiment: Cut yourself a strip of ordinary paper, say 11 inches long by about two inches wide. Put a half-twist in it and tape the two ends together as shown in Figure 13-1. You will now have a weird-looking ring known as a Möbius strip. Now, paper has two sides to it, right? Try drawing a line of arrows down the center of your strip. The arrows go all the way around (covering the entire strip, crossing over from what used to be one side to the other) with the arrows continuing to point the same way. You have created a piece of paper that has only one side! Is that possible? How can paper only have one side? But there it is—you have it in your hands. If you color one side before you tape them up, you can see that nothing magic happened—the scribbled-on side just meets the other side, as you would expect. Try coloring one edge. What happens? Now try cutting it in thirds. What happens? Is that possible? A scientist would find this exciting and would play with it for a while.

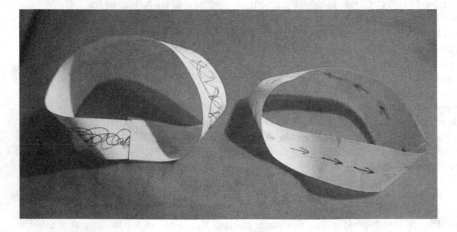

*Figure 13-1.* Möbius strips

This experience (presuming you have not seen a Möbius strip before) is similar to what happens when scientists see a piece of data that does not fit any existing theory. How can they broaden their theory to take in this new data? Do they have to come up with a new theory? Did you like the feeling of discovering what a Möbius strip could do, or did it make you vaguely uneasy? By the way, this phenomenon was discovered in 1848 by August Möbius, a German mathematician, and, at nearly the same time, by Johann Benedict Listing. It led to a burst of new mathematics that continues to be important to theoretical physics today.

# Different Ways of Doing Science

Scientists can be split into three very broad types: observers, experimentalists, and theoreticians. In addition, some scientists curate collections or protect rare resources, as you will see in a later section. In practice, most are a bit of each type. As the names would imply, *observers* look at the world around them without trying to change anything. *Experimenters* try to change something about the world in a controlled way to see what happens. *Theoreticians,* on the other hand, look at the data collected by observers and experimenters and (usually using math and computers) try to decide what is going on and to predict what will happen in the future (if a particular experiment were to be performed, for instance).

In the example about finding your keys, you were a theoretician when you stopped to think about where your keys might be and why. Then you defined some observations and experiments that needed to be done to find them. All types of scientists have to be careful observers of the world. They must be very conscious of their assumptions so that if they make a mistake, they do not assume right away that they've discovered something new. (Well, OK, they might get excited for a while, but then they calm down and start paying attention again.) It can be pretty embarrassing if a scientist announces a "new discovery" to the world, only to find out it was all a mistake. Scientists hate it when that happens.

How do scientists check that they have not made mistakes? They first double-check how they made each observation—was anything unusual going on that day? Could anything have affected their measurements? If you buy shoes on a hot day, and your feet tend to swell, you know you should keep that in mind when choosing a size. In the same way, scientists also have to allow for outside effects and check their experimental process, conditions during the experiment, and whether they might have missed something.

If you are balancing your checkbook and the amount of money you think you have does not match what the bank says you have, a few things could have gone wrong. You may have added or subtracted wrong, you may have written down the amount of a check wrong, or you may have forgotten to write in a check altogether. As you go through figuring out what happened, typically you first check your addition and subtraction. If they are not the problem (or if fixing your math made the problem different or worse), you go back to the original receipts for the month to see what was going on. So, first you check the process you used to get to your result (your bank balance), and then you start to check your errors of omission—the things you left out or wrote down wrong. Eventually, you get everything to balance out (hopefully, since even banks make mistakes).

Scientists do not get a handy statement from the universe each month telling them what their answers should be; instead, they check each other—a process called *peer review.* When a scientist is pretty sure he has a good observation or experiment, he writes a paper about it. Then he sends that paper out to a scientific journal. The editor of that journal then has other scientists review it (often anonymously). These reviewers look carefully both at how the experiment or observation was done (like checking addition in our checkbook example) and whether the authors forgot anything. Then, if the conclusion about how the world works is different than people thought it was before, the reviewers think hard about what else may have gone wrong. Reviewers will make suggestions to the editor (including, sometimes, having the author re-do the experiment, analyze data in alternative ways, or do other additional work). If everyone agrees that the experiment was done correctly and it does seem that something new was discovered, the paper is published in a science journal. This process is not perfect, and, people being people, sometimes an innovative idea does not make it into print, or a bad one does. By and large, it serves science well as a way of questioning assumptions and getting more than one pair of eyes on a particular problem.

---

■ **Note**    This continuous questioning also leads to a culture that, broadly speaking, tends to encourage some degree of nonconformity and doubts about authority. If you visit any science department at a major university, you are highly unlikely to see a suit or tie. This is true, of course, for laboratory scientists who wear lab coats (or more esoteric protective gear). However, many scientists just use a computer, whiteboard, and paper all day long and so have a tendency toward jeans and sweatshirts. More significantly, if you try to tell scientists what to do, most of the time they will decide whether you're right, and, if not, will ignore you. Scientists expect this from each other, and when someone with different norms and expectations attempts to collaborate with them, oftentimes misunderstandings occur. But perhaps scientists are not so different from the rest of us. What would your response have been if early in your search for your keys your spouse had asked, "Looked on the top of the car, honey?" As you might imagine, this is another thing that scientists share with the hacker culture.

---

## Observing

In many ways, the oldest activity in science is observing how the world works and then developing a story about why it works that way. Yet scientists, like the short person who could not have seen the keys on the car roof, sometimes cannot solve a problem with existing instruments in their own fields. They have to wait until they figure out how to invent a new instrument, or until someone in a different field happens to turn something built for a different purpose into a potential solution to their problem. (Or they wait until a new hypothesis is put forth that explains a set of observations that did not make sense before.) This is why scientists want to know a lot about how precise a measurement is that a particular instrument makes. If you want to see how many fleas are on a dog, a picture of a dog a mile away showing the whole dog as a dot is not very useful. It's true that you counted zero fleas on the dog in the picture; it's also meaningless to say so.

Some scientists have to deal with observing things that happened a long time in the past, or reconcile observations taken with instruments of varying quality, such as rainfall measurements taken in 1600, with ones made today. Climate change researchers need the longest possible record of weather to find out how much warmer the world is now than in the distant past. However, thermometers have only been around for 400 years or so, and good ones for far less time than that. Some people have it even worse. Astronomers must always view their quarry at unthinkable distances and come up with ways to predict behavior that might take millions or billions of years to occur. How do they make progress in the face of such literally astronomical odds? Astronomer Stephen Unwin guides engineers developing telescopes that will fly in space to look for planets around other stars. New discoveries these days usually require large and complex telescopes to see the subtle effects, for example, of a small planet orbiting a big, distant star.

Astronomers as a community have to argue and compete to figure out what equipment should be built, what astronomy is best done in space, what is best done on the ground, and so on. Because very few new, professional-grade telescopes are built each year, either on Earth or in space, scientists have to know what kinds of experiments they want to do long before anyone starts polishing mirrors. It's like deciding what kind of new car your family will buy: some people might want a two-seater to zip around in, but you might need to haul things and so you get a truck instead. No matter what sorts of telescopes are ultimately built, astronomers cannot alter the sky—they can only observe it. Or as Unwin puts it, "I have to take what sky gives me."

Astronomy is largely an observational science. This means that astronomers cannot change anything in the sky and see what happens to validate their theories about how the universe works. What they have to do instead is figure out ways to make the effect they are looking for at any given time stand out clearly. Once they have all that figured out, astronomers still have to do a lot of thinking to interpret what they are seeing and pick the right things to look at in the first place. For example, Unwin explains that if you were looking at stars at all different distances and trying to figure out how bright they were, the distance would distort this measurement because closer stars (like one flashlight closer to you than another) would appear brighter. Instead, you would use your knowledge of the sky to find a cluster of stars that are all more or less the same distance from the Earth. Then you can look at all the stars and see whether there are more bright ones than dim ones among stars all at the same distance. "You learn how to read them," Unwin says.

One of the cornerstones of science is the ability to do an experiment more than once and get the same result, a trait scientists call *reproducibility*. If an experiment can be reproduced, the outcome is less likely to have been a freak result due to some weird circumstance or something measured incorrectly, which can happen in science just like anyplace else. Because astronomers cannot start the universe over and make the exact same measurement twice, how can they know their data is reproducible? They make measurements multiple times; of course, if the sky is changing, astronomers have to do the best they can with data from other, similar objects in the sky. For that reason, astronomers, perhaps more so than other scientists, can't take any one piece of data by itself but must view all the known data in context. That context itself changes continuously as more data is collected. This raises the question of what happens if a piece of data is measured incorrectly, due to equipment failure or human error. Does it matter?

Unwin says, "Because you can't actively do experiments, it's very hard in astronomy to build a coherent picture based on a single event or single piece of data. So, testing of a theory requires collecting more data, which will either verify or contradict that theory." In other words, it's back out to the telescope dome for the observers to see whether they've discovered something new or just made a mistake. A balance has to be made between how an observation appears to not fit into established theory (which might mean a new discovery) versus the chances that the data is just plain wrong. "Bad data is worse than no data" is a truism in astronomy (in all science, really) because bad data can waste your time and raise your hopes of a new theory when you may just have recorded some unfortunately timed interference.

## Curating and Protecting

Science careers can be all-consuming. As a result, a scientist may find himself explaining to his wife why he needs to make a late-night foray to count rare toads splashing their way down a rain-lashed road. Some avoid these explanations (or, more likely, lengthen them enormously) by marrying another scientist. Husband and wife Bob Cook and Mary Hake, currently working at Cape Cod National Seashore in Massachusetts (shown in Figure 13-2), have made studying and advocating for endangered species their collective life's work.

*Figure 13-2.* *Cape Cod National Seashore*

Cook and Hake work for the National Park Service. They live and have brought up two daughters far out on the Cape, where just a couple of miles of land separate the Atlantic from Cape Cod Bay. The rhythm of Hake's life is driven by the migrations of the piping plover, a small, endangered shorebird that nests on undeveloped beaches. The birds depart in late August or September and return to Cape Cod from their winter migration around St. Patrick's Day. During the six months the plovers are around, Hake is as frantic as she would be during a visit by a picky houseguest. The plovers lay their camouflaged eggs on the sand, vulnerable to being accidentally crunched by a visitor's foot (or a dog's paw). So, the first step is to fence off the beach each year with what Hake calls symbolic fencing—just a line of string intended to warn people off, but not actually to stop them. Once the plovers start laying eggs, "there are never enough hours in the day," Hake says, because the birds need protecting along 20 miles of shoreline.

Once the eggs are laid, she places wire boxes over each nest, open on the bottom and held down by stakes pounded into the sand. These predator exclosures have openings large enough for an adult plover to come and go, but they are too small for foxes or larger predatory birds. No subtle, expensive instruments here: Hake's tools are a shovel, chicken wire, stakes, and a sledgehammer, which she wields with impressive gusto.

Just as important as the aerobic part of her job is her presence on the beach in a National Park Service uniform, explaining to people why they need to keep their dogs away from the plover nesting area. She realizes that she typically has only one to three minutes before people lose interest and wander off. If the time of year is right, she shows them a plover chick: "If someone has an off-leash dog, I show them how vulnerable that chick is." Once they see an actual cotton ball of a chick, she says, their dog usually goes on a leash thereafter. "We'll get an injured gull on the beach, and 20 people will gather around it," she says, but because the plovers are out of sight, a chick killed by a dog doesn't get the same sympathy.

Hake says that it's important not just to inform people about rules, but also to empower them so that they know they can make a difference. She says her greatest frustration is the small number of visitors who resist her attempts to protect nesting plovers. (The extreme version of this attitude manifests itself on local cars sporting bumper stickers that read "Piping Plover: Tastes Like Chicken.") Educating the public is important to her, but she realizes that if a person is 50 or 60 years old, their attitudes are harder to change. "But that doesn't stop me from trying," she says. "I do change some, and it's so rewarding," as when local kids excitedly tell her about how they are watching out for plovers. "That's what makes our salary priceless."

Her husband Bob Cook is a PhD scientist who develops reports and statistics about the Cape's fauna, with stints before that having taken him as far away as American Samoa. His is far from a desk job, though: it can involve going out on rainy nights to close one of the park's secondary roads to protect the spadefoot toad, which is listed as threatened by the state of Massachusetts. Rainy nights are a particularly good time to collect information on the number, sizes, ages, and sexes of the toads, which are brought out by what they apparently regard as fine travel weather. "What I end up doing," Cook says, "is collecting pilot data on subjects of interest that may have bearing on management issues." This data can be used to entice graduate students from universities to come and do a more thorough project for their thesis, and spend more time than he can realistically on any one issue.

How do Hake and Cook think about the need to save species? They do not really think of it in those terms. Cook says that that in the national parks, "We're trying to preserve not necessarily individual populations or individual species but the ecosystem and ecological processes that go with it." Cape Cod, for instance, has various rare environments, such as its deep freshwater kettle ponds, salt marshes, and the like. The reality, though, is that as soon as you build roads and parking lots in a national park, you have impacted natural processes within the park. Even when the environmental judgments do not involve people, difficult management issues can arise. For example, Cook says, "We have a habitat that was altered 100 years ago that one group of people are trying to restore, but the complicating factor is that some state-listed rare species are making use of that habitat in its present condition."

To decide what to do in cases like that, he would consider how abundant the two different competing species are within the park. He might expand his analysis beyond the boundaries of the park to a regional and state level, taking into account lots of factors. "The truth is, with landscape management, any decision you make to do something, even if the decision is to not do anything, is going to affect some population." If you have a species that builds nests in fields, you have to keep in mind that, over time, wild fields will become shrubs and then woodlands. As the land goes through succession, it is occupied by one group of species and then by another. You may have to decide to sacrifice the field species to save woodlands, and your decision would depend on other fields and forest and how much of each remains available to any rare species.

Are all species created equal, then? For wildlife biologists like Cook and Hake, they are. However, for the general public, big, furry animals that can't be missed when they stand in the middle of the road command more attention than, say, bugs. (Animals with a cuddly factor advantage are referred to as *charismatic megafauna* by biologists, with a bit of tongue in cheek.) Cook points out that most animals are small and spend most of their lives hiding because otherwise they would be easy pickings for predators. For an extreme example, imagine the lot of the endangered bug. Cape Cod, for instance, has an endangered species of beach beetle, which occupies the same habitat as piping plover. It can be a hard sell to convince people who want to use vehicles on the land that a beetle and a small bird need saving as part of preserving the larger ecosystem.

Why are Hake and Cook spending their lives working to keep these creatures alive? Why not let endangered species die out? Cook says he wants to prevent extinctions caused by the impacts of industrialized human beings. There may be pragmatic reasons for this—sometimes a plant or animal has medicinal or other immediately obvious economic value, and extinction cannot be reversed. Beyond the pragmatic, though, Cook says that for many people, there is a spiritual and inspirational reward in being able to see animals and plants in their natural habitats rather than in a zoo. "Ultimately, the long-term survival of wildlife is not going to be based on squeezing the last animal out of a piece of land. It's going to be based on educating people about the effects of their lifestyles on the natural world." He hopes that people will become more aware of population growth's effects so that they will make wise decisions about housing and transportation that are harmonious with the land. Perhaps the couple's work will someday result in a world in which, as he puts it, "wildlife isn't relegated to something that's only in preserves, but wildlife is part of the world wherever one lives."

# Science Philosophy

As with every other human achievement, someone had to invent an orderly process of observing and explaining the world. The critical pieces of this process are the ability to question existing knowledge and to develop new explanations as inconsistencies are developed. Someone somewhere had to dream up a system of keeping track of which facts could be used to draw which types of conclusions. In that respect, philosophers probably developed the very earliest pieces of the puzzle.

Suppose I say, "If I use an expensive shampoo, my hair will be gorgeous." Does that mean that if my hair looks great, I must have used an expensive shampoo? Actually, no—advertising aside, I might just be lucky and have good hair days all the time. The statement did not imply that the only way my hair might look great was to use an expensive shampoo. Keeping track of what one can actually infer from observations underlies a lot of what scientists do. The example here goes by the fancy name of *hypothetical syllogism:* I develop a hypothesis (if I use an expensive shampoo, my hair will be gorgeous), make an observation (my hair looks great), and draw a conclusion (therefore, I must have really splashed out on shampoo). However, as mentioned, I actually can't draw that conclusion from the hypothesis and facts given, so this particular syllogism is also a *logical fallacy*—logic that might lead me to an incorrect conclusion.

These ways of looking carefully at cause and effect are thought to have first been written down by Aristotle about 2,300 years ago, in Classical Greece. It's very easy to develop all sorts of cause-and-effect relationships if you're a casual observer of nature—but scientists make mistakes if they're not very careful about what has to be the cause of an observed effect and what might be coincidence. People have probably been doing experiments of one sort or another since well back into prehistory. Developing experiments that follow what we today understand as the scientific method, however, was first clearly articulated in print in Western society by Francis Bacon in the 1600s, and shortly thereafter by members of the Royal Society of London.

Officially founded on November 28, 1660, the Royal Society was developed for "natural philosophers" (forerunners of today's scientists) to get together once a week and witness science experiments. Early members included Christopher Wren, Robert Hooke, Robert Boyle, and, later, Isaac Newton. Some credit Boyle's vacuum pump as one of the first modern pieces of experimental equipment, and his discovery of what is now called Boyle's law (the relationship between pressure and temperature of a gas) as one of the first experimental discoveries.

For centuries before the founding of the Royal Society, the ideas of ancient philosophers and religious texts were accepted without question, and it was considered heretical to actually observe nature and draw conclusions about causes of natural phenomena. Once it became acceptable to observe and measure the world directly and publish the results, science began to advance at a rapid rate.

# Indirect Measurement

Sometimes scientists cannot measure what they want to measure directly, either because an event happened in the past and was not recorded at the time or because the thing they really want to know is hard to measure. Imagine that you have a black metal box with a powered light bulb inside. You cannot tell from looking at the box whether the light bulb is on, but if you put your hand on the box, you might well be burned if the light is on. However, if the box is hot, you cannot tell whether the light has just been turned off, and the box is still hot because the light was on for an hour. And if the box is cool to the touch, you have no way of telling whether the light was just turned on (and thus the box has not had time to heat up yet). Therefore, the temperature of the black metal box is not a perfect indicator of whether the light is on, but it is a generally accurate indicator.

If you could measure instead whether any current is flowing into the box, then you would know with far more certainty whether the light is on, because there is no appreciable time lag between the current flowing or not and the light turning on or off. Therefore, measuring current would be a better *surrogate measure* of whether the light bulb is on or off than feeling the temperature of the box. Using a surrogate measure means that you have to thoroughly understand the process that ties the surrogate to what you want to measure, or you might wind up with misleading data. Coming up with good surrogates is one of the key creative skills of a scientist and is critical in many fields. Clinical medicine uses surrogate measurements all the time. An electrocardiogram (ECG) measures different electrical voltages on your skin and then creates a squiggly line that is interpreted to see whether your heart is functioning well; ditto for electroencephalograms (EEGs) that measure brain function. Doctors take a long time to learn how subtle differences in these surrogate measures mean particular diagnoses for their patients.

## Beyond What We Can See

Another way to make observations is by using measuring tools that can see what we normally cannot with our eyes. Anyone who has ever wondered how on Earth a dentist can tell that a dark blob on an X-ray is a cavity knows how hard it can be to learn to read a type of image that isn't a normal photograph. For one thing, images like X-rays are not really pictures per se; they're *transmissive*, which means things that block X-rays (like bones) appear bright, and things that let the X-rays through (like skin) appear dark. A shadow is the simplest type of transmissive image, in the reverse way of an X-ray—if light passes through, it's bright; if light is blocked (from your hands making a dragon, for example), then there is a dark shadow. A problem with transmissive images is that if, for instance, one bone is in front of another, the X-ray will show just one bright pair of crossed bones—not very useful if you are trying to see whether there is a crack at that very spot.

Other kinds of light we cannot see with our eyes let scientists gather data, too. A rainbow contains all the colors our eyes can see, from violet through blue, to green, yellow, and then red. If you keep going off the red side of the rainbow, you get to infrared light. Infrared energy is given off by just about everything—you cannot see it, but you can feel it as heat if it is strong enough (another surrogate measure). Infrared cameras show things that are warm as bright and things that are cold as dark. This allows scientists to measure the temperatures of objects they cannot easily check with thermometers, such as the tops of clouds. Infrared images of the Earth show clouds with cold, high tops in contrast to the warm ground or sea, allowing for good cloud images even at night. (By and large, higher cloud tops are colder, and probably imply bigger storms—more surrogate measures.) Infrared images of hurricanes and other weather systems allow meteorologists to make predictions that would have been impossible before the development of weather satellites.

## Designing Good Experiments

Suppose you are lucky enough to be in a field in which you can do good experiments to determine how the world works. The word *experiment* brings up visions of bubbling beakers (and, in Hollywood, often maniacal laughter from a "mad scientist"). In real life, though, scientists have limited budgets, and often experiments are expensive to perform. Thus, it is pretty rare for someone in a lab to randomly try things to see what will happen. An experiment can involve months if not years of planning, not to mention a great deal of time finding someone to pay for it.

Normally, scientists will spend a long time figuring out what question(s) their experiments will answer. So how do scientists figure out which experiments they should conduct? A large part of science is posing questions. Very often, a good experiment will open more questions than it answers—and, to scientists, that's a good thing. To design that great, field-opening, Nobel-prize-winning (well, OK, science-fair-honorable-mention-winning) experiment, you have to figure out what you are trying to learn and why.

The question you are asking ("Why did it snow more this year than last?") has to be posed in a way that can be answered concretely. It is also important that others can repeat the experiment and get the same result. Different types of scientists have different problems trying to measure things when they do an experiment. For example, some types of physics experiments are very easy to do because our ability to measure relevant things is very mature. It is very easy to measure how much someone weighs at a given moment because accurate scales are widely available.

However, pity the poor medical researcher trying to figure out whether a new diet helps people lose weight. Not only are there a lot of things that affect how much a person weighs, but the test subjects will probably fib about what they actually ate, might exercise more than usual because they will know they are going to be weighed in front of other people, and so on. In other words, it is difficult in many areas of science (including medicine) to conduct what physicists would consider a controlled experiment. A *controlled* experiment is one in which only one thing changes at a time (the *variable*), and the variable varies in a way that is understood as well as possible—hopefully, in a way that can be measured accurately.

If you've ever tried to get a robot with a lot of components to work, you can appreciate that it's hard to figure out why something that is supposed to be moving is not moving if you change several things every time you try a new fix. Better to leave all but one knob alone and try moving that, then go on to another, then maybe move a cable, and then turn the power on and off and start over.

Scientists try to do the same thing, but sometimes turning only parts of the universe on and off is hard. Biologist Charles Mobbs is a researcher at Mount Sinai Medical School in New York City. Mobbs studies the link between being skinny and living longer by studying mice, which get old and fat in ways similar to humans (although a lot faster) and thus are good models to use for studies like this. The fact that many factors affect how long mice live sensitizes scientists working in fields like this to craft experiments very carefully.

Mobbs says a good outcome is one from which you learn something, even if it's not what you had in mind. Mobbs emphasizes carefully thinking through all the possible outcomes before the experiment starts. For example, he wanted to test a drug that might make mice lose weight (and, in the process, get some insight into how the drug works). First, he made some mice fat by feeding them a high-fat diet (doubtless they became the envy of their cousins, gnawing out a living on the other side of their Manhattan laboratory walls). Then he injected the drug into half of the obese mice. The other half were injected instead with a chemical that he knows does not make mice lose weight. (This removes the possibility that just giving them the injection is what makes them lose the weight.) Mobbs asks, "But you might say, why do we have to do that? Why not just inject the drug into obese mice and see if they lose weight?" Many unlikely things could go wrong, though—the caretakers could forget to feed the mice, for example, which would make them lose weight.

"Always do controls to pick up the things you didn't think of," he cautions. This type of controlled experiment is called a *negative control*—it helps analyze the cases in which the drug did work and makes it reasonably clear that it's not just some sort of accident that would have happened anyway. If the drug failed to work, though, you might not have had enough insight to know why—did the drug not get to the part of the body where it needed to go, for example?

Therefore, it's a good idea to have a *positive* control too. Maybe the drug should have worked, but something went wrong. In order to rule that out, you would divide the mice into three groups and inject one-third with the drug under study, one-third with something you know does not make mice lose weight, and one-third with something you know does make mice lose weight. No matter what happens, then, you would learn something—Mobbs's definition of a good experiment. He concludes: "Controlled experiments are built into the way that a scientist thinks. I couldn't do an experiment without a control any more than I could go to bed without brushing my teeth."

---

■ **Rich's perspective** Learning to do controlled experiments also enhances the learning process. The abundance of kits, tutorials, and example code available today enables you to start making things by only making one change and seeing what happens, rather than needing to learn everything about a subject before you get started. My generation is often derided for needing instant gratification, but I think there's real value in being able to quickly see the results of what you've done, whether it works as intended or not, and act on that feedback. In this case, your hypothesis is that you have correctly understood how to do *X*. Being able to test that hypothesis as quickly as possible, by changing one thing in an otherwise working program, circuit, or mechanical assembly, allows you to either move on to the next topic or see where you have misunderstood and try again to understand.

For example, I tried to teach myself the C programming language in my first year of high school. I carried around books that were thicker than my arms, reading whenever I had the time to do so. These books failed to teach their subject because all the computers I used were Macintosh computers, in the days before Mac OS X, when the Mac operating system did not include a way to run basic text-based programs directly. The barrier to entry for creating a program on a Mac was high because in order to run a program, it had to have a graphical interface, which is a more advanced concept than what I was trying to learn. I could write some code and try to compile it, but in order to create a program that I could actually run, I would have to build up so much foundation that if it failed, it would be difficult to understand why.

In contrast, before that I had created web pages using the HTML language, and had found a few codes that could make a page do interesting things in response to the user. These bits of code, which were embedded in the HTML but looked and acted differently, turned out to be little bits of JavaScript. JavaScript is a language that looks and behaves similarly to C, but can function within the context of a web page in such small snippets that it's possible not to recognize them as a language independent from the HTML that they're embedded in. These bits of code are able to make changes to what is displayed on the page. I was able to start with a bit of JavaScript copied from another page, modify that code, and then see if it worked as expected just by reloading the page. With Mac OS X and the Arduino, I was eventually able to use C in an environment where I could start simply and build up.

---

Sometimes, though, doing orderly experiments is not possible. Referring to his earlier discussion about well-thought-out controls, Mobbs says, "In reality, though, you can't actually do a lot of science that way." Science can't really proceed without what he characterizes as "fishing expeditions"—casting a wide net to make some real progress without knowing how to do a thoroughly controlled experiment in a new research area. Because the experiments are not controlled very well, if you find nothing, you may not learn a lot. But if you do discover something during a fishing expedition, you can push a field forward in a hurry. However, you still will need controlled experiments to verify any potential findings.

The classic fishing expedition example Mobbs offers is the discovery of the antibiotic streptomycin. A specialist in the biology of soil-dwelling microscopic life, Selman Waksman got the idea that because mold lives in soil in successful competition with faster-spreading bacteria, mold must be producing a chemical that kills off competing bacteria. He sent his students (including Albert Schatz, whose contribution was later controversial as noted in the next paragraph) off to various places to find mold that produced materials poisonous to bacteria. Finally, one day the group discovered one mold that killed off the bacteria that caused tuberculosis.

This was important because other antibiotics available at the time could only kill certain kinds of bacteria (called gram positive), and tuberculosis was a different kind of bacteria (gram negative), against which there was no defense. These fishing expeditions landed a big catch indeed—and saved many lives. In a somewhat controversial honor, Selman was awarded the Nobel Prize for the discovery, but many thought others who helped troll for the fish, notably Schatz, should have gotten some of the recognition as well.

## Developing a Theory

The word *theory* has developed a somewhat different common meaning than the one scientists mean when they use it. For most people, *theory* and *guess* mean the same thing. However, to a scientist, *theory* is as high a level of certainty as is possible. Scientists are trained never to think of anything as absolutely correct (or not). They are trained to think of any body of knowledge as "the best information we have now." After all, it is their job to question and to move the line between what we do and do not know.

Therefore, at any given time, there are the best theories that constitute biology, physics, and so on. There is nothing else. Scientists cannot magically check the back of the universe's book to see the answers. Therefore, they continually question their theories to see how they can prove various parts wrong or incomplete and thereby move the frontier forward. This is the point that is alien to most of us, but fundamental to science, and is the point at which our looking-for-lost-keys example begins to fail us.

Scientists never feel they know an absolute, true-for-all-time answer about how some part of the world works. If they did, they would be out of a job. However, the best theory in a field has been questioned and tested and turned this way and that by the smartest people around. That means it is most likely right. Guessing, inventing other theories, or otherwise developing completely new ways of explaining the world need to be tested in the same ways as the currently accepted theory, and any new hypothesis must be proven to explain the world better than the existing theory.

Even better, a good theory has predictive power: we can say that if our theory is true, we can go out and look at thus and such and it should be a certain way. If that works out, our theory is stronger (and the new theory will supplant the old). Note that this method requires a culture of openness, sharing of data, and disclosure of limitations of any observation to work. It also means that no one has the ability or right to declare something true—the data and the observable world have to support the theory.

Somehow we have to guide experiments and all that data-taking. We can take all the data we like, but the exciting part comes when we can predict what the next data should be. Will it be a warm or dry summer? If we measure the number of birds along a stretch of coastline after wetlands have been restored, exactly how many more should there be ten years from now, and why? If we turn the biggest telescope ever developed on a particular area of sky, how many stars will we see? Scientists develop a hypothesis to explain things they have seen and to predict what they should see when they do new experiments and make new observations.

A hypothesis, loosely speaking, is a scientist's best estimate about how things work, but it probably has not been tested yet by seeing whether it fits data that was not available when the hypothesis was developed. Scientists develop experiments or plan new observations to test and refine a hypothesis into a theory. Some fields—like seismology, the study of earthquakes—have particular difficulties in testing their hypotheses. Because earthquakes are (fortunately) few and far between, it takes a long time for any given hypothesis to be proven correct (or not). Some scientists can use an animal to model a human being. Just like an architect creates a little model of a house before building one, scientists have a variety of ways to test theories when it is not feasible to experiment directly on their ultimate subject. For example, medical researchers like Mobbs use mice to test the effects of drugs in order to avoid exposing humans to possible toxic effects. But even experiments on mice are usually approved by an ethics panel at the university or hospital in question, because no one wants to sacrifice any living thing without good reason.

The other way to test a hypothesis is to develop computer models, or simulations. Meteorologists take data all over the world and feed it into big computer programs that have been developed to model the physics, chemistry, and history of weather all over the globe. Data is fed into these programs all the time, and periodically new theories about how the oceans and atmosphere work (or bigger and faster computers) lead the models to be tweaked to be more accurate as time goes by. However, to build a computer model, the underlying science must be understood pretty well. Forecasting weather depends on computational fluid dynamics (CFD) models. We understand fairly well what happens if we heat a little cube of air, add moisture to it, and so on; that kind of physics is easy to measure and analyze. What gets complicated is trying to understand what happens when you have a gazillion little cubes of air piled next to one another. The air is also being heated, cooled, and humidified as it interacts with water, lakes, trees, desert sand, and so on. What happens when one little cube of air has some sun heating it and another does not? Computer models divide the Earth's atmosphere (or a part of it) into many, many, tiny cubes of air. Then, one cube at a time, these giant computer programs mix "real" data (from weather balloons, ground stations, and so on) with predictions to forecast how warm or cold, wet or dry, each of those cubes is going to be and whether wind and clouds will flow through them. Over time, steady improvements in computers (these weather models take a lot of memory and processing), as well as more robot measuring stations in more places, have improved these models (and therefore improved forecasts).

There are always a lot of assumptions, though, as well as things that have to be averaged and estimated to make it plausible to run these programs even on the biggest computers. Professional meteorologists usually run several programs (with different underlying assumptions, strengths, and weaknesses) and then use their experience to combine the results into a forecast. Once you have a weather computer model you believe, you can also use it as the basis of experiments. You can start out with a weather model and add more effects to it so that it can make more accurate predictions. These models, however, are only as good as the data and assumptions in them, and for something that models the entire Earth, deciding what to include accurately and what to estimate requires some deep knowledge of physics and other fields.

Scientists can and do disagree about what is important to include in computer models—disagreements that ideally result in experiments to measure the quantities in question, observe how they vary, and see the resulting effects on weather and climate when they do. Scientists have to spend a lot of time prioritizing what to go out and measure in these complicated situations. For many sciences, however, we are still learning so many basics that we really can't yet develop a computer model, and we have to ask mice or yeast cells to stand in for us for a while longer. In all cases, though, a model is never perfect; but each model and experiment gets a little better than the last one, and gradually we learn more and more about how the world (or the universe) actually works.

## Science at All Ages

I am often asked to be a science fair judge. One of the things I find most intriguing about this is seeing how students go about learning the scientific method. Because of the limited science and mathematics young students typically know, projects tend to be oriented mostly toward experimental science rather than theory. All too often, science fair projects come off as something more appropriate for a cooking show: The process takes precedence over asking new questions. Yes, you can measure some quantity with great care—but you need to know why you are measuring it. Nothing is more frustrating to a scientist judging a science fair than a well-executed project that appears to be an exercise in mixing chemicals with no obvious question answered by the student. Good scientists spend a lot of time posing questions (and then spend more time trying to see whether anyone else has already posed and answered these questions, referred to by scientists as "keeping up with the literature"). I always get excited when a student has asked a good question, even if it is imperfectly answered. I get even more excited if I discover that the student knows she has an imperfect answer! Learning to ask good questions and develop experiments to answer those questions is a key skill that is taught far too rarely. I try to start my young friends off as early as possible—all you have to do is let them ask questions, which is the essence of the hacker mentality, too.

---

■ **Note**   With the Internet, it is easier than ever to find materials to answer novel questions, as Rich has noted many times in this book. I will give the caveat here though that one has to consider the source carefully, because a lot of the science material online is flawed, particularly for controversial topics, and there are no hard-and-fast rules on how to tell whether a source is authoritative The best bet is to take a look at the author's qualifications and ask, just as you would in real life, "Who is this guy?" (An academic scientist? Does the source claim to be peer-reviewed?) There are now many open-access journals (like the ones at `www.plos.org`) that are both free and peer reviewed, and these can be a good place to start. Consider the source: a scientist from a well-known research institution is probably giving good information; someone who just acted in a film about the topic, perhaps not so much.

---

# Summary

In this chapter we have explored the different ways that scientists think about their work and compared it with the hacker's learn-by-doing ethos. We have seen that questioning assumptions and trying to see the world in as hands-on a way as possible are tendencies both groups share. However, there are also caveats about finding good background information for those cases when you cannot get all your own data—which scientists work hard to keep in mind, and which hopefully inform hacker style learning as well. In the next chapter, we move on to seeing what a sampling of scientists and other technologists actually do all day.

■ ■ ■

# CHAPTER 14

# What Do Scientists Do All Day?

In this final part of our exploration of how professional scientists work, Joan visits working scientists and engineers. Most people do not often get to see these people at work, either because the work requires a lab that would be pretty disrupted if people visited all the time, or in some cases because a lot of their work takes place in regions that are remote, dangerous, or both. In other cases, the work is just largely internal, with interaction between colleagues from time to time for inspiration. First, though, you need to understand the difference between a scientist and an engineer.

## Science vs. Engineering

When I still worked as a rocket scientist, relatives would ask me, "So, what exactly is it that you do all day?" It's hard to describe within most people's attention span. After I fumbled out an answer, the usual reply was, "That's so nice, dear," and a change of subject. The old joke is that a scientist like it when the results of experiments are surprising, while an engineer does not. Scientists are explorers—sometimes literally, in the case of Antarctic researchers and astronauts. When scientists use and apply existing knowledge in novel ways rather than creating new areas of study, they may be called *applied scientists* or sometimes engineers.

To understand the difference between a scientist and an engineer, think about the difference between a research biologist and a doctor. The biology researcher spends a long time coming up with new questions and might have a research plan spanning years. The doctor, on the other hand, has a patient for a few minutes, in which time he has to use all the existing knowledge in his field to develop a diagnosis. The researcher might find a cure for cancer and save millions of lives years in the future. (If that does not work out, more than likely he will learn something else and that will still be OK.)

Doctors usually have immediate responsibility for patients and may be legally liable if they do not figure out what is going on. Scientists vs. engineers have a similar split. Scientists pursue new knowledge for its own sake. Engineers have to know a wide range of current knowledge and often need to figure out how to apply new knowledge generated by scientists. Depending on a scientist's or engineer's training and overall interests, the lines between them can be very blurry. Often engineers are, like doctors, responsible for decisions that immediately affect lives and property, and they develop new solutions for problems on tight deadlines. Often engineers wish they could use things just discovered by scientists to do something new. More often than not, though—to avoid surprises—engineers have to go with what is known and has been used before, unless they are designing something that is impossible with current technology. Then engineers and scientists have to talk to each other.

■ **Rich's perspective** The distinction between a scientist and an engineer is very much like that between a hacker and maker. Both the scientist and the hacker are in it mostly for the thrill of discovering something new or figuring something out, whereas engineers and makers are trying to apply something with an eye on the end result. These descriptions are not mutually exclusive, though, and someone fitting any one of them probably fits the others to some lesser extent. Being well rounded in these interrelated fields will make you better at all of them.

## The Business of Science

Science is fiercely competitive, and scientists sometimes find themselves underemployed (in the United States, anyway) because of the lack of research funding and the specialization that makes openings in some fields scarce. The National Science Foundation (NSF) reported in 2000 that over the previous ten years it funded 30–34% of submitted proposals overall. By 2010, this had fallen to 23% overall. Teaching typically covers nine months of an academic researcher's salary. The rest is found through grants or consulting. Academics must also obtain grants so that they can do high-quality research leading to publication in the science journals in their field. If they do not succeed, they may find themselves unemployed.

Even in a corporate laboratory, scientists need to convince executives that their research will bear fruit for the organization down the road. Those executives, in turn, need to predict the future: do I believe this guy in the lab who says he might have a new product for our company in 5 (or 15) years? Will the new product cannibalize the market for our existing products? If so, are our competitors working on the same thing anyway, and do we need to do this research to stay ahead of them? Researchers in this environment also have the disadvantage that, for competitive reasons, they often cannot talk freely about their work to their colleagues elsewhere. This tends to mean that corporate research and development labs need to be big enough so that there is a real community (if a partially closed one) for those scientists and engineers.

■ **Rich's perspective** This kind of secrecy is damaging to the field of science in general. Competing laboratories can do parallel research in an arms race to try to stay one step ahead of one another, or they could share information and learn twice as much. There is an *open science* movement that parallels the open source software and hardware movements, trying to make research and data freely available to anyone. The practice of *open notebook* science even makes this data available as it's being collected. Sharing information is the only way for scientists to build on one another's work to advance their field, and I hope to see broader support for open science in the coming years.

Sometimes a scientist or engineer who fails to convince his employer that an idea is worthwhile quits and negotiates to take some part of his research to start a new company, which then means the scientist has to talk to venture capitalists and other investors. Everyone has to agree on which part of the not-quite-invented potential discovery is owned by the scientist and which part the former employer retains. As Rich notes, science proceeds quickly when everyone shares results, but sometimes this just is not realistic because labs do, in reality, compete with each other for limited grant resources. For science to be truly open, there will need to be more money to support most good researchers, instead of the handful that are supported now.

Science and engineering require tremendous focus and attention to detail. Many scientists are also talented musicians, since learning to play an instrument takes concentration, memory, ability to recognize patterns, and sheer doggedness similar to that required in rooting through data, debugging computer programs, or writing 50-page grant proposals. The sometimes-tedious legwork behind great insights requires physical and emotional stamina. Keeping up with new developments is a never-ending task and usually requires work in the evenings and on weekends—reading, talking to colleagues, and bushwhacking through the forest of interesting new things that appear daily in all fields.

## The Daily Grind

Science is similar to many other creative fields in that people develop a small cadre of collaborators. Most science projects require specialists from several disciplines. Teams might be scattered around the globe, but modern communications (and the occasional airplane) hold projects together quite easily. In that sense, science is similar to the film industry. There, too, teams come together for the project and might split up and reform years later for the sequel to an earlier success. A producer, director, and writer might live in Los Angeles, New York, and Topeka, respectively, most of the time, but might go to live together in the forests of New Zealand for six months to shoot a film.

Because it is relatively easy to make off with a new idea when it is being fleshed out, a culture of trust must develop, and peer pressure generally prevents theft of science ideas. Properly giving credit on published papers and patents and recognizing the primary inventor can accelerate (or wreck) careers. Both scientists and filmmakers are always raising money for their next project. In both professions, you're as good as your last success, and the quest for funding for the Next Big Thing takes up a lot of time that in an ideal world would be spent creatively instead.

Even though working with a group of people you know is comfortable, grazing the edges of other fields and finding new paths often becomes necessary. A new chemistry insight might have implications for biologists, and fundamental discoveries frequently jump across several disciplines. So, it is not enough for a scientist merely to keep up with his own discipline, and new people must be added to a scientist's lists of collaborators over time. More than other scientists, field scientists depend on their logistics crews, pilots, and mechanics. Even those who are working with more abstract ideas, like mathematicians, need to compare notes with each other or people in other fields.

Scientists tend to work long (and sometimes odd) hours, too. If a scientist is out in the field, she is probably more or less working all day—making measurements, packing samples, and so on. Work in a lab might be driven by the process the scientist is exploring. If a chemical reaction takes 12 hours to complete, going home after 8 hours is not an option. If data on a biological process needs to be taken every 4 hours, often that means that a scientist (or assisting grad student) is going to be coming in every 4 hours, 24 hours a day, 7 days a week, until the experiment is done. Academic scientists usually need to teach classes as well, and scientists in industrial jobs might need to meet with colleagues in other departments. All in all, the work tends to lead to lots of nights and weekends taking data or writing it up for others to study. All this raises the question: why would anyone become a scientist or engineer?

The years of training are a big investment, followed by a life of long hours and a continual need to prove yourself. Most do it because they cannot imagine doing anything else. The thrill of exploration, and of seeing something for the first time, are experiences that cannot be given up easily. All scientists share the explorer's drive—but use very different tools to survey their lands, literally or figuratively.

# Some Typical Scientists (and Engineers, and Mathematicians…)

My career has been focused on helping teams of experts work well together. I sometimes say that I specialize in being a generalist, or that I am a translator between people in very different fields. Rather than give you specific examples of things I have done, in this section I introduce you to a few very different types of scientists, throwing in a couple mathematicians and an engineer for variety. My intent is to give you enough of a view so that you can imagine them working on your team every day, seeing just a bit farther than the day before.

## Southern Crossings

In their explorations, scientists push forward the boundaries of what we know. Sometimes this is physically, literally true, as is the case for David Vaughan, a British Antarctic Survey (BAS) scientist who studies the interaction between polar ice sheets and Earth's climate. Most of the time he is in Cambridge, England, at BAS headquarters. However, for many years he went South, as they say, to Antarctica every three years or so. Vaughan has visited some of the more isolated areas of Antarctica, which explorers call the *deep field*. Figures 14-1 and 14-2 show some pictures he took in the field.

*Figure 14-1.* *David Vaughan takes a selfie in the field*

*Figure 14-2.  In camp. (Photos courtesy of David Vaughan.)*

He says, "We do work pretty hard when we're down there. When you're out in the field, it's the top of the logistics pyramid. We have the two bases, and they're halfway up the pyramid getting things from the U.K. to the deep field." Because a lot of resources are expended to get to these distant places, once a scientist is in place, the workload is intense.

There are some things—like certain foods—that polar explorers miss when they're in the field for months. "You get used to the food that you've got—all you want is food," says Vaughan. "You need the calories and you get that release from whatever you've got available. When you're out in the field with one other person for weeks at a time, it's pretty relentless. You're so focused on that one job that there's very little real break. You have to find a release. For me, it's reading books."

A benefit of working in Antarctica in the summer, when the sun shines 24 hours a day, is reading in the tent at night without needing a light. "I've spent many months over the course of years in those tents," Vaughan says, "a comfortable little womb in the middle of the white expanse." In principle, Antarctica could have all 24 time zones arrayed around the South Pole, and sometimes this can create a lot of confusion. To give structure to the day, they schedule a particular time to call in to their base station.

Usually they make this call their first action item of their day, and no matter how late they went to sleep the "night" before, they get up at that time and say, "We're going to get up and start a new day and call in." In many ways, these explorers have lives similar to astronauts on a mission. What else does Vaughan miss? "One of the things that we look for in people we're interviewing is that they have to be able to handle no solitude. Your buddy is only going to be 100 meters away. If anything, it's quite a crowded space. You have to stay close to people. One of the nice things [about] being back in the U.K. is being able to walk out and not have someone on your shoulder. It's usually a good relationship, but there's always somebody there. And for ten weeks it might be exactly the same person."

On his last trip to the Pine Island Glacier, on Antarctica's western side, he remembers, "We were nine people and we had sleeping tents, but our whole lives centered around one living tent and one science tent. Very much we were living on top of one another. We were out there for 60 days, and we got very used to one another's company. It was a whole lot more sociable than going out with two people or four people."

Does Vaughan take accounts of early British explorers with him to read in the tents? No, he reads novels. Vaughan says that a couple of years ago, his expedition was attempting to get into Pine Island Bay. "We didn't get into Pine Island Bay because it was blocked by sea ice. When we came back, we were reading a book about Cook's expeditions. He probably got to almost the same point as we did. The explorers that went down there 100 or 200 years ago were so tenacious and so brave. I appreciate how tenacious and goal oriented [they were]. I find it very hard to read the accounts of what they did; it makes you feel very unworthy and small in comparison. The level of personal commitment is so much greater than what I can bring to it I find myself being embarrassed reading of what they did with so little. I tend not to read that sort of book when you're in the Antarctic. It's hard not to draw comparisons. These guys really did it. They laid their lives on the line just to explore. When they were down there, the thing that must have pushed them on from day to day to day was not knowing what was there."

## Mental Frontiers

Exploring a glacier is one way to extend the frontiers of what we know. At the other extreme, the expedition occurs entirely in the abstract, using paper, pencil, brain cells, and perhaps a computer. Probably the one scientific discipline we find the hardest to think about is mathematics. Is math a science? There are many types of mathematicians, ranging from statisticians who develop methods to understand whether bird populations are doing well in an ecosystem to those doing very abstract work that might someday enable new ways of thinking about physics or chemistry problems.

There are a lot of mathematicians. As one indication, the American Mathematical Society, a professional organization, reports 30,000 members. Many mathematicians are brought in as part of a larger team for their ability to propose ways to organize complicated problems. But what does it all mean? If someone develops a new piece of mathematics, so what? Fundamentally, one can think of each new development in mathematics as a new tool that engineers and scientists can use to better understand and predict the world, just like inventing a new physical instrument such as a microscope.

In the late 1600s, Isaac Newton and Gottfried Wilhelm Leibniz developed different mathematical techniques that collectively became what we call calculus. A few hundred years later, the tools of calculus allowed pioneers to understand electricity and magnetism. Calculus underlies almost all engineering work today, and there probably is not an office building, car, or airplane that did not require calculus during its design.

Good mathematical tools can vastly cut down on the need to hunt and peck around to find out how something works; a testable prediction can be made and a hypothesis proved (or disproved) using a mix of mathematical tools and shiny instruments. If you imagine how hard it would be to use just addition for your daily life without ever using multiplication, you can get an idea of how useful a full box of mathematical tools can be for people who use them daily.

Mathematician Niles Ritter points out the key distinctions between mathematics and the other sciences: "They call mathematics the queen of the sciences, but it differs from other sciences because it is not empirical. You can do mathematics completely in your head. Where's the world you're experimenting on?"

Ritter has been a math professor and a researcher figuring out ways to process images from space, and now he's a problem solver for a software company, who lives far out in the Utah desert (see Figure 14-3). Ritter continues: "Imagine you had a cube made from wire and you put it on the ground out in the sunlight. The wires of the cube's frame would create a complicated shadow on the ground. If an ant wandered by, it would not be able to tell that the pattern of light and shadow on the ground came from the wire cube above."

*Figure 14-3.* *Niles near Virgin, Utah. Courtesy of Jean Krause*

When mathematicians solve problems that look complicated in two or three dimensions by thinking about them in more abstract realms, they call it *lifting*. Maybe a problem that looks too hard and complicated to develop mathematics for is a shadow of something that is quite simple in a higher dimension. Mathematicians think of the view from above—the broader view—as their world, in which the best understanding of how things work can be found.

What becomes possible when mathematicians and others think beyond three dimensions? Mathematicians have a hard time developing good mathematics, for example, when something—poof!—changes from one thing into another. When a particle inside an atom splits in two, it gives mathematicians fits. Looking at things in higher dimensions lets a physicist look at the particle from a point of view as different as ours is from an ant's. Ritter allows, though, that this can tend to make mathematicians a little otherworldly. If mathematicians create these worlds in their heads, how do they know that the cloth they are spinning has at least some threads tied to reality?

Ritter notes that mathematicians have developed precise rules for understanding things. In the early 1900s, people like David Hilbert tried to prove (using math) that some simple areas of math were completely consistent. After some decades of unsuccessful wrestling with this, Hilbert (and later Kurt Göedel) came up with *metamathematics*—theories about mathematical theories. He proved that even simple math could not be proven to be completely consistent. This situation continues to worry mathematicians, who have to depend on their own self-consistency for things too complex to observe in the real world.

How do mathematicians solve problems? Do they close their eyes and sit in a darkened room? Actually, one of the things they do is talk to other people—sometimes to other mathematicians, sometimes to other specialists, depending on the problem at hand. If they get stuck, they might say to each other, "I've tried this and I've tried that," and another mathematician may talk about similar problems he has seen solved a different way.

Scientists looking at data that is subject to interpretation have it harder. In biology or other physical sciences, a researcher may get to a certain point only to discover he cannot take data to answer a question with current instrumentation, because the instrument is not sensitive enough or there are other problems. It's also possible for tools to limit a mathematician, though this problem comes up less often. From the point of view of helping other scientists, mathematicians want to see whether the math is "right enough" to provide data within a certain range. They then have to delineate when this kind of math will work without misleading results.

Why are people afraid of math? Learning mathematics is mostly learning how to think a particular way, which takes practice. However, as discussed in Chapter 12, it can often be crucial to find a good coach so that your practice is effective. As a specialist in problem solving, Niles Ritter's opinion is that most people could be mathematicians, but phobics had a bad math teacher who did not understand mathematics. People with math anxiety develop a picture in their heads that math is like a ladder. Down at the bottom rung is learning how to count, the next one up is multiplication, and then algebra, and so on. Not a good picture, he says; math is much more an art rather than an empirical science.

There are as many different kinds of mathematicians as there are artists, and different mathematicians develop different problem-solving styles. Some mathematicians think visually, and others think about the exact same objects in a verbal way. To solve the same problem, one person might immediately go to a whiteboard and draw a sphere, circles, and so on to get a feel for how the problem might appear if physical objects were interacting. Someone else would do nothing but draw letters, symbols, and arrows.

It's like drawing versus writing to explain an artistic idea. But in the end, they're all abstract—and all mathematicians love the abstract and the ability it gives them to lift above the real world and fly around, looking down on us mortals and helping to solve our problems. If I am helping someone with a math problem and they get stuck and start hyperventilating, I ask: "If you knew the answer, what would it be?" Amazingly often, people answer that question with the correct answer, given the implied permission to be wrong.

---

■ **Note**   Rich perceives math as an exercise in logic. To him, it is more an extension of common sense than an art, at least in the range from counting to algebra. He also sees an even greater perceived disparity in ability in art than in math, at least for adults, and thus doesn't see this description as making math less intimidating. However, I felt differently. To me, all math is an art form—a great one, in some ways even more so at the basic insight level. I see math as a great achievement that people often do not appreciate either for its beauty or the sheer leap that someone had to take to come up with arithmetic. When I have taught algebra to adult math-phobes, I have found that, sometimes, seeing math as art—something to be admired and approached as not all that easy to understand—makes them feel less inadequate and more comfortable taking some time to make themselves the equal of that long-ago genius.

---

To learn a discipline like math or science, you must be willing to try things and fall down sometimes, just like an athlete learning a new move. Mathematicians have a certain amount of faith that if they try enough avenues, they will ultimately find answers, but there sure can be a lot of crumpled paper in the meantime. The reward at the end—knowing that you have the unambiguously correct answer—is a powerful motivator.

## Bird Societies

Earlier in this chapter, you met a scientist who explores a literal frontier and a few who work in more abstract realms. Even the discipline of biology encompasses a huge range of topics and styles of problem solving these days—from analyzing DNA at the molecular level to trying to understand entire ecosystems.

Dave Moriarty, a professor of biological sciences at California State Polytechnic University in Pomona, sits between these extremes. He studies why certain species of birds live together while others aren't in a particular community. He says, "That tells us about evolution, about how the world came to be the way it is. On the more practical side, it tells us about conservation. If we want to save something, we need to know the rules about its assembly."

There are some bigger questions out there right now about how birds are related to other species on Earth. For example, based on unique features shared by bird and dinosaur skeletons, most scientists think birds are avian dinosaurs. Moriarty's research group at Cal Poly studies birds and their habits using a combination of statistical analysis and fieldwork. One area that has received a lot of attention lately is how birds elect to set up housekeeping.

DNA evidence has allowed scientists to establish the paternity of chicks in a nest. This has shown that the prevailing theory—that most birds are monogamous—is not necessarily true. Sparrows will form a seasonal pair bond and build a nest, but there is a fairly good chance the babies weren't fathered by that male, even though both parents are engaged in caring for the young. "Theory," he says, "has fallen behind the empirical evidence."

To catch up, more fieldwork is required to get more data about how things work. *Mist nets* (which Moriarty describes as "hairnets gone wild") are set up to catch the birds without hurting them. The nets are taller than a person, about 12 meters long, and arranged in a way that resembles four shelves. The nets are black and normally placed where vegetation is thick. Birds fly into the nets, and researchers such as Moriarty's grad student put bands on the bird's legs to identify them later. With the bands in place, Moriarty says, "She could recognize who was hanging out with whom and take a blood sample."

When the babies hatch, Moriarty's student also takes samples from chicks. If she finds eggs broken, she tests DNA from the eggshells as well; because birds have lots of predators, there are lots of broken eggs. Blood samples are analyzed back in the lab with more or less the same technology used by crime labs to develop DNA profiles. She also keeps track of how many chicks are female and how many are male to see if any population imbalances occur. Over time, this new data provides an understanding of how bird populations evolve in an area, and how to protect populations when changes due to natural or manmade causes disrupt a bird's environment.

Moriarty guides many budding scientists through their studies. Some may become employees of federal or state fish and game agencies. Those students learn how to do fieldwork, and also have to learn how to do a lot of background research on what is known about the animals they will manage and their habitats. They have to know about current laws protecting the creatures they are studying, and may have some work to do getting various permits before grabbing the binoculars. A developer may want to build 50 houses at a particular location and need biological surveys done. Scientists trained by Moriarty might be assigned the task of doing the survey to see whether any state or federally protected birds, mammals, reptiles, or amphibians would be affected by the development.

How is Moriarty's area different from other scientific disciplines? "The scale of the problems is quite different," he says. "We're interested in chemical processes but want to know how it plays out at the level of organism." In other words, he tries to find the big picture of an ecosystem in the DNA of a bird's egg.

## Robot Crew

This chapter has covered a range of scientists and has even gone on a foray into mathematics. To complete our tour of different kinds of scientists, we need to ask: what does an engineer do? The introduction to this section lays out some of the differences between a scientist and an engineer. What does an engineer who considers himself a researcher actually do all day? An associate professor of engineering, Chris Kitts rides herd on undergraduate and graduate students—and robots. The robotic inhabitants of his gizmo-stuffed lab space have been to the bottom of Lake Tahoe, to trenches off the California coast, to a wide variety of places on land and sea, and even into space.

Floor-to-ceiling whiteboards at his Santa Clara University lab, located in California's Silicon Valley, are covered with diagrams, scribbles, and to-do lists—a reflection of the frenetic activity that almost never seems to slow as students raised on video games move on to controlling a machine in the real world. Developing and building these robots teaches Santa Clara engineering students how to design and build complex machines. It also teaches them to work in teams to create something bigger than any one student could possibly make.

This is a crucial lesson to learn for their professional careers, since most engineering projects require teams, sometimes with thousands of participants. Kitts and his student crew can provide low-cost exploration services to scientists. For example, the Triton remotely operated underwater robot has explored the depths of Lake Tahoe, allowing scientists to see what they think might be evidence of ancient landslides.

For Kitts, the difference between engineers and scientists is simple: "An engineer's ultimate goal is to build stuff." Sometimes that means working in an environment very close to that of a scientist—determining how feasible new technology might be without necessarily aiming it at concrete problems. Engineering research gives more tools and options to those who are oriented to solving specific problems. Kitts, like so many others in this book, believes that "tinkering" is the key to getting kids excited about science and engineering. Hands-on experience lets students go through the whole process of hypothesis testing and enables them to go off on their own tangents. Is tinkering enough? No, he says. "A next crucial step is catching it up with the real engineering analysis." Tinkering, in short, works better if you know what you're doing.

---

■ **Rich's perspective**   Hackers and makers elevate tinkering to an art form. When you get really serious about a project, you need some real engineering, but I consider looking up that type of information when you need it to just be part of the process. Just like the ubiquity of calculators made learning to do calculation less important than knowing how to work with equations to figure out what needs to be calculated, the ubiquity of information on the Internet makes memorizing facts less important than knowing how to recognize when you need them and find them when you do.

---

# Looking Back, Looking Forward

About a decade ago, I had an opportunity to visit the town of Plymouth, Massachusetts, where the Pilgrims landed in 1620. Even though it was June, it was chilly and rainy—one of those New England early summer days when all you want is a bowl of chili and some dry place to eat it. There is no shortage of such places in the tourist part of Plymouth, but it seems only right to earn your food and warmth by walking around for a while first.

Plymouth's waterfront looks out onto Cape Cod Bay, a chunk of the Atlantic protected by the curve of the Cape. The water on this drizzly day was flat under a low gray sky. A full-scale replica of the Mayflower rests in the harbor, absurdly small and with the odd bit of plastic sheeting covering parts presumably under repair (see Figure 14-4). (What would the Pilgrims have given for a big plastic tarp, one wonders—not to mention outboard motors?)

*Figure 14-4.* *The Mayflower replica on a gray day*

A little way around the curve of the shore stands an enormous, mausoleum-like edifice. In the middle of its imposing grayish columns there is an opening in the floor. I peered through the columns and down the hole and discovered that the structure is designed to frame a bit of rippled beach and Plymouth Rock (see Figure 14-5). The memorial is wildly out of scale for what is left of the Rock after nearly 400 years of erosion, tourists, and other insults. After all, it is not just about the small Rock but memorializing all that has unfolded since the Pilgrims' buckled shoes first stepped here. I decided to walk up to higher ground to look out over the city and the bay. I went up past the tourist shops and restaurants, past the church, and found I was walking uphill into a wooded graveyard. The only sounds were the trees dripping from fog condensing into drops on their branches, and my footsteps on the path.

*Figure 14-5.* *What is left of Plymouth Rock, now just about 6 feet across*

I paused where a sign announced I was standing at the grave of the colony's leader, William Bradford, and looked out through the nearly illegible mossy nubbins of tombstones, the misty trees, and wisps of fog that closed out the bay below (see Figure 14-6). It was easy to imagine the early days of the colony, with black-clad figures making too-frequent trips up this hill. What would Bradford make of me? What would he make of my airplane trip in five hours from Los Angeles to Boston? Would he approve of my time working at the Jet Propulsion Laboratory on robot spacecraft that sailed alone to other planets? What would he think about a United States with over 316 million people in it, and cures available for nearly all the common diseases of his time (but not for some new ones)? What about Massasoit, the leader of the Wampanoag tribe living here then? What would he make of me?

*Figure 14-6. William Bradford's grave, about 350 years after his death*

Statues in town honor both men, and it was not hard to imagine either of them walking out of the mist to ask me what my business might be: Bradford in his black Pilgrim hat and swinging cape, Massasoit wearing a breechcloth. I imagined showing them spacecraft images of Saturn and Venus and telling them what we now know about those places. Even photographs would be surreal for them, much less images captured by a robot flying on its own to other planets.

What would Bradford and Massasoit ask me? If they saw a tourist bus go by on the road below, would they think the world had been taken over by witches and was now run by magic? Would they ask whether people still had wars and poverty (and how disappointed would they be when I answered in the affirmative?) Would the Pilgrims recognize that they were part of a long heritage of exploration, now reaching out toward the edges of the solar system? The scientific method was developed in Europe just around the Pilgrims' time, the start of a period of rapid changes in politics and technology. And what would Massasoit think of how things worked out for his people? It is easy to stand on their land in modern raingear and think romantically of their simpler time, but they certainly could not walk down the hill always assured of a meal whenever they felt like it. Nor could they predict the world as it is today. As for me, I shook off the water pooling on parts of my raingear and headed back into our present, imperfect though it may be. It was finally time to leave the fog-shrouded cemetery behind and get that bowl of chili.

What would I ask if I had the opportunity to come out of the graveyard mists above Plymouth 400 years from now? A Plymouth visitor in the year 2415 would presumably be musing over events 800 years in the past. What events from our time would be remembered 400 years from now? Will the park visitor in 2407 be wearing outlandish but warm clothes, or will he be hungry and draped in homespun of lower quality than that available in 1600? Will he be 200 years old and in better shape than I am now, or will he be 35 and dying of a bacterial infection? Will he be one of a few survivors—or one of billions of humans living both on Earth and on other planets?

I would want to ask him whether my team won: did science and its methods survive, or did so few people become scientists and engineers that the world could not manage its problems? People of every era must think that theirs is the critical time for humanity, but the hazards now are particularly great. We have developed incredible technologies using the scientific method—but we are not making it a high priority to train new scientists and engineers to tend to what exists and make improvements where needed. Will enough voters understand the tough choices (and the need to invent solutions to problems) that we face regarding climate change and our use of energy? Science's core message is that we can always learn more: what we know will always continue to change and grow. That message makes it hard to have a comfortable routine that we know will never change, but routine is a luxury in a world that is rapidly adding people.

I would like to think that the park visitor in 2415 will be 200 years old, and on vacation from his home on Mars. I would like to think that he will be clothed in a fuchsia and green leisure suit (hey, the future cannot be too perfect) that was not made by people living in poverty. (Rich thinks that if clothes are still made by people at all in 2415, that will be a failure of intervening generations.) And I would like to think that it will still be misty and cool in Cape Cod in the summer, and that Plymouth Rock and the beach walked by Bradford and Massasoit will not lie submerged below a risen sea.

All of us—scientists, students, citizens—hold in our hands the power to choose whether the visitor to Plymouth in 2415 has to arrive by boat, or whether he has the resources to do more than survive. Think about what has made the changes since 1620 possible and consider: what is the best way to honor those long-ago Plymouth residents and the many scientists and other world-changers who have come along since then? The best way is to become a bit of an explorer—a part-time scientist—yourself. There are plenty of questions left to ask. Get out there and ask them until you believe the answers.

---

■ **Note**    Large universities and science labs often have open houses with staff available to talk about their work. If you live near one, you might look on its website for opportunities. Such an institution might at least offer occasional lectures or perhaps webinars if you would like to see how someone actually does science all day.

---

# Summary

In this chapter, you have seen some of the everyday activities of several scientists, engineers, and mathematicians, and learned how they think about their activities. The chapter also compared the distinctions between these professionals and argued that there are often blurry lines among them. This three-chapter section concluded with a bit of reflection on the last 350 years and how our current progress may look 350 years from now.

**PART IV**

# Tying It All Together

This last section of the book ties together the concepts built in the earlier parts of the book, comparing the world of the hacker and maker with that of the scientist and engineer.
Chapter 15 goes over the central concept of both worlds—that we learn more by failing than we do by succeeding, and that true progress is getting up after a failure and moving your field forward.
Chapter 16 ties this to the process of learning science, and finally, Chapter 17 reflects on what a scientist might learn from a hacker.

# CHAPTER 15

■ ■ ■

# Learning by Iterating

One common thread in this book has been the virtues of actually building something and seeing what goes wrong. A lot of traditional education is focused on walking through the "right way" to do something, heavily implying that the body of knowledge that a teacher is describing sprang up originally in just that form. Anyone who has worked on a real engineering project of any scale knows that it is never that way. Good managers put "margin" in their budgets just for the things that they either did not think of or realize they *cannot* think of ahead of time because the project is exploring new territory, literally or figuratively. Many big failures occur because someone was surprised by something previously unknown, and so an equally big discovery may ultimately arise from the failure. In Chapters 12 through 14, Joan talks a lot about science and serendipity and how sometimes a scientist is just in the right place at the right time (and trained and disciplined enough to recognize what was going on).

The teaching-only-success style has another issue, too, in that it is designed to impart knowledge to a passive learner sitting in a chair. Joan has taught a lot at the college level and can relate to this: you figure out how to break up the material the first time you teach it, and then you talk through it, have the students do something to show they learned that much, and repeat the next time. This has the side effect that subjects often look pretty intimidating since it feels like a lot of smart people had to be way ahead of you to come up with all this stuff. It is a pretty efficient way to learn many subjects, at least if you can learn well by listening to someone and reading. You learn what works, an expert (presumably) teacher frames it for you, and the idea is that you take it all in, apply it, and in turn add to it.

But if you do not learn about failures, are you doomed to repeat them? It would be hard and probably impractical to talk about all the blind alleys that anyone has ever encountered. But what about incorporating some classic failures? This chapter tries to give the person who (like Joan) grew up learning traditionally and who might be trying to teach in a hands-on, hacker-y way some ideas on how to get started. This chapter is mostly Joan talking, given that she is trying to be a guide. Rich pops in occasionally and also talks through a situation where he (and others collaborating with him) iterated repeatedly before they finally arrived at a design that worked really well for them.

## Failing and Frustration

If you are used to learning traditionally, how do you get started in these areas where some of the point is that you are intended to teach yourself? In this book we have tried to point you to books and other more conventional sources of information and, where those do not exist, to online open source community resources. The reality is that maker technologies are evolving very rapidly, and the communities are welcoming as long as it is clear you have made an attempt to master the basics and read the materials that are out there before asking a question. You do not need to be an expert to start hanging around a makerspace or reading messages on a forum (see Chapter 9). But it can be hard to figure out where to get started.

Chapter 8 talks about some "beginner" technologies that might give you some insights and make it easier for you to get started with coding and electronics. You may or may not find this intermediate step helpful; Rich feels strongly that it wastes time that would be better spent trying out the simplest possible projects with Arduino and a common coding language instead of learning a hypothetically easier smaller system. If you try to do something with these artificially constrained systems that they are not capable of, you might waste a lot of time trying to figure out why things are not working, or find yourself needing to learn a whole new system just to get access to a slightly more advanced feature.

Simplicity usually comes at the price of limited functionality and some artificial boundaries—it's a bad idea to try diving headfirst into a 2-foot-deep kiddie pool, and you should not expect to learn to swim there, either. But on the other hand, there is nothing wrong with playing with all sorts of construction toys, and certainly lots of kids spend a lot of time learning the innards of a game world. We do not want to imply that the *only* thing we approve of is coding in C and using an Arduino. Anything that involves problem solving and, even better, playing with a physical object has advantages.

If you do not have time to try out anything yourself—if you are a teacher wanting to learn enough to try some projects with a student, for example—you might consider just empowering a student who has the time and the "hacker inclination" to get started. You can then have that student summarize for you and the traditional learners in the class, and correct any misconceptions that crept in along the way. It is just reality that high school students probably have more time to try things out and mess with a technology than their teachers do. We are familiar with a lot of situations that have worked out like that, and they have the virtue that if a student leads it, it isn't "schoolwork" in quite the same way.

---

■ **Rich's view**   Get comfortable admitting that there are a lot of things you do not know. Learn to ask questions that will move you a small step in the right direction (or a large step, if you are lucky). For a lot of situations in 3D printing, I find myself asking questions that have no answers (a state a scientist would recognize immediately as a good thing). My process looks something like this:

Ask a question. Do you know how to go about finding the answer? If not, the question is probably too complex. Rather than directly looking for an answer, look for ways to break it down into several simpler questions. Repeat this process until you have questions you can answer (ideally they should be polar questions—ones to which the answer is either yes or no) and then work your way back up the chain until you have the answer to your original question. You're likely to find information along the way that will allow you to answer other, related questions more easily.

If you're working at the edge of your field, you may find that your problem boils down to questions that nobody has an answer to. This is where the scientific method (see Chapter 13) comes into play. Rather than formulating a question that you can look up an answer to, you'll need to design an experiment, which is just another type of question that includes a procedure for testing to find the answer (or at least to suggest which question to ask next). Breaking your questions down to their simplest forms is important for creating a controlled experiment, where you're only testing for one thing.

---

# Failures vs. Iteration

The hacker community has embraced the word *fail* as a positive thing, describing a certain attitude and ability to keep trying things until all problems are solved. Some others prefer the word *iterate* instead, which perhaps has a more neutral connotation. Engineers always expect to iterate their designs. Otherwise, why would anyone test a new product? We never like it when a test fails, but the process of figuring out why can turn into a detective story. Some even go so far to say that you never fail—you only succeed at learning what doesn't work.

John Umekubo of St. Matthew's School (see the section "The Younger Set" in Chapter 5) likes to talk about "learning by iterating," rather than learning by failing, and that difference really clarified the concept for us. It is a great way to think about the professional design process, too (discussed later in this chapter) because no design leaps whole out of the designer's mind.

## Grand Failures

Usually failures happen during tests, more or less in private in the inventor's garage or a company's test lab. But sometimes failures happen spectacularly and publicly, and sadly can result in loss of life or a great expenditure of money and effort. To make up for it, in a way, we often learn a lot from those failures, and systems are safer afterwards (the Titanic comes to mind).

When I was an undergraduate, a lot of what I studied were things that had gone wrong. Yes, we learned all about what had gone right, but we were often given scenarios of actual failures and told to go away in teams and figure out what had happened, or at least analyze what sort of tests or experiments would be needed to figure it out. This was long before the Internet, of course, so you could not just search the commission's report online. It is harder to do now as a pure discovery exercise, but if you are teaching an engineering class you might still consider some role-playing along these lines. Here are some classic failures that might be interesting for you to use as studies of what happens when things go seriously sideways:

- *The Tacoma Narrows Bridge*: This bridge over Puget Sound opened (and tore itself apart) in 1940. It was built in a way that made it vulnerable to resonance—a phenomenon like the one that lets you push a child on a swing and get a pretty big arc out of a relatively small amount of force. In retrospect, the designers realized they had fixated on other aspects and had not analyzed what would happen when wind gusts pushed sideways on the bridge, like a person pushing a child on a swing at just the right frequency. You can see a video and get more details in the Wikipedia article at http://en.wikipedia.org/wiki/Tacoma_Narrows_Bridge_%281940%290. Be sure to watch the video of the bridge's collapse. It's hard to forget once you have seen it!

- *Space Shuttle Challenger*: Space Shuttles are terrifically complex systems, and the margins for error are small. The late Caltech professor Richard Feynman famously did some experiments that were worthy of any hacker, asking for ice water at a formal hearing on the Challenger disaster and doing a small experiment right then and there to make a point. This story is wonderfully described in Feynman's book *What Do You Care What Other People Think? Further Adventures of a Curious Character* (W.W. Norton, 1988) or you can search for video of Feynman telling the story himself. If there was any doubt that scientists are at heart hackers and makers, reading this book will dispel it for you.

- *Bhopal Disaster*: In 1984, in Bhopal, India, a Union Carbide pesticide plant experienced a series of failures (http://en.wikipedia.org/wiki/Bhopal_disaster) that resulted in a cloud of toxic gas killing many people outside the plant. It has been described and analyzed in many places, but particularly well in Nancy Leveson's work (see Tip after this list). It is often considered the classic "multiple cause" software, hardware, and process interaction failure.

- *1940s and 1950s aviation*: The early days of "routine" passenger aviation had a lot of failures as people learned how to design reliable aircraft. Searching around a bit for aircraft of that day and lists of accidents might give you a lot of ideas for structural analysis problems (or, perhaps, make you never fly again!). Search on the names of aircraft listed at http://en.wikipedia.org/wiki/Category:United_States_airliners_1950%E2%80%931959 plus the words "accident" or "failure." You might start with the Lockheed Electra structural issues that made a few of those planes lose their wings in flight, which turned out to have fairly complex causes, similar in a way to the Tacoma Narrows failure.

---

■ **Tip** A classic book about engineering failures is *To Engineer is Human: The Role of Failure In Successful Design* by Henry Petroski (Vintage, 1992). When Joan arrived at MIT in the late 1970s, every student was sent a copy of an earlier edition of the book. Another great book about (averting) failure in software systems is Nancy Leveson's *Safeware* (Addison-Wesley Professional, 1995). Also check out her MIT website at http://sunnyday.mit.edu.

---

## Problem-Based Learning

Learning by solving a big problem or analyzing what designers should have known about a system that failed has been around for quite a while (obviously, since I am in part quoting my long-ago undergraduate experience!). Project-based learning (PBL) is at the heart of (controversial) academic standards in the United States called the Common Core (www.corestandards.org/about-the-standards). The Buck Institute (http://bie.org) has a lot of examples of curriculum ideas that are based around PBL.

At the undergraduate level and above, the premise of a lot of design education (for product designers, engineers, and the like) is often to give a "design brief" that students then have to work through to create a product or service that solves the problem or market need. Typically these problems require a student to use material from several traditional academic disciplines at once, so a course may be team-taught by several teachers, or by one generalist who likes to cross discipline boundaries.

### Iteration for Robust Design

This section has focused on failures of completed, nominally operational systems. But would having lots of mini-failures and explorations be a good way to avoid the big ones? If you start with an imperfect but somewhat workable prototype and iterate it from there, will you naturally tease out some of the problems? Is it even a failure if you have a working design but then raise (or otherwise change) your standards so that the design is no longer adequate? The next section is a case study of iteration in 3D-printer design as an example of design by iterative exploration.

## Case Study: Bar Clamps

As we have mentioned many times, Rich designed some of the early 3D printers (Chapter 3), and in particular, RepRap open source ones (see the section "Free Speech vs. Free Beer" in Chapter 9—Figure 9-1 shows the Wallace printer he designed, and the Mini-Mendel he used as the starting point design is shown in Figure 15-1). In this section, Rich describes one particular part he decided to improve during the evolution from the Mini-Mendel to the Wallace.

***Figure 15-1.*** *Rich's Mini-Mendel (which he evolved into the Wallace, shown back in Figure 9-1)*

One problem 3D-printer designers have before they build their first printer is that they cannot make parts for it, because they do not yet have a printer to build parts with. Early printers were designed to be made with some 3D-printed parts (which you would need to obtain from someone who had already had a printer) and other simple parts, like threaded and smooth metal rods. The following is Rich's story about some of the design experiences he had in the early days of these printers, around the latter half of 2010. As a bit of background, the printers we are talking about here are "Cartesian"—they move in three linear directions, designated $x$, $y$, and $z$. Usually the platform the objects are built on move in one or more directions (in the case you will read about here, it moves in the $y$ direction), and a printhead that extrudes plastic is moved somehow in the remaining dimensions. (There are designs where the platform is stationary, too, but we are not talking about those here.)

When I first started building a 3D printer (a Mini-Mendel, later renamed RepRap Huxley, http://reprap.org/wiki/Huxley), a number of things struck me as needlessly complicated. These printers used smooth metal rods to allow their axes to slide linearly, and the first thing I wanted to simplify was the clamps used to mount the linear rods for the $y$ axis (in this case, the platform, which moves between the front and back of the machine) to the threaded rods used to build the frame. These were designed as two pieces intended to be clamped together with four screws and additionally clamped in place by a pair of nuts on the threaded rods going through them (Figure 15-2). This was too many parts for such a simple task, and as I was assembling them, I quickly realized that the parts could serve their purpose with two screws just as well as with four.

**Figure 15-2.** *The Mini-Mendel's original bar clamps, using two screws instead of four*

Still, the design was needlessly complex, especially in light of the RepRap project's goal of using as few non-printable parts as possible (and my own personal goal of also reducing the *printed* part count, so that a machine could reproduce itself faster and less expensively). I realized that the two nuts used to locate the clamp on the threaded rod could also be used to apply tension to a single piece that wrapped around the smooth rod to clamp it in place (Figure 15-3). This was one of my first attempts to 3D print something, and you can see that a lot of evolution in print quality was still to come (achieved by improving printer designs and expanding my own knowledge, as well as significant advancements in the software used for printing).

**Figure 15-3.** *The first version of my bar clamp design, and one of my first attempts to 3D print*

I designed a replacement, and posted it online for others to try before I even had a printer to attempt to make it. Others did try it, and the response was positive and constructive. Not having printed anything yet, I didn't know that the tensile strength of the bond between layers was a concern, and another user helpfully suggested printing it in a different orientation to reduce its vulnerability to that weakness. When I was finally able to print it, I saw how right that was, and the second version, which I had designed in the meantime, was a big improvement (Figure 15-4).

***Figure 15-4.*** *The new, stronger clamps I designed. Side note: back then, this was considered acceptable print quality*

These new clamps were significantly more effective, and Josef Prusa, one of the most well-known RepRap designers, later used the same design (which he seems to have discovered independently) in the design of his Prusa Mendel printer, which quickly became the most popular RepRap printer design of its time.

Fewer parts isn't always better, though. My next printer was a Makerbot CupcakeCNC (http://en.wikipedia.org/wiki/MakerBot_Industries). The Cupcake had a wooden frame, so it used a different method of mounting the bars. At opposite ends of the frame were holes that the bars slid into, and additional pieces of wood were bolted over these holes to keep the bars from sliding out. These holes needed to be loose enough to slide the bars through, and the motion of the printer would often drag the bars so that they would rub against the holes and hit the ends when changing directions. This was just one of the things that made the Cupcake an extremely noisy printer. The movement of the bars also had a tendency to wear out the holes, making them looser and less effective at holding the bar in place as the machine was used.

At the time, many different parts on Thingiverse (a database of 3D-printable objects, www.thingiverse.com) were designed to solve this problem. My first solution was to trap pieces of foam in the holes to stop the rods from moving and hitting the ends, but it wasn't a pretty solution. One design that became popular was based on the same principle as the clamp I had previously designed, using a screw to tighten a clamp that wrapped around the bar, but I didn't like this solution because it was vulnerable to shearing forces on the bond between layers where it was mounted. In the end, I came up with an even simpler design that still used a screw for tightening, but rather than wrapping around the rod and flexing the plastic to tighten, it used a set screw to push the rod against the side of the hole to hold it in place (Figure 15-5).

*Figure 15-5.* *My bar clamp for the CupcakeCNC*

When I designed the RepRap Wallace, I used the same set screw design for the $z$ axis but returned to the wraparound clamp design for $x$ and $y$. I wanted to use as few screws as possible in the design, so I found ways to use those screws for multiple purposes, such as clamping multiple components with one screw, and also using that screw to connect another component to the clamp, such as a belt pulley or even a motor. By this point, I was iterating so quickly that I often had a new revision of a part ready to print before the printer was done producing the previous one.

Today, many designs are moving away from these smooth rods in favor of linear motion components that are designed for easier mounting. The number of people building 3D printers has created a market for these higher-quality components, many of which just weren't available (at least not in reasonable quantities, or at a reasonable price) in those early days. Some designs still use smooth rods, though, and their methods for mounting them evolved from these earlier designs. Instead of screws, the Printrbot Jr. and Simple designs began using zip ties to press the rods and bearings into slots, and the Prusa i3 uses a similar method. With access to precision machining tools and printers now also capable of making much more precise parts, some designs are even relying on the ability to produce press-fit parts, or ones that are springy enough to clamp without fasteners.

Each step of the way, my designs and those of other users were shared online. Because they were open source (see Chapter 9), we were able to try one another's designs, give feedback, and often get inspired to design a modified version. The RepRap project was started with the intention that mechanical designs would evolve like an organism. Designs that worked well would become popular, and subsequent revisions would be based on them, while others would inevitably turn out to be evolutionary dead-ends. Biological evolution uses a process of random mutation with natural selection to produce life that is so complex and well suited to its environment that some people find it difficult to believe that those environments weren't designed for it, and the same process, with a little forethought given to the changes, can produce the best designs for the job and the tools available much more quickly.

■ **Joan's View**    I find this case study intriguing for a few reasons. One is just to see how fast the field has progressed. This book was written just four or five years after the events described here, and all of the hardware looks ancient. The other is to ponder that in my experience working as an engineer in a big organization, failure stories tend to mostly be oral traditions, of the late-night, over-a-beverage variety. There might be "lessons learned" documents (and formal reports if Something Really Bad Happened, but blessedly I never was close to one of those). Any story that is captured is framed and tidy—as we traditional learners like it. But one of the things the hacker tradition does is to record a lot of failures and blind alleys, since they are not viewed as negative.

It is annoying as a beginner to wade around in this maze, and doing so probably would get unwieldy for really big systems. However, it is interesting to speculate on just how complex an engineering system could be and still be iterated the way the RepRap machines have been. The visibility of all the evolutionary branches means that anyone designing something new can browse around and maybe avoid repeating mistakes. I know that I reach for paper and often an old textbook to solve engineering problems. I always see Rich raise his hands to his keyboard when faced with just about every question he can't answer off the top of his head. Which approach is "better" is something we good-naturedly debate all the time, and doubtless hybrids will evolve in the upcoming generations who grow up online.

## Iterative Problem Solution as Career Training

Chapter 11 includes a case study in learning-by-making at Pasadena City College. More broadly than that, though: how does solving iterative design problems iteratively translate into workplace skills? For one thing, the current workplace is becoming more iterative, and so learning this way is direct training for environments where prototypes may be 3D printed and electronics prototyped with consumer-level components.

The Minimum Viable Product (MVP) concept, is discussed in (among other places) books about the Lean Startup concept, such as Ash Maurya's *Running Lean* (2nd edition, O'Reilly, 2012). An MVP is what it sounds like: a minimal version of a product that you can take to customers to get feedback and then iterate upon. A lot of software development methodologies encourage similar strategies. Until the advent of the technologies in this book, frequent iteration was more the realm of software than hardware. Now, though, it is possible to iterate hardware easily as well, and many of these concepts that one associates with phone apps and websites apply to hardware, too. Students brought up on iterative learning will be very valuable employees (or perhaps successful entrepreneurs).

## Summary

In this chapter, we started the process of tying together the process of learning through making (and breaking), discussed in the first 11 chapters, and seeing how it is similar in many ways to the scientific method, discussed in Chapters 12 through 14. We reviewed a design case study from the early days of open source 3D printers to see how a collective, iterative design process with small failures and small successes can converge to a good solution.

The next two chapters explore these similarities further and suggest how they might be applied. Chapter 16 looks at learning science by making, and Chapter 17 talks about what scientists can learn from the maker/hacker community.

# CHAPTER 16

■ ■ ■

# Learning Science By Making

Chapter 15 talks about learning by trying things out and gradually overcoming small failures. Chapters 12 through 14 look at a lot of stories of working scientists, engineers, and mathematicians and explore how many of them started out by taking something apart or doing something to see what would happen. In this chapter, we discuss how to harness some of this to teach various subjects, either in a formal classroom or elsewhere. We admit that we have not ourselves taught K-12 students directly. However, we have been consulting on how to use the technologies described in this book and as such have helped teachers and administrators think about how to effectively deploy 3D printing, Arduinos, wearable tech, and the like in a formal educational setting. We have interviewed teachers at several schools for this book (and reported on some of those interviews, particularly in Chapters 5, 8, and 10), and so you have seen some of our anecdotal evidence. We also discuss learning by making at the community college level as a case study in Chapter 11.

*Making* has become trendy with many buzzwords and acronyms. Joan particularly dislikes the acronym STEM (science, technology, engineering, and math) or the even more unwieldy STEAM (add art to STEM) because it seems more useful to just say *learning* instead of *STEAM learning*. (What about history? Political science? Learning how to camp in a forest without having your food eaten by bears?) In this chapter we talk about *science*, but use that term broadly to include anything that requires you to think critically and keep teaching yourself new skills as time goes by. Because Joan has been teaching for many years as an adjunct at various universities, she narrates most of this chapter, but Rich weighs in from his perspective some as well.

Currently, use of the technologies described in this book is still very much in the early-adopter stage in schools. Education is notoriously and significantly behind other industries in adapting to change, and so it will take a while for 3D printing, Arduinos, and wearable tech to become mainstream in education. Joan cringes when she hears people talk about things like "the maker movement in education." Calling making things a *movement* is counterproductive and polarizing, because it implies an all-or-nothing adoption of a belief system. (Rich expresses a different opinion below). She thinks that most educators are using making to varying degrees whether they call it that or not. The important thing is to figure out how to use a technology to expand what is possible for a student rather than just do something you have already done before using a different, cheaper tool, because that is a pretty fast way to make a technology purchase look frivolous.

Curriculum based on 3D printing, for example, should not be based on printing things that could far more easily be made out of cardboard. As we have advocated throughout the book, start simple to get some intuition (the classic thing to make in 3D printing is a keychain fob with your initials, which is a great introduction) but then *keep going*. Think about what being able to use 3D printing or a programmable microprocessor lets you do that would not have been possible a few years ago. We hope that this book will help people get past the hump between printing a keychain or something downloaded from Thingiverse and really designing something new—with all the learning that implies. If something fails in front of your students, that's great! Have them see (and participate in) the debugging process. They will learn far more from that than they would from following a foolproof recipe to make some tchotchke.

■ **Rich's view**   Education's tendency toward very late adoption of new technologies is a huge systemic failure, which affects the capabilities of the next generation. I'm already inclined to believe that formal education isn't of much use (education being something that is done to you, while learning is something you do), but being perpetually out of date makes it downright detrimental. The maker movement might offer some hope. I do hope and believe that it's a shift rather than a fad, and I don't think that the term *movement* implies that it is a fad in the way that Joan does. The movement itself may cease to be one because it has achieved its goal, the same way there isn't a women's suffrage movement today because women already have the vote.

# Learning the Science of Making

There are several ways to think about making things as a way to teach science, math, and other technical subjects. The first is to teach the science of making things per se—how a circuit works, how heat is dissipated in a heat sink, how to code, how to figure out how much material you will need to make something. In the past, this endeavor probably would have been called an "electronics lab," and everyone would expect to sit down with a lab partner and bend wire and connect things. It is not so different now, except that the projects probably can be more ambitious than they could have been not so long ago, and instead of making a circuit with a battery, a switch, and a light bulb your students can program just about anything they have time for (see Chapters 2, 3, 4, 6, 7, and 8). *Anything they have time for* is the catch, of course. One of the challenges of making things is that it takes longer than just reading about it and is more unpredictable than watching a video of someone else doing something. But, of course, you learn more along the way.

## Learning by 3D Printing

I found that I learned a tremendous amount in my first days in the 3D-printing universe. I was trained as an aeronautical engineer, and as time went by I became a generalist and more focused on software and on coordinating the efforts of others. Chapter 1 talks about trying to find starting points in the sea of open source documentation and forums, particularly without much experience doing things with modern component-level electronics or using 3D CAD systems.

The thing that helped me the most was an ability to organize knowledge and debug things systematically, changing just one thing at a time. I also had the advantage of working for a 3D-printer manufacturer, so I could ask questions as I needed to if the online information universe had too much information for my patience at any particular moment. (Rich was the most frequent target of these questions, 3D-printing "old-timer" that he is.) Once I became competent, I spent a lot of my time explaining printing to people and seeing what metaphors worked well. With that experience in mind, the following list outlines some things that might naturally be taught by making, as opposed to adding maker technologies to existing curriculum (which talk about in the next section). Refer to Chapter 3 for the 3D-printing workflow and issues that we mention in passing here.

- *3D CAD*: To do anything beyond printing something someone else has developed, you need to learn CAD or use a scanner system. This also assumes reasonably good computer and mouse skills (for most programs) and/or some coding (for CAD programs like OpenSCAD). Scanners still tend to be rather hard to use and have complex "clean up" programs.

- *Design principles*: Design principles like leaving adequate clearance become more memorable when you have an object that does not work in your hand. A 5 mm insert needs a hole bigger than 5 mm to fit into, and knowing how much bigger it needs to be in a given situation is sometimes more art than science. 3D printing allows for cheap iteration compared to using machine tools. The ability to iterate a part over and over (see Rich's example of a bar clamp design in Chapter 15) creates a lot of opportunity for students to try out different design options both analytically and empirically.

- *The limitations of the virtual*: 3D printing starts with an object in the virtual world and makes it real. The fact that this transition is neither automated nor entirely reliable is often shocking to people and can make for a good teachable moment in the limitations of computer models, the properties of materials, structural integrity, and thermodynamics—or, if you are feeling more philosophical, in the difference between the real and virtual worlds in general. Just because it looks wonderful on the screen does not mean it will be a gleaming, perfect print. Figuring out why not is a great exercise in critical thinking and perhaps patience.

- *Materials properties*: Anyone who is doing a significant amount of 3D printing will learn rather a lot about the behavior of plastics in varying temperature regimes and will likely do some tweaking of the print temperatures. How a 3D print is oriented on a print bed makes a big difference to both how hard it is to print and how strong it is (because printed objects want to fail along layer boundaries most of the time, at least with regard to filament-based printers).

- *Robotics*: The printers themselves are robots, and many are still sold as kits. Close observation of a 3D printer and empirical discovery of how various adjustments are reflected in prints are good for building mechanical intuition. Building a printer from a kit, if that seems within reach, will of course go a lot farther along these lines. Most kits have online instructions; you can take a look at those before you buy to see if you can handle it.

- *Design aesthetics*: This section is primarily talking about science and math, but obviously you can teach the aesthetics of design through printing as well (at least, through art projects that can be developed in a 3D CAD program).

---

■ **Rich's view**    It feels to me that some of Joan's discomfort with open source documentation is that the information doesn't have starting points because it's meant to be *used*, not *studied*. When you are using the information, you necessarily already have a starting point—you have a goal and something you need to figure out to achieve it. Trying to learn information without the context of the reason for learning it is like trying to make sense of a sentence without a subject. We more or less agree on the points above as good things to learn while 3D printing, but significantly Joan uses the point of view of "teaching," whereas I think of "learning."

---

On the negative side, 3D printing is slow, so any demonstration will probably extend well past a 50-minute class period. Having a separate makerspace that can handle monitoring prints if the students cannot be there for the whole printing time is one option, or finding ways to schedule longer blocks of time.

---

■ **Tip** If you ask students to just pick something out of a database to try printing on a first outing with a 3D printer, they often will see something they want to try but have no idea whether it might be hard or easy to print. Then they get upset when the 3D-printing workflow seizes up at some point. Quite often beginners pick out a file that is very hard to print or that might not print at all. Sometimes people post a model to a database but do not actually try to print it first.

If you are teaching a class, you may want to curate some models ahead of time and test whether they work. Let your students start from those so that they are not fighting too many unknowns at once. Finding a database model that has a lot of positive comments or notes by people who have made one is a bit of insurance. Some even allow users to add pictures of their own prints. Links to some databases are in Chapter 3, in the section "Downloading an Object To Print." Alternatively, loosely define something that they can make themselves in a simple CAD program (see Chapter 3's section "Creating a Model to Print").

---

## Learning by Using Arduinos, Wearable Tech, and Sensors

It is a little more obvious how to incorporate Arduino-ecosystem sensors and other electronics into curriculum, since electronics classes have been around for a while. How each component works, how to test it, and (in the case of sensors) how to see the way in which the component interacts with its environment are the most straightforward ways to learn. Depending on the age and sophistication of the students, teaching them the basics of the kinds of components you have decided to have available and then giving them a problem to solve might be the best way to get them to delve into the component capabilities. Wearable tech, as mentioned in Chapter 7, may also be a good back door to interest students who otherwise think they are not interested in learning technical subjects. The next section talks about adding making to the traditional science curriculum. Using Arduinos and sensors to make instrumentation is a great way to do that (see Chapter 6 for more about citizen science).

# Adding Making to a Traditional Science (or Math) Curriculum

People tend to view science teaching as very structured and built up like a pyramid: first you learn this, then you "build on" it by learning that, and so on. The system works reasonably well, and it is one way of organizing a fairly complex body of information that needs some tightly integrated math. However, science also has a tradition of labs and class demonstrations, and adding the technologies described in this book to a traditional lab opens up hands-on capabilities and real research options, instead of the usual follow-the-recipe school science lab.

## Creating Equipment for Experiments

Tom Haglund, a teacher at the Windward School in West Los Angeles (also discussed in Chapter 5) wanted to see whether saltwater aquarium fish would react differently to 3D-printed and real coral. The coral was scanned and then 3D printed in natural ABS plastic (the plastic that LEGO bricks are made of). The prints needed support structure, as do many 3D prints. Figure 16-1 shows one of them just after it finished; you can see the supporting structure, which was removed later.

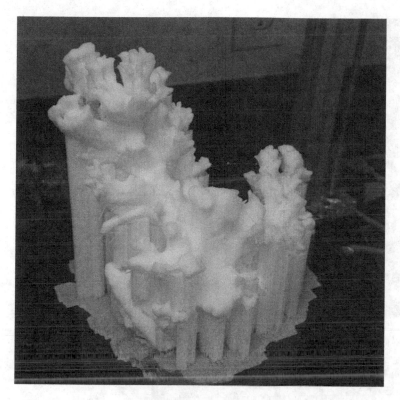

***Figure 16-1.*** *The coral just after it printed, with support*

The print needed support because the object is built up from the platform, and pieces that stick out more than a small amount need to have support built under them all the way up from the platform so they are not printed in thin air. Coral, of course, is "additively manufactured" itself, although building underwater is a lot easier and avoids the need for support in the same way.

Figures 16-2 and 16-3 show some side-by-side comparisons of the original and printed coral. You can see that the resemblance is pretty good, but the set in Figure 16-3 did not have quite the same fidelity. It is tricky to scan objects with a lot of nooks and concave crannies, because the light beams the scanner uses to illuminate the object to scan it cannot always get into all the corners.

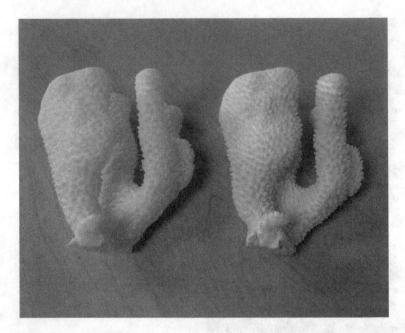

**Figure 16-2.** *One set of 3D-printed copy of coral (L) and the original (R)*

**Figure 16-3.** *Another set of 3D-printed copy of coral (L) and the original (R)*

As of this writing, the coral was soaking in two buckets of plain water, one each for the real coral and the 3D-printed one, to leach out any impurities or unwanted salts before putting them in the tank (Figure 16-4). The printed coral was created in natural ABS, as the material thought most likely to be stable in the environment. If the test is successful (and the fish cannot tell the difference), this might be an interesting first attempt in creating custom mini-ecosystems either in captivity or in the wild that are more robust and accurate than the current ones that are available for students to study.

***Figure 16-4.*** *The coral soaking, with real coral in one bucket and the 3D-printed coral in the other*

In this case, students will use objects created for them, as opposed to ones they create themselves. Having a designated teacher, staff member, or small group be the ones primarily using these technologies to create devices or instruments for students is one way to take advantage of the technology.

Some of the teachers and school staff that we interviewed found teacher and staff mediation to be a good near-term solution that allowed the students to explore areas they would not have realistically been able to experience any other way. The idea, though, is that gradually other students and teachers will become familiar and climb up the learning curves, informally or through classes or after-school activities, and then branch out into a range of projects.

## Visualizing Difficult Concepts

Chemistry is often difficult to master because of the many abstract structures that arise in the process of modeling molecules, distributions of electrons in the molecules (called "orbitals"), and so on. Chapter 11 describes some 3D-printed models made to teach blind students about orbitals. The concepts are not easy for sighted students either, and we are seeing a variety of chemistry models at all levels of sophistication. Some are simple enough that a student can print them out, and some are very complicated but still available to print and assemble from 3D-printed and other parts (such as Peppytides, www.peppytides.org, which are physical models of polypeptide chains). There is a lot of chemistry modeling software out there, and in some cases the software can output files that can be 3D printed (or perhaps files that can be 3D printed after some translation).

We have also seen some early attempts to 3D print histology models (for example, Mike Kolitsky of Atlantic Cape Community College) and "DNA origami" models (Matt Gethers at Caltech and collaborators). Right now the process of truly making 3D models is still a little slow and labor-intensive. Hopefully the tools will start to catch up with the need soon!

## Mechanical Learning

It can also be difficult to imagine how gears and other mechanisms will work together. Rich designed a set of planetary gears that have been very popular just as a "fiddle toy" that people love to play with; they come off the printer assembled and move freely with just a little bit of flexing. They are shown on the cover of this book and in Figure 16-5. The design and instructions are freely available on the Youmagine repository, at www.youmagine.com/designs/quick-print-gear-bearing. Creating a mechanism that will actually work in a CAD system and then determining end-to-end how to print it out seems to us to be a really good use of the technology and a great "next challenge" for a student who has gotten past the keychain fob stage. If you search in the popular 3D-printing repositories (see Chapter 3) for "gears," you will find a lot of options to get you started.

*Figure 16-5.* *3D-printed planetary gears*

## Creating Instrumentation

Chapter 6 discusses citizen science and open source labs, including a lot on instrumentation. We will not repeat ourselves here except to note that many, many sensors can be managed by an Arduino. If you want to measure something in the lab or in the field, there may be low-cost sensors available. Be sure to read data sheets carefully to be sure that the instrument is measuring what you think it is.

## Making Learning Aids for the Visually Impaired Student

Chapter 11 describes projects to create objects to teach blind students chemistry and to assist them with navigating their schools. Teachers of the visually impaired have always created tactile models out of whatever was lying about for their students, but readily available fabrication means that it is now a lot easier for these teachers to make what they need (or have it made far more cheaply) than was possible before.

The DIAGRAM (Digital Image And Graphic Resources for Accessible Materials) Center, http://diagramcenter.org, is run by Benetech (www.benetech.org) to find ways to create more accessible electronic media generally. Recently, the Center has become interested in 3D printing and has collected some research recommendations on its site at http://diagramcenter.org/3d-printing.html.

# Overcoming Barriers

Change is never easy, and that often goes double in education. There is rarely enough money to do everything a teacher wants to do, and teachers have packed schedules as it is. Sending a teacher to be trained in using a new technology means the school has to find a substitute, or the teacher has to give up some rare personal time. Another challenge with adding self-directed learning to the curriculum is how to assess that students have learned what they need to and deal with the students who choose not to learn this way.

One good option is to gather a diverse group of colleagues to try out some joint interdisciplinary projects. An art or shop teacher may have some experience with the hands-on aspects, and a computer science or math teacher may be comfortable with the computing aspects. The Castilleja School (www.castilleja.org, discussed in Chapter 10) and its Bourn Idea Lab (http://bournidealab.blogspot.com) have had students do projects in a variety of disciplines, including making da Vinci machines, modeling the circulatory system, and making holiday card that light up.

---

■ **Tip** We have seen that the best approach for us as technologists has been to ask teachers what they would like to do if they could do anything with their students and then walk back from there what is possible. If people do not (yet) understand what is possible, they often aim too high and are disappointed, or too low and wonder why they did not just make something the traditional way.

---

# Just Make Something!

The bottom line of all this is that learning by actually having a new experience is very effective. A couple of years ago, I had the experience of trying out glassblowing with an artist colleague. In a beginner one-day class, the stereotypical thing to make is a paperweight (sort of the equivalent of 3D printing a keychain fob). Figure 16-6 shows glass paperweights and a vase I made. To see what the process looks like, try doing a search for videos with the keywords "glassblowing class."

*Figure 16-6. Joan's paperweights and vase*

I learned more about glass as a material in those six hours or so than I could have in days of reading about it. Hot glass is about the consistency of taffy, but taffy that is so hot that it is glowing. You are hanging around open flame so hot that you have to be careful to avoid wearing any synthetic clothing, which can spontaneously "flash" and catch fire. One thing that is not obvious at all before the experience is that creating a handmade glass object requires very rapid, precise movements; the very experienced teacher moved like a disciplined classical ballet dancer. Every move gets captured in the glass as it hardens. He had to grab the thin-walled vase you can see in the background of Figure 16-6 away and finish it for me. I had inadvertently got it to a point where it was too delicate for someone with my limited experience to complete it without shattering it.

As an adult learner, even one with an engineering master's degree, I learn a great deal every time I try making something new. I did not really try out making *anything* physical for many years, but the hot glass experience led to me become interested more in how things are made, and eventually led me to cross paths with 3D printing and now with many other technologies. Try making something, and you will never look at the objects around you the same way again!

# Summary

In this chapter, we talked about how to learn traditional academic subjects, particularly science, by making things. First we talked about using the technologies in this book for their own sake to teach subjects like science and math. Then we looked at using these technologies instead as tools to supplement existing curriculum. In Chapter 17, we close out our book by looking at what professional scientists can learn from hackers and makers.

■ ■ ■

# CHAPTER 17

# What Scientists Can Learn from Makers

In this book we have often talked about the similarities between scientists and makers or hackers. The previous chapter discussed how to teach someone science by making things. But what happens if we turn that around? What can a scientist learn from a maker or a hacker? This concluding chapter looks at this aspect in two ways. First, the pragmatic: what technologies and techniques from the maker community might be useful in the scientific community? And second, philosophically: how are makers and scientists alike—or different? Because we will be jumping back and forth between experiences we each have had and some that we experienced together, we conclude our book together and call out our individual experiences.

## Practical Things Scientists Can Learn from Makers

Scientific instrumentation tends to be very expensive, so labs tend to keep it for a long time and design experiments around the capabilities of the existing equipment. However, we feel that this is the wrong way around. Scientists should be able to design instruments that do what they want to do, rather than bend experiments to what is available. Chapter 6's "Open Source Labs" discussion touches on this. There are some challenges making this work, though. Scientists are experts in their science and not necessarily in the details of how their instruments operate. This means it can be pretty easy for them to over– or underestimate the complexity of their machinery.

Usually people are a lab's most expensive and overcommitted resource, so hacking for hacking's sake to try to build something typically is not the first option a lab will pick, because it takes staff time. If you are the world expert on some aspect of DNA's structure, becoming an expert on stepper motors might not be a good use of your time.

In some cases, though, there is no commercial option, and then becoming a bit of a hacker might enable an experiment that is not otherwise possible or that otherwise might be impossibly time-consuming to set up. In one case, things worked out very well, and the scientists were able to use 3D printing to create some insect traps that would have been challenging to make otherwise.

## 3D-Printed Insect Traps

Entomologists have it tough. They have to try to study (and sometimes outsmart) living creatures that live in swarms (or maybe alone) in inaccessible places. They may have to find and manage research subjects that are the size of biggish dust particles. They frequently need to make a lot of very small, relatively simple devices to track where a particular insect is going, how they move around, and what attracts them or keeps them away. To get a sense of the types of insect traps out there for educators to use, see `www.bugdorm.com`, or just search on "insect trap" to see the fantastic array of gadgets designed to catch bugs that interfere with people's activities in some way.

When professional entomologists are on the trail of a newly identified and potentially economically destructive insect—like the polyphagous shot hole borer (PSHB) described in Chapter 6's section "Citizen Science Case Study: Invasive Species"—they often need to get creative and whip up novel equipment.

Joan had been making various local groups aware of the possibilities of 3D printing for scientific applications. One of the people she met was Dan Berry, Nursery Manager at the Huntington Library, Art Collections and Botanical Gardens. Berry had been working with UC Riverside on the PSHB problem and put Joan in touch with Richard Stouthamer's lab there (`www.entomology.ucr.edu/faculty/stouthamer.html`).

Stouthamer, Berry and a group of collaborators had been researching PSHB and realized that 3D printing some specialized traps would be a fast way to get some data about the beetle's behavior. Making a few dozen or even a few hundred specialized, small beetle traps is a really good job for a 3D printer, particularly compared to people cobbling (and thus assembling) pieces to create them instead. Deezmaker 3D printers in Pasadena (where Joan and Rich worked at the time) collaborated closely with the group to design and prototype a complicated trap.

The first few traps were the result of many design iterations as everyone learned about what was needed and what was possible. Eventually the lab bought a 3D printer of its own and will be designing and developing its own traps going forward. Figure 17-1 shows Stouthamer Lab postdoc Roger Duncan Selby starting up a print in the lab. As we are writing this book, they are getting ready to deploy the first traps in the field with a hope of learning a lot about how the beetle lives in and emerges from trees.

*Figure 17-1.  Printing insect traps in an entomology lab*

■ **Note**   If you are a scientist trying to do an experiment for which there really is no commercial equipment, it is getting increasingly easier to prototype and program simple little robots using an Arduino (see Chapter 2) or similar device as a controller. Chapter 4 talks about robots in more depth, and Chapter 6 covers combining those with sensors. It is also now very easy to hook up a camera or proximity sensor to keep an eye on something remotely. Many scientific disciplines are being transformed by the option of leaving instrumentation in the field indefinitely and collecting data.

The Arduino user forums have a board just for "Science and Measurement." Go to http://forum.arduino.cc and under "Topics" take a look to see what is available. The National Institutes of Health has a repository of various 3D-printable labware and visualization models at http://3dprint.nih.gov.

## One-off Lab Automation

The parts that make up an open-source 3D printer can pretty easily also be rearranged to make simple lab automation devices. One scientist needed to move two small devices around precisely in three dimensions in a particular pattern. To that point, the laboratory staff had been doing these very repetitive, tedious motions by hand. The machine that the group designed in collaboration with a 3D-printer company moved the instruments around just fine, but then it turned out that one of the devices could not be used as many times in a row as the new automation enabled without having some other maintenance procedures inserted into the automated workflow. This required programming some other maneuvers, and by the time this was worked out the staff had just done the procedure by hand because they had a deadline. They subsequently did use the machine for some other purposes, but the lesson learned there is that we would not suggest trying a hackerish solution for a time-critical problem, because by definition these things tend to be somewhat exploratory.

## Using Maker Technologies to Visualize (or Teach) Abstract Concepts

Scientists, engineers, and mathematicians have always built physical models to help them think about abstract concepts, or to see what a design might look like before committing to building a full-scale or hard-to-build real model. For example, paleontologists have been early adopters of 3D printing, scanning bone pieces that can then be replicated (instead of creating plaster casts as was the case in the past). 3D printing enables collaborators to share models very easily (just email a file around instead of mailing physical objects) and to iterate them quickly. People can hold a 3D-printed model in their hands and discuss it with others in a way that just is not possible with an image on a screen.

---

■ **Tip**   As discussed in Chapter 11, chemistry molecular models have been early targets for 3D printing, too. The ones in Chapter 11 were designed from scratch to represent particular molecules. If you are a scientist and want to print out molecular models, check to see whether your favorite visualization program outputs files formatted for 3D printing (such as STL files). Joan's book *Mastering 3D Printing* (Apress, 2014) has a chapter about using 3D printing in scientific visualization and gives examples. More generally, if you use a 3D-visualization program that can create a "surface model," it may create some sort of mesh that can be converted into something 3D-printable. If your software cannot export to an STL file, you can always search on "convert (whatever your program puts out) to STL" and see whether a conversion program exists.

---

Some scientific papers now make a 3D-printable model available for download as a companion to the traditional paper and its illustrations. A group of NASA scientists created an image of the Homunculus Nebula, a region of gas and dust around the binary star Eta Carinae. The group used a ground-based telescope to image a series of strips of the nebula's surface, which they then put together using astrophysics modeling software. The data, combined with a computer model, gave them a 3D model of the nebula's surface. They also included a link to a 3D-printable version. 3D visualizations on-screen are not new, but being able to easily and cheaply allow anyone with a 3D printer to also have a 3D model available has a lot of possibilities for collaboration and teaching. Details are available at www.nasa.gov/content/goddard/astronomers-bring-the-third-dimension-to-a-doomed-stars-outburst/.

# How Hackers and Scientists Are Similar (and How They Differ)

Clearly there are practical, technological ideas from the hacker/maker community that can contribute to a scientist's work. But in this book we have tried to also show the parallels. What aspects of the hacker ethos itself (as Rich introduced in Chapter 1 and commented on throughout the book) might be something that scientists could think about as somewhat different perspectives on the same problems they try to solve? We give a few examples in this section. First Rich talks about how hackers have an equivalent of peer review. Then Joan talks a bit about how science might benefit from adopting some of the hacker views on taking risks.

## Hacker Peer Review

The peer review process is essential to science. The open source community of makers and hackers has its own form of peer review that may not be as rigorous, but is just as essential to us. When a project is released as open source, everyone has access to the code used to create it. This access allows rapid development of very complex things, such as the Linux operating system, if the project is one that will get enough hackers interested in contributing.

With the number of developers involved and the loose ties between them, you might suspect that one bad apple could introduce malicious code, such as adding a "back door" to bypass security features. On the contrary, in the computer-security community, open source is often considered a prerequisite for *trusting* a piece of software. A back door can be exploited by the malicious hacker (or government agency) that put it there, but it also creates a weak point in the security and can also be exploited by anyone else who discovers it. Encryption algorithms in particular must be open source for the algorithm to be provably secure. Any program can have a back door, but proprietary code can't be audited, whereas open source code can.

## Truecrypt Case Study

One example of this involved the Truecrypt program. This software allows users to encrypt entire hard drives, including the operating system, to keep all of their data secure. Obviously, having a back door in such a broad security product would be disastrous. In 2013, a crowdfunding campaign began to audit the code to ensure not only that there were no back doors, but to have professional cryptographers analyze the cryptographic procedures and look for weaknesses. As of this writing, their report has just been released. The auditors found no major problems, but did identify several areas that may be vulnerable to attacks under specific, abnormal circumstances, which can be improved now that they have been identified.

In cases like this one, it's less important that such an audit occurs than that it *can* be done, at any time, by anyone with the knowledge and inclination to do so. Some pieces of code, or other information such as a Wikipedia article, are curated by individuals who audit every change as it comes in. For others, the fact that a deliberate error (sometimes called defacement) could be discovered and fixed at any time is enough of a deterrent to prevent them from being added.

## How Does a Hacker Decide What Is "Right"?

There isn't always a "right" and "wrong" way to develop a piece of software or hardware. Hackers, though, have their own criteria to judge projects against. The first definition in the *Jargon File* (mentioned in Chapter 1) for *hack* is "Originally, a quick job that produces what is needed, but not well," and the second, ironically, is "An incredibly good, and perhaps very time-consuming, piece of work that produces exactly what is needed." A kluge may work just fine, but an elegant solution is better, and the difference between the two is sometimes ineffable.

When you browse one of the repositories of 3D-printable objects, it may be difficult to tell which designs are better than others before you have much experience. There are many factors, depending on what the design is for, but printability is always an essential one. A good way to see if an object is printable is to read the comments, but a better one is to look at the pictures that other users have posted of their prints. If nobody has successfully printed it and posted a picture, that's a bad sign.

Rather than relying on rigorous duplication of a study or in-depth review of a project by two or three anonymous referees, hacker peer review is based on the aggregated review, comments and adaptations of many people who build on the work. It is sort of like an incremental version of the all-at-once formalized review that scientific papers go through. If there are no comments and no one built on the work, it is sort of like a scientific paper being rejected by a journal. Both failures doom a project to obscurity, at least for the time being, but perhaps the hacker version makes it easier for the "author" to correct the work and try to interest people again.

---

■ **Note**    Just because a project doesn't get the attention of hackers, that doesn't necessarily mean it's poorly executed or not useful. It may just be "uninteresting" to other hackers. The *Jargon File* defines an "uninteresting" problem as one "for which a solution would neither advance the state of the art nor be fun to design and code." The *Jargon File* goes on to say that "Hackers regard uninteresting problems as intolerable wastes of time, to be solved (if at all) by lesser mortals. Real hackers (see toolsmith) generalize uninteresting problems enough to make them interesting and solve them—thus solving the original problem as a special case (and, it must be admitted, occasionally turning a molehill into a mountain, or a mountain into a tectonic plate)." Scientists have been known to resemble hackers in their definition of "interesting" problems!

---

In the next section, Joan looks at how scientists and hackers look at risk. Can scientists take chances and fail? We have said in this book that many great ideas have come out of failures, but can scientists still expect the public to accept failures?

## Taking Risks

Throughout this book we have drawn a lot of parallels between the maker, hacker, engineer, scientist, and mathematician. Early in Joan's career, in the 1980s, being a scientist or engineer was kind of cool— sort of like a maker or hacker is today. Somewhere along the line, though, the image of science became either sort of vaguely corporate and evil, or boring. Joan asked a scientist friend to tell her the first adjective that came to mind to describe a scientist. His answer was "methodical." (Asked to do the same to describe a hacker, he said, "creative.") Joan finds this very depressing, accurate, and just plain not how things should be.

## The Scientific Funding Problem

Some risk aversion has been a result of the scientific funding environment, at least in the United States. Scientific funding has gotten a lot more competitive and harder to get, and the perception in some fields is that you pretty much have to propose experiments you know will have positive results before you do them, because stuff that is likely to fail probably will not get funded. Anything really groundbreaking probably has to be done nights, weekends, or when no one is looking, and with labor done by undergraduates who need a few extra credits. If it fails, it will quietly go away—which means other people may waste time going down the same path. In other words, the scientist has to act like a hobbyist hacker to get something novel done but may not have the hacker's advantage of being part of a community where everyone lets everyone else know about his great fails.

Similarly, to do anything in the United States in the medical realm typically requires a lot of money for FDA approval and testing once things start heading toward trials on humans. This usually means that any new idea being tested needs to be trussed up in patents and otherwise very narrowly defined to attract the investors needed for the process. If someone is at the front end of an approval process that might cost hundreds of millions of dollars, the answer to the question "Is this going to work?" really can't be "Maybe..."

## Low Startup Costs Drive Innovations

A counterexample of sorts is the 3D-printing world. Initially 3D printing was an academic invention and was licensed that way to a small number of firms. The companies with the key patents elected to keep the technology expensive (and thus the market relatively small). Then, as described in Chapter 9, as the patents ran out, the open source community moved in and created a wild variety of 3D printers. The companies that had been holding the technology close to the vest (Stratasys and 3D Systems, which bought early player Z Corp) grew enormously, too, even though they no longer had the protection of some of their key patents.

Stratasys's stock price (symbol SSYS) peaked in 2013 at over 730% of its ten-years-ago price, and 3D Systems (DDD) peaked at about 1200%. As of this writing (in the second quarter of 2015), both have fallen from their peaks but are still at over 250% of their stock prices from a decade ago.

A lot of the energy came from the hacker community, which was able to invent and try things at very low cost and get a lot of new projects crowdfunded on platforms like Kickstarter. Now that there is a lot of competition in these low-end printers, some competitors are trying to fence in some pieces of the space with patents again. How this will play out remains to be seen. But it says that when the hacker mindset is set loose in an area that has been growing in the "grown-up" business world, a lot of good things (and of course, a lot of silly things) can happen.

Certainly, the hacker mentality never left the software world, precisely because starting a software business is cheap, so the constraints and adult supervision that come with massive funding are not there, at least not early on. It is our hope that because hardware prototyping cost is plummeting due to the innovations described in this book, perhaps hardware and scientific startups will be able to become more like software and web ones. That is, these startups may be dominated by people able to take chances and fund themselves on their own or with just a few thousand like-minded crowdfunding friends and family members. We need scientists to be able to do wonderful things on the margins of major projects and start exploring things that might fail. That is the best way to ensure really big successes down the road (other than dramatically increasing science funding, which seems unlikely to happen anytime soon).

# Making Change

A lot of very difficult problems in the world have a mix of scientific and social solutions, like combating climate change, ending hunger, and finding ways to bring education to people who do not have access to it. The American Midwest has endured some brutally cold winters (see Figure 17-2), and the Southwest is drying out.

*Figure 17-2.*  *Chicago winter, February 2014*

These problems probably will not be solved by any one person. They will need many incremental solutions, contributed by scientists working on large research projects, but also by hackers and makers inventing things, failing, and continuing to try. We hope that this book has given you ideas about how to be creative, take risks, and keep going if your first solution does not work out.

Above all, we hope that if you start projects around some of the technologies in this book, you bring a kid along when you start making things, whether your projects are simple or complex. It may start them on the path to being a scientist (see Figure 17-3). As we have seen in this book, that path can begin in a lot of different places, but, with luck, the path will always go someplace no one has traveled before.

*Figure 17-3.* *Foreword co-author Coco working to save the world. Photo courtesy of Mosa Kaleel*

## Summary

This chapter discussed what scientists might learn from hackers and makers, both by using the technologies described in this book and from the risk-glorifying hacker culture. It also tied in many of the earlier chapters in the process of making these points, with the goal of showing the reader how a scientist might benefit by being just a bit more of a hacker now and then.

# APPENDIX

■ ■ ■

# Links

This Appendix aggregates all the links in the book in one place for ready reference. If a link appeared more than once, it is just listed in the place it appeared first.

## Author and Foreword Sites

Joan and Rich's company site, Nonscriptum LLC: www.nonscriptum.com

Joan's blog: www.joanhorvath.com

Rich's blog: www.whosawhatsis.com

Coco Kaloo's blog: www.veryhappyrobot.com

## Chapter 1: 21st Century Shop Teacher

*Jargon File*'s definition of a hacker: www.catb.org/jargon/html/H/hacker.html

Sparkfun Electronics: www.sparkfun.com

Adafruit: www.adafruit.com

Common Core Initiative: www.corestandards.org

"The Death Of Shop Class And America's Skilled Workforce" from *Forbes*, by Tara Tiger Brown:
www.forbes.com/sites/tarabrown/2012/05/30/the-death-of-shop-class-and-americas-high-skilled-workforce

"Is the Era of Mass Manufacturing Coming to an End?" from *Harvard Business Review*, by
Peter Acton: https://hbr.org/2014/12/is-the-era-of-mass-manufacturing-coming-to-an-end

## Chapter 2: Arduino, Raspberry Pi, and Programming Physical Things

Ardusat, a small Ardunio-controlled spacecraft: www.ardusat.com

Processing tutorials: https://processing.org/tutorials/overview/

Processing IDE interface reference: https://processing.org/reference/environment/

Arduino: http://Arduino.cc

Instructables project site: www.instructables.com

Qtechknow electronics: www.qtechknow.com

Fritzing circuit software: www.fritzing.org

123D Circuits: www.circuits.io

Raspbian, a Linux distribution for Raspberry Pi: www.raspbian.org

Raspberry Pi: www.raspberrypi.org

Circuit Stickers: www.circuitstickers.com

LittleBits: http://littlebits.cc

LightUp: www.LightUP.io

Arduino forum: http://forum.arduino.cc

Let's Make Robots: www.letsmakerobots.com

Hackaday: www.hackaday.com

The Maker Shed: www.makershed.com

# Chapter 3: 3D Printing

Wikipedia's article on 3D printing: http://en.wikipedia.org/wiki/3D_printing

The RepRap open source 3D-printer project: www.reprap.org

MIT's *Technology Review:* www.technologyreview.com

The open-access scientific journal *PLOS ONE*: www.plosone.org

*3D Printer World*: www.3dprinterworld.com

3Ders 3D-printing community: www.3ders.org

Tinkercad 3D modeling site: www.tinkercad.com

Solidworks 3D modeling software: www.solidworks.com

OpenSCAD 3D modeling programming language site: www.openscad.org

Blender 3D modeling site: www.blender.org

Maya 3D modeling software: www.autodesk.com/products/maya/overview

Z-Brush 3D modeling software: www.pixologic.com/zbrush

FreeCAD 3D modeling software: www.freecadweb.org

Thingiverse 3D printable objects site: www.thingiverse.com

YouMagine 3D-printable objects site: www.youmagine.com

Leopoly 3D modeling and printable objects site: www.leopoly.com

The U.S. National Institutes of Health's centralized database of medical-interest 3D-printing files: http://3dprint.nih.gov

MatterControl 3D-printing software system: www.mattercontrol.com

Shapeways 3D-printing service bureau: www.shapeways.com

iMaterialize 3D-printing service bureau: http://i.materialise.com

Sculpteo 3D modeling software: www.sculpteo.com

Solid Concepts 3D-printing service bureau: www.solidconcepts.com

3D Hubs 3D-printing community/service bureau: www.3dhubs.com

Makexyz 3D-printing community/service bureau: www.makexyz.com

# Chapter 4: Robots, Drones, and Other Things That Move

FIRST Robotics: www.usfirst.org

Wikipedia's entry on electric motors: http://en.wikipedia.org/wiki/Electric_motor

Pololu: www.pololu.com

Hobby King: www.hobbyking.com

3D Robotics: www.3drobotics.com

Robot obstacle course: www.instructables.com/id/Qtechknow-Robot-Obstacle-Course

Crazyflie, an open source programmable quadcopter: www.bitcraze.se

FAA's draft rules for hobbyist drones: www.faa.gov/uas/model_aircraft/

Botball: www.botball.org

Fuzzbot robot instructions: www.instructables.com/id/FuzzBot

# Chapter 5: What's a Makerspace (or Hackerspace)?

Meetup.com: www.meetup.com

Crashspace hackerspace: www.crashspace.org

Machine Project: www.machineproject.org

Vocademy, The Hackerspace: www.vocademy.com

Artisan's Asylum: http://artisansasylum.com

The Fab Lab network: www.fablabs.io

Fab Lab governing foundation: www.fabfoundation.org/about-us

Fab Academy: www.fabacademy.org

TechShop: www.techshop.ws

LA Biohackers: www.biohackers.la

"How to Make (almost) Anything" class at MIT: http://fab.cba.mit.edu/classes/863.14/

The Tech Museum of Innovation in San Jose: www.thetech.org

Tinkering Studio at The Exploratorium in San Francisco: http://tinkering.exploratorium.edu

Kidspace Museum in Pasadena: www.kidspacemuseum.org

LA Makerspace: www.lamakerspace.com

The Windward School in Los Angeles: www.windwardschool.org

The Center For Early Education in West Hollywood, California: www.centerforearlyeducation.org

Scratch programming environment: https://scratch.mit.edu

St. Matthew's Parish School in Pacific Palisades, California: www.stmatthewsschool.com

St. Matthew's Parish School's Project Idea & Realization Lab (PIRL): www.creatorsstudio.org

# Chapter 6: Citizen Science and Open Source Labs

SETI@Home: http://setiathome.berkeley.edu

The Galaxy Zoo project: www.galaxyzoo.org

Zooniverse citizen science site: www.zooniverse.org

The Old Weather project: www.oldweather.org

The Christmas Bird Count project: www.audubon.org/conservation/science/christmas-bird-count

Cornell University Ornithology Lab: www.birds.cornell.edu

The Port of Los Angeles: www.portoflosangeles.org/about/facts.asp

Polyphagous shot hole borer (PSHB): http://ucanr.edu/sites/socaloakpests/Polyphagous_Shot_Hole_Borer/

PSHB observation collection site: www.inaturalist.org/projects/scarab

Weather stations category on Instructables: www.instructables.com/howto/weather+stations/

Sensors category on Instructables: www.instructables.com/howto/sensors/

Tekla Labs project at University of California at Berkeley: www.teklalabs.org

"Build My Lab" contest on Instructables: www.instructables.com/contest/buildmylab/

Michigan Tech Open Sustainability Technology Lab's optics lab equipment: www.appropedia.org/Open_source_optics

"Open-Source 3D-Printable Optics Equipment" in PLOS ONE: http://journals.plos.org/plosone/article?id=10.1371/journal.pone.0059840

Public Lab: www.publiclab.org

# Chapter 7: Cosplay, Wearable Tech, and the Internet of Things

Anouk Wipprecht, fashiontech designer: www.anoukwipprecht.nl

Particle Dress open source wearable tech project: www.instructables.com/id/JOIN-OUR-OPEN-SOURCE-ELEMENT-DRESS/

Becky Stern, wearable tech designer: www.beckystern.com

Adafruit tutorials page: http://learn.adafruit.com

Limor "Lady Ada" Fried, the founder of Adafruit: www.adafruit.com/about

Sparkle Skirt: https://learn.adafruit.com/sparkle-skirt

LED goggles tutorial: https://learn.adafruit.com/kaleidoscope-eyes-neopixel-led-goggles-trinket-gemma/

Mathematical knitting: www.toroidalsnark.net/mathknit.html#smmk

MIT's self-assembly lab: www.selfassemblylab.net/ProgrammableMaterials.php

The GlowCap: www.vitality.net

MIT Media Lab researcher David Rose's book *Enchanted Objects:* http://enchantedobjects.com

Ravelry: www.ravelry.com

Amateur costuming website: www.costume.org

# Chapter 8: Circuits and Programming for Kids

The Lifelong Kindergarten Group at the MIT Media Lab: https://llk.media.mit.edu

Kickstarter: www.kickstarter.com

The Transformative Learning Technologies Lab at Stanford: https://tltl.stanford.edu

Bird Brain Technologies: www.birdbraintechnologies.com

The CREATE (Community Robotics, Education And Technology Empowerment) lab at Carnegie Mellon University: www.cmucreatelab.org

KitHub: http://kithub.cc

Indiegogo: www.indiegogo.com

Circuit Scribe: www.electroninks.com

MaKey MaKey: www.makeymakey.com

MaKey MaKey piano: www.makeymakey.com/piano

Squishy Circuits: http://courseweb.stthomas.edu/apthomas/SquishyCircuits/

ElectronInks: www.electroninks.com

Bitlab: http://littlebits.cc/bitlab

Chibitronics, makers of Circuit Stickers: www.chibitronics.com

LEGO Mindstorms: www.lego.com/en-us/mindstorms/

FIRST LEGO League: www.usfirst.org/roboticsprograms/fll

Hummingbird robot controller: www.hummingbirdkit.com

S4A (Scratch For Arduino): http://s4a.cat

Ardublock: http://blog.ardublock.com

## Chapter 9: Open Source Mindset and Community

A teletype machine: www.quickiwiki.com/en/Teletype_Corporation

The RepRap Wallace: www.reprap.org/wiki/Wallace

RepRap project evolutionary tree: http://reprap.org/wiki/RepRap_Family_Tree

GNU licenses: www.gnu.org/licenses/license-recommendations.html

Creative Commons licenses: http://creativecommons.org/licenses/

Github: www.github.com

National civic hacks site: http://hackforchange.org

## Chapter 10: Creating Female Makers

"You're a good man, Dr. Smurf" by Martha Beck: www.salon.com/1999/02/16/feature_378/

Parable of the Polygons: http://ncase.me/polygons/

National Science Foundation, National Center for Science and Engineering Statistics, Scientists and Engineers Statistical Data System (SESTAT), 2010: www.nsf.gov/statistics/wmpd/2013/tables.cfm

Society of Women Engineers' report on the status of women in engineering professions: http://societyofwomenengineers.swe.org/index.php/trends-stats#activePanels

The Laurel School in Ohio's Center for Research on Girls: www.laurelschool.org/page.cfm?p=625

The National Center for Women and Information Technology: www.ncwit.org

The Anita Borg Institute's "Why Women Leave" infographic: http://anitaborg.org/insights-tools/why-women-leave/

Intel's "MakeHers" report: www.intel.com/content/www/us/en/technology-in-education/making-her-future.html

*Los Angeles Times* article "Toy makers learn that construction sets aren't just for boys anymore": www.latimes.com/business/la-fi-girls-toys-20141214-story.html

*The New York Times* article "How Elementary School Teachers' Biases Can Discourage Girls From Math and Science": www.nytimes.com/2015/02/07/upshot/how-elementary-school-teachers-biases-can-discourage-girls-from-math-and-science.html

The Marlborough School: www.marlborough.org

The Castilleja School: www.castilleja.org

Bridgette Mongeon's blog: http://creativesculpture.com/blog/

Roominate: www.roominatetoy.com

Goldieblox: www.goldieblox.com/

DIY Girls: www.diygirls.org

# Chapter 11: Making at a Community College and Beyond

Pasadena City College: www.pasadena.edu

The DIAGRAM (Digital Image and Graphic Resources for Accessible Materials) Center: http://diagramcenter.org

Benetech: www.benetech.org

# Chapter 13: How Do Scientists Think?

*PLOS* open access journals: www.plos.org

# Chapter 15: Learning by Iterating

"The Tacoma Narrows Bridge" on Wikipedia. http://en.wikipedia.org/wiki/Tacoma_Narrows_Bridge_%281940%29

"Bhopal Disaster" on Wikipedia: http://en.wikipedia.org/wiki/Bhopal_disaster

"United States airliners 1950–1959" category on Wikipedia: http://en.wikipedia.org/wiki/Category:United_States_airliners_1950%E2%80%931959

Nancy Leveson's MIT website: http://sunnyday.mit.edu

Common Core standards: www.corestandards.org/about-the-standards

The Buck Institute: http://bie.org

RepRap Huxley: http://reprap.org/wiki/Huxley

"Makerbot Industries" on Wikipedia: http://en.wikipedia.org/wiki/MakerBot_Industries

# Chapter 16: Learning Science By Making

Peppytides peptide models: www.peppytides.org

Rich's set of planetary gears: www.youmagine.com/designs/quick-print-gear-bearing

DIAGRAM Center's 3D printing research recommendations: http://diagramcenter.org/3d-printing.html

The Castilleja School's Bourn Idea Lab: http://bournidealab.blogspot.com

# Chapter 17: What Scientists Can Learn From Makers

Bug traps: www.bugdorm.com

Richard Stouthamer's lab at UC Riverside: www.entomology.ucr.edu/faculty/stouthamer.html

3D model of the Homunculus Nebula: www.nasa.gov/content/goddard/astronomers-bring-the-third-dimension-to-a-doomed-stars-outburst/

# Index

# Get the eBook for only $5!

Why limit yourself?

Now you can take the weightless companion with you wherever you go and access your content on your PC, phone, tablet, or reader.

Since you've purchased this print book, we're happy to offer you the eBook in all 3 formats for just $5.

Convenient and fully searchable, the PDF version enables you to easily find and copy code—or perform examples by quickly toggling between instructions and applications. The MOBI format is ideal for your Kindle, while the ePUB can be utilized on a variety of mobile devices.

To learn more, go to https://www.apress.com/index.php/companion or contact support@apress.com.

Apress®
THE EXPERT'S VOICE™

Printed in the United States
By Bookmasters